ECONOMISTS AND THE
FINANCIAL MARKETS

This book explores how economists operate effectively in financial markets. Using events as diverse as the Wall Street Crash of 1929 to European monetary union and Japanese earthquake damage the author traces the responses of the market to a variety of financial events. In so doing, he shows how a knowledge of economics, correctly applied, can enhance investment performance.

This book is divided into sections dealing with a wide range of issues, including:

- The valuing process;
- Interpreting the news;
- The challenges of long-term business scenarios;
- The business and growth cycle;
- The economist as strategist.

Throughout, the importance of scenario building is emphasized, along with illustrations of how the economist can build practical skills in the marketplace. Written in an accessible style, the book will be a valuable guide for students wishing to broaden their knowledge of economics away from the theoretical. It will also appeal to experienced market economists interested in a fellow professional's approach.

Brendan Brown is head of research at London-based Tokyo-Mitsubishi International and has been a market economist specialising in currency and international bond markets for more than twenty years. He is also the author of a number of books about the market.

ECONOMISTS AND THE FINANCIAL MARKETS

Brendan Brown

London and New York

First published 1996
by Routledge
11 New Fetter Lane, London EC4P 4EE

Simultaneously published in the USA and Canada
by Routledge
29 West 35th Street, New York, NY 10001

Typeset in Garamond by
Poole Typesetting (Wessex) Limited
Bournemouth, Dorset

Printed and bound in Great Britain by
TJ Press (Padstow) Ltd, Padstow, Cornwall

British Library Cataloguing in Publication Data
A catalogue record for this book is available from the British Library.

Library of Congress Cataloging in Publication Data
A catalogue record for this book has been requested.

ISBN 0–415–02080–8 (hbk)
ISBN 0–415–06721–9 (pbk)

To
JUDITH, AARON, and JOSHUA

CONTENTS

FIGURES

FOREWORD

This is a book about what economists can really tell you about financial markets. As such it is best written by an economist and by one who has practised in markets. The subject belongs to a family which includes 'What can lawyers really say about your rights?'; 'What can doctors really say about healthy living?'; 'What can the art expert really say about beauty?'; 'What can a minister really say about your soul?'. All of these works could be written by the outsider looking in. But as such they would bear a superficiality, and at their worst be no more than a sniping, albeit humorous, commentary about failures of the particular profession. By contrast, the books written as confessionals by insiders out of the full wisdom of experience have a potential quality which no outside narrative could possess.

The cynics might say that the best confessional, from the viewpoint of maximizing the number of readers, is one which explodes the myths of what the insiders are really capable of. Other members of the profession should be a good market for such a book. But the person looking back in despair or disillusion, who has concluded that his talents were dissipated in a fruitless venture, is not a reliable source of a serious opinion as to what his profession – practised and used optimally – can achieve. Rather, the disillusioned is at best seeing his mission as warning would-be users or practitioners of the profession in question from getting trapped.

In writing this book I am a market economist who has definitely not lost faith. Indeed, I would describe the course of my journey through the marketplace in the last two decades as one of continually finding new ways in which economic knowledge can be applied. Yes, there are areas where as a beginner I had exaggerated views of the power of economics alone as a tool for interpreting markets. Twenty years later, I am more prepared to incorporate ideas of 'group psychology' and 'information failure' into the analysis of market price behaviour. Also how to use appropriately the laboratory of historical experience has been a preoccupying theme for me.

In the early and mid-1980s I combined my work as a practising market economist in the City of London (specializing in currency markets) with researching for and then writing my two 'history books' – *Monetary Chaos in Europe (1914–31)* and *Flight of International Capital (1931–86)*. These were not history books in the traditional sense but rather an attempt to re-create the environment of investors' decision-making at various key stages of market crisis. What were the possible scenarios which investors were looking at or which the skilled analyst should have been drawing to their attention? Where can investors and analysts be criticized during these historical episodes for sloppy assembly of information and careless use of their powers of probabilistic vision?

The driving interest behind writing the two histories was a clear antecedent of that behind composing this present work. In the histories I was examining the record of past generations of investors and analysts. Here I am seeking to generalize the lessons learnt both from re-creating scenarios at crisis points several decades or more away and also from my own living experience.

It is indeed as a scenario-builder that the market economist should largely be seen, so long as 'building' is understood as a broad term. Building requires much preparatory work. The market economist has to use intelligence sources to find out what buildings are out there in the minds of big actors in the marketplace. How secure are the structures? What are the probabilities attached to the various scenarios built and how could these shift?

Economists, when they leave university with their degrees in pocket, are totally unskilled at scenario-building. That is a skill which they have to learn on the job, and I hope that they will find the present book an eye-opener to practising their new knowledge in the financial marketplaces of the world. By contrast, experienced market economists reading these pages are most likely to be interested in how a 'fellow-worker' deals with many of the same problems which he or she encounters.

Those are two of the potential classes of readers. I have written this book, however, with a much broader interest in mind. The output of market economists reaches a wide audience, made up largely of investors. Many of these are paying (implicitly or explicitly) for the service of one or more market economists. They have a potential interest in reading a confession by an 'insider', especially if it offers insights on how to better use the market economist's output and how to better judge which market economist to follow.

Then there are at least three main groups that the market economist communicates with in the course of his information-gathering. They might well be curious to read more about the 'dynamics' behind their inter-relationship. First, the officials 'inside the Castle' from whom the market economist regularly extracts ideas and analysis can read about the problems and the complimentarities intrinsic to their encounter. Second, financial economists and journalists can see how similar and yet dissimilar their function is to that of the market economist. They might even be prompted into reconsidering whether scenario-builders should not get a greater space allocation in their pages! Third, academic economists (in universities and research institutes) might well have an interest in discovering how far a practising economist can be guided by principle.

Some academic economists, like some members of all the other groups mentioned, may in fact be less interested in the subject of market economists than the principles which they are applying and in what form. Investors who would like to be their own market economist rather than relying on outside advisers are an important example of this segment of the book's potential audience. I do not offer them magic. But I would hope that in this narrative, which winds through markets in currencies, bonds, equities, real estate, precious metals and collectables, they gain important insights on their way to developing a framework of thought within which their investment performance should improve.

1

THE MARKET IS MORE THAN
A STATE OF MIND

No one would deny the importance of psychology in the market-place. But many market-participants, and surely all economists, would stop far short of giving 'psychological factors' the lead role in a history of price movements. Arthur Miller's quip that 'the market represents nothing but a state of mind', and that stock market speculators 'believe that nothing is real; that if it is Monday and you want it to be Friday, and enough people can be made to believe it is Friday – then by God it is Friday', was aimed at a theatre audience. The successful investor, however, with a long track record realizes that there can be no short cut which excludes the process of 'value-assessment'. Political and economic projections cast in the form of alternative scenarios with attached probabilities of occurrence are indispensable.

Financial market prices are driven by how the future appears to present investors. They cannot hope to see all that is important in an artist's sketch or in an 'executive' forecast summary such as is prepared by various econometric services. The future is a span of all possible realities. The most probable outcomes are at the centre of the focal range. At the perimeter of our vision are poorly defined scenarios of low probability. The span of possible scenarios becomes ever wider the further we look ahead into the future. And even the central scenario (the most likely outcome) becomes less and less distinct.

Psychology can help to explain shortcomings and distortions in our 'probabilistic vision' (the portraying to oneself of the future in terms of a widening span of possible scenarios each with a determined probability of occurrence). Why, for example, do markets sometimes tend to concentrate on a focal point many years into the future (illustrated by a particular hypothesis about the long-run future, whether it be ageing populations, capital shortage, or the state of the budget ten years from now, tending to dominate short-term price movement)? Are there sometimes biases towards optimism or pessimism? Is it possible for there to be brief periods of 'probabilistic blindness'? Do investors show varying degrees of fright through time before their vision of the future? In their search for refuge are they impressed excessively by previous experience? Is vision distorted or over-influenced by the media and by a shifting population of 'gurus'? Are news events over-dramatized in general? What are the mental circuits which link a changed perception of the future to a decision to act in the marketplace and what are the outside catalysts which can help make the connection?

All of these questions are relevant to the work of appraisers of market value, but first they must themselves have looked into the future, using whatever aids are available. Trained political economists should be at an advantage in portraying the future. But in linking those portraits to present market value, sometimes critically, they must often draw on characterizations of the present and past 'state of mind' in the marketplace. Thus psychology enters the appraisal process.

Note that we are discussing here the appraisal of market 'averages', not the prices of small individual component parts. Is the overall level of the equity market about right? What about land values in general and long-term bond yields? And what about currency rates? In the answering of all these questions the economist has a vital contribution to make. It is quite different with respect to micro-valuations. You don't ask an economist to value your home, your office-building, or your Renoir on the wall, or even your shareholding in XYZ corporation. For these tasks you turn to a skilled appraiser who can rank one asset against others within the same class and draw on a reliable database of recent price information for transactions which have been concluded. How many pluses and minuses does this house have compared to other similar ones sold in the past twelve months? And on the basis of the appraiser's experience, what should be the price tag or discounts for these differences?

These micro-valuations are relevant to individuals who have already decided to enter the marketplace, whether to buy a house, or place so much of their portfolio in equities, bonds, real estate, or art. But at one stage further back in the decision-making process a different type of appraisal is required. Is the price-level for the asset-class as a whole reasonable? Should investors be in the equity market at all at current price levels? Should they be liquidating all their real estate holding? It is at this stage of the decision-making process that economists, familiar with aggregate demand and supply functions, and trained in the specification of present and future possible realities in aggregate terms, should hope to market their services.

ARE EQUITY PRICES TOO HIGH?

The question of whether equity prices in general are too high or too low is perhaps the most widespread preoccupation of investors. Central to answering that question is a macro-economic assessment – including both business cycle analysis and longer-term projection of economic trends. Having 'established' where the economy is in the cycle, a bold forecast might be made of what lies ahead. How far off is the next peak or trough? What will be the behaviour of corporate earnings over coming years, both within this business cycle, and as a long-run trend? What is the likely opportunity cost of other investments, particularly bonds? Investors should realize that no two cycles are identical. And they must not become obsessed with the cycle to the exclusion of hard thinking about secular trends which might dominate market performance.

We all know that a record of good business cycle forecasting does not make a history of good equity market forecasting. Whilst the correct forecasting (several months in advance) of a major turning point for the economy should yield good profits (if acted on!), a good track-record on projecting minor fluctuations in the pace of growth may be worth little in terms of performance. One particular difficulty is that equity market valuation depends as much on 'bottom-up' as 'top-down' work. The problem of aggregation besets equity market analysis.

Towards illustrating the problem, let us suppose that there were an asset, called PROFEX, whose income were perfectly correlated with total profits of the corporate sector calculated net of taxes (except for any element which can be credited directly against investors' overall tax liability) before the deduction of interest payments but adjusted already for inflation (with respect to depreciation and inventory valuation changes). In fact, during the early and mid-1990s, the inflation adjustment was a source of added profit over what was shown in the historic cost-based data.

The replacement cost of much machinery and especially computers was falling and so less had to be set aside for renewal than the accounting statements suggested. An adjusted corporate profits series, as described, is reported in the US national data on gross domestic product; in this particular series only profits generated within the US economy are included. The US Bureau of Commerce produces data on the so-called inventory valuation adjustment and capital consumption (depreciation) adjustment which allows the conversion of the profits series into an inflation-adjusted aggregate. Unfortunately this type of information is not so readily available for many other economies.

The price of a unit quantity of PROFEX would be set so that the spread of its yield below the real yield on bonds would reflect the expected long-run growth of profits less a factor to take account of risk and liquidity disadvantages (compared to bonds). The value of a portfolio invested in PROFEX would tend to fluctuate by a greater margin than one invested in money and bonds, at least where measurement were over short and medium periods of time (income reinvested within the given portfolios). Potential cumulative losses and gains (including both changes in the quoted price of PROFEX units and income earned) measured over the short and medium term would be greater on PROFEX than on the mixed money and bond portfolio, at least in a normal low-inflation environment. PROFEX would be less liquid than money market instruments or US Treasury bonds.

Good analysts of the given index would be skilled in forecasting corporate profits as shown in the national GDP data, and in forming a view on how profits expectations of investors would change. They would also have to judge well the likely evolution of the liquidity and risk premiums through time and forecast the path for real bond yields. Views on the 'risk premium' would involve in considerable part an assessment of market psychology – attitudes towards risk and willingness to bear it are conditioned by the 'state of mind'. Another element in the risk premium is the nature of the risk, as determined by economic and political fundamentals (for example, uncertainty with regard to future US corporate profits might well have been greater in the 1970s than in the 1990s). The forecasts of profits and real bond yields would be largely based on economic considerations. From these ingredients the analysts could project a price path for PROFEX.

A period of only mild fluctuations in the pace of economic activity (as compared to one of violent changes in direction) should go along with a lowered perception of risk as regards the stream of profits in the short and medium term. But uncertainty about profits growth over the long-run might well be dominated by other considerations than the cycle – capital scarcity (reflecting perhaps a secular fall in households' propensity to save), terms of trade gains (a fall in import prices – particularly of oil – might not be passed on fully to consumers), immigration (an inflow to the labour force might hold down real wage rates), demography (an ageing population might bring a scarcity of labour, meaning lower profitability) and shifts in the frontier of investment opportunity (a big technical innovation might be a source of new profitable activity).

The yield on PROFEX would be below the real yield on bonds – providing that its risk and liquidity disadvantages (compared to a portfolio of bonds) were outweighed by the growth potential of profits. Indeed, PROFEX could be a highly desirable asset – not least because there would be no need to incur the transaction cost of continually re-weighting components as in a conventional equity portfolio. In reality, an asset such as PROFEX is not to be found. The nearest equivalent, a well-diversified portfolio of equities approximating the relevant overall market index, is in fact different in several important respects.

First, the profits earned by the corporations represented in the portfolio are not wholly available in the form of disposable income to the equity holder – a substantial share (the non-dividend component) is forcibly retained for further investment. Indeed some, if not all, of the growth in corporate profits over the long-run can be attributed to such reinvestment. (As illustration of this point, suppose corporate earnings are running at around 6 per cent of total equity outstanding and that there is a 50 per cent retention ratio. The retained profits reinvested at 6 per cent would in themselves bring a 3 per cent growth of earnings in the next year. And 3 per cent is near the 'steady-state' growth rate of earnings over the long-run, assuming productive potential growth for the US economy of near that amount and a long-run constant share of profits in GDP.) The PROFEX holder, unlike the equity investor, can obtain his/her share of the increase in corporate profits without having to forgo income in the present. If indeed the implicit returns on reinvested profits are excluded, the equity holder would have little basis for looking forward to a substantially rising trend in real income from the portfolio (meaning that the earnings yield on the equity portfolio should be higher than the real yield on bonds even before making allowance for risk or illiquidity).

Second, the composition of the portfolio must be changed through time. Equities in corporations which are on 'the way out' have to be discarded once they are eliminated from the market index. Equities in new successful corporations have to be acquired, once they cross the threshold into the index. The passive investor who follows this rule would inevitably suffer loss from the process of 'creative destruction' which Schumpeter saw as the dynamic element in capitalist economies. Successful corporations, by the time they become represented in the index, have already recorded their highest growth rate in profits. Dying corporations, when at last they are discarded from the index, have usually produced a stream of disappointing results.

Third, most corporations issue debt (including bank loans) as well as equity. Thus a substantial share of income which would have accrued to the hypothetical asset PROFEX does not come to holders of the market index, even in the indirect form of retained profits. The leverage of the corporate sector means that its net earnings fluctuate by much wider margins than gross profits as reported in the GDP data (the latter is the income concept relevant to PROFEX). The correspondingly greater risk of the equity port-folio (than PROFEX) also justifies it having a superior yield.

Fourth, only a share of domestically generated corporate profits comes to investors in publicly quoted domestically registered equities. The rest goes to the owners of non-quoted private corpo-rations or to parent corporations which might be quoted on a foreign stock market (and so not included in the earnings accruing to a portfolio of domestic equities). Moreover a large share of the earnings of domestically registered corporations may come from abroad and form no part of corporate profits estimated in the GDP data (in contrast to GNP).

In sum, the obstacles in the way of a 'top-down' approach to equity market analysis (starting with an estimate of an aggregate – say net corporate income – and working down to an overall valuation of equities versus bonds) are immense. It is no wonder that the general method of proceeding in large equity brokering houses is 'bottom-up'. The analysts in each sector project income for 'their' corporations – albeit on certain macro-economic assumptions fixed 'centrally' (by the economics department) and these are then aggregated.

6

The macro-economist can usefully be called in to examine the implications of the 'bottom-up' projections. He/she should also check whether the projections in aggregate can be reconciled (allowing for a considerable margin of latitude) with GDP data, both actual and projected. If the 'bottom-up' projections prove to be irreconcilable, then the individual analysts can be sent back to the drawing board with a scale factor to be applied.

For example, at the start of 1992, a consensus of US analysts was looking for net earnings growth (for corporations included in the S&P 500) of around 20 per cent. In practice, given the sharp fall in interest payments made by the corporate sector (in line with a declining trend of US interest rated during 1991/2), that was consistent with a less remarkable inflation-adjusted growth in net corporate income (generated inside the USA) of about 11 per cent – a result which should have been seen as well within a realistic range by macro-economists for a second year of recovery from the business cycle trough of early 1991.

Similar earnings growth (around 20 per cent) being projected in early 1993 by a 'consensus' of analysts seemed less credible to many economists, who were taking as their central scenario a slowing of productivity growth and a 'bottoming' of interest rates. Some warned that even if 20 per cent plus growth in earnings were to occur, the earnings yield on the US market portfolio (after applying an adjustment for the effect of inflation on depreciation and inventory valuation) would be around 6.25 per cent, compared with a present 10-year real yield (in early 1993) on Treasury bonds of say 3 per cent. That did not seem like a generous yield pick-up. Note, however, that there is no ready-made series of historical data for the spread relationship. Empirical research on the 'excess return' from equities has been based on portfolio returns (capital gains plus dividend or coupon income). Over long periods of time (30-year averages) the excess return (otherwise called equity risk premium) has varied between zero and 12 per cent. A 4 per cent 'norm' is widely assumed by finance specialists.

Some pessimistic analysts in early 1993 saw the small spread as evidence of a speculative bubble forming in the US equity market – many retail investors being drawn into mutual funds by concern at the low level of money market rates – and encouraged to do so by banks who welcomed the opportunity to boost earnings from off-balance sheet activities (earning commissions on selling 'in house' mutual funds). More optimistic analysts, however, pointed to the likelihood of rapid profits growth continuing into 1994 (buttressing this view with the hypothesis that the revolution in information technology and 'globalization' would bring unusual productivity gains yet keep labour costs down). A further reason for optimism was the prospect of economic recovery outside the USA taken together with the fact of 40 per cent of earnings for S&P 500 companies coming from investments outside the USA.

Whether 'bulls' or 'bears' on the equity market, most 'fundamentalist' analysts couch their appraisals in terms of earnings growth potential and the yield spread over bonds. However, the application of this method to the Tokyo equity market is often questioned. The exceptionally low level of dividend and earnings yield in Tokyo are hard, albeit not impossible, to reconcile in any fundamental sense with the much higher yields in foreign markets, even when allowance is made for various special factors, including the prevalence of interlocking shareholding and the high value of land in Japan. Perhaps the Tokyo equity market is indeed more a 'state of mind' than any other.

The influence of interlocking shareholdings can be illustrated with a hypothetical example. Suppose the fifty biggest corporations (measured by stock market capitalization) listed in Tokyo agree to issue an additional 25 per cent of equity capital, the proceeds to be used towards acquiring other equity (within the group of fifty). No actual cash exchanges hands on a net basis; all accounts are reconciled through the mutual exchange and issuance of shares. Underlying earnings of the corporations are unchanged. Reported earnings (in total) of each corporation would be bolstered by the receipt of intercorporate dividend, but this would be small compared to the implicit share of say corporation A in B's earnings and conversely. Thus reported earnings yield per share could fall to near 80 per cent of the previous level.

Yet in the assessment of equity market valuation, making comparison between one market and another (for example Tokyo equities versus New York equities, or Tokyo equities versus Japanese government bonds) requires the correction of the distortion due to intercompany shareholdings. Some estimates put the adjustment factor for the Tokyo market's overall earnings yield as high as 20 per cent (an actual earnings yield of 1.6 per cent would be marked up to 1.9 per cent). Behind the large size of the adjustment factor in Tokyo lies the pervasiveness of the so-called *keiretsu* relationships. These exist within a family of companies across a wide spread of industries tied together by interlocking shareholdings. The companies exercise some preference for each other in business relationships.

Alongside the problem of interlocking shareholdings analysts, in appraising fundamental values in the Tokyo equity market, must consider accounting practices which lead to profits being depressed by Western standards (but not in the case of the banking sector). In particular, depreciation deductions are exceptionally high. Analysts should also 'weigh up' the land factor as an explanation for low earnings yields in Tokyo and here they should look beyond accounting standards.

Land is typically a low earnings yield asset (the ratio of current rent for prime properties to capital value is usually less than the earnings yield on the equity market). Thus Japanese corporations owning large amounts of the space they use for business purposes could be considered as in part real estate investment companies and in part 'business corporations', and the low earnings yield on the investment component would drag down the overall ratio. In the aftermath of the bursting of the bubble economy (from 1990 onwards), the sharp fall in real estate values (and thereby rise in rental yields) has made the 'land element' less significant (maybe irrelevant) to explaining the exceptionally low earnings yields in Tokyo.

LAND – THE THIRD ESTATE

According to neo-classical economics, land is the third factor of production. Yet it is the other two – labour and capital – which have been the main preoccupation of those involved in macro-economic analysis. Unemployment, wage-rates, natural rates of unemployment, interest rates (nominal and real), and cost of equity capital, are all the conventional material through which the analyst – especially the business economist – sifts. Rent levels, unoccupancy rates (for buildings), and yields on real estate investment, are usually at most a marginal consideration.

The frequent overlooking by macro-economists of land as the third factor of production stems in part from theoretical considerations. Neo-classical economists themselves acknowledge that the distinction between the three factors becomes blurred in highly developed economies. For example, many types of labour include a large element of so-called 'human capital' – investment in education and training. (Capital itself provides formidable measurement problems. Its market valuation depends on interest rates – yet in the neo classical model the interest rate is itself determined in equilibrium as the marginal productivity of capital.)

What is termed real estate usually includes a large element of capital (in the form of buildings). The pure land content can vary from a near zero proportion (for example, a warehouse in an unpopular site) to near 100 per cent (a shop in a prime city-centre position). The original formulation of land as a separate factor of production goes back to the so-called classical economists of the eighteenth century. These economists had in mind primarily agricultural land, whose productivity was a function of its fertility.

In the modern economy, land values are to a great extent dependent not on the fertility of the soil but on the capitalization of scarcity rents. Urban dwellers pay a premium for residential space in pleasantly situated neighbourhoods within easy commuting distance of facilities concentrated in the city centre (for example, entertainment and work). Retailers pay a premium for space in a popular shopping mall to enjoy custom from the concentration of shoppers there (in competition for space, the successful bidders are potential users who can realistically derive the most profit per square metre, subject to the prospective return – net of rent paid to the landlord – being above their cost of capital). Office users pay a premium for space well situated in a prestigious business district.

Thus commercial and residential land values stem from a combination of negative and positive considerations. Under the negative heading come the sum of commuting costs and other nuisances of urban congestion avoided. Under the positive heading come both man-made benefits – for example, attractive shopping malls, the easy comparison of alternative merchandise and services on offer which consumers and businessmen can make in well-designed and accessible marketplaces – and 'natural' benefits (for example, a view over a lake or mountains).

A country whose economy is highly concentrated in geographic space will tend to have higher land values than one where economic activity is well dispersed. The high valuations in the former country are in considerable degree a measure of congestion costs. They can also stem, however, from the benefits (in terms of range of choice for consumers – both business and private – within one small area) of metropolitan life.

For example, Japan stands out as having the most geographically concentrated economy – 30 million population within 30 miles of

Tokyo's city centre. Hence it is hardly surprising that Japanese land values tower above those in other advanced industrialized nations (even after taking account of 'price destruction' in the aftermath of the bubble economy years). But the high land values should not – in the main – be considered as part of national wealth. Any additional benefits to the Japanese consumer from concentration (compared to, say, his US counterpart) are likely to be outweighed by additional congestion cost.

Congestion is not, of course, entirely a natural phenomenon, especially in Japan. Zoning policy is also important. For example, where the authorities severely restrict the expansion of a metropolis so as to protect the agricultural use of surrounding land, upward pressure is put on real estate values in a central location (the cost of commuting to cheaper more spacious accommodation is increased). Rents which stem from scarcity of land created by such zoning are a measure of sacrifice (in terms of space availability) which city dwellers must make towards avoiding the 'sprawling out' of the urban mass. In effect, private landowners amongst their many possible roles are collectors of taxes on space imposed to bring about an officially favoured allocation of its use. The amount of tax to be collected depends crucially on the particular set of laws regarding land use. In the appraising of the general level of prices in the real estate market the economist must be sensitive to how that set of laws might change.

The heterogeneity and illiquidity of the land market make any aggregative type of analysis more difficult than for equities. Yet this does not mean than the economist should leave the field in despair. He is in a better position to make an overall commentary about the *level of the market in general* than the real estate broker or psychologist, so long as he has sufficient humility to gather 'grass roots' information about current trends.

The key ingredients for appraising the level of the real estate market are projections on the likely growth of net rental income and judgement on the appropriate yield which investors should expect (taking account of such factors as risk, growth, liquidity). In their work, appraisers divide the real estate market into several general classes – offices, warehouses, shops, apartment, and houses, for example. These classes may be further divided into broad regions, and within each a distinction can sometimes be made between prime and secondary quality. They can make use of indices calculated for both recent and historical growth of rents in

11

each category put together by independent property research institutes and also published by real estate or equity brokers (their research departments). Similarly they should have access to data on 'rental yields' for each category and their movement through time.

The data must be treated gingerly. In a rapidly moving market many of the indices would be far behind the times. Moreover, changes in rent levels might be understated due to failure of the statistician to capture rent discounts in the form of long rent-free periods during recessions. But there is no better data source. In gathering background information such as the amount of empty space as a proportion of the total stock, analysts will often have no better sources than hearsay and newspaper commentary.

The so-called 'rental yields' quoted in real estate statistics are not directly comparable with earnings yields in the equity market. The rental yield is calculated as the current rent payable divided by capital value. But the rent is considerably larger than the net income to be received by the owner. Deductions must be made for management costs, legal expenses, sinking fund to cover normal amounts of non-occupancy when outgoings including local taxation become payable by the landlord, and depreciation (calculated on a replacement cost basis). Assuming, for example, a building with a 40-year life, where land value is only a small proportion of the total value, a rental yield of 8 per cent might convert to a net earnings yield of 4.5–5 per cent. By contrast, a piece of prime agricultural land for which the above deductions would be very small would have a rental yield and net earnings yield which were very close to each other.

What relationship should the net earnings yield on a particular class of real estate bear to that on the equity market index? Historically the spread between the two has been quite variable, whether in Europe, Japan, or the USA. At times when prospective rental growth has appeared as much greater than net earnings growth for listed corporations (adjustment must be made in the comparison for the fact that corporate earnings growth is in part due to reinvestment of earnings, whilst rental growth comes without reinvestment of net rental income), the net earnings yield on property might well be below that on equities. Even the so-called rental yield (before making the various deductions listed above) in the case of prime retail properties has sometimes fallen below earnings yields.

How can analysts discover the average forecast in the market for rental growth? There is no survey of brokers' predictions to which they can turn, analogous to the IBES survey for the equity market (Institutional Brokers Estimate System). Analysts can take note of brokers' opinions, but there is no alternative to forming an independent view based on hypothesized relationships between economic growth (consumer spending in the case of retail rents, service sector activity for office rents, industrial production for warehouse rents), employment growth, profits, and demand for space. They must also take account of the amount of empty space overhanging the market, changing trends in space usage (are standards of acceptable amount of space per office user increasing?) and the cost of producing additional space.

In general, net earnings projections for real estate are even more hazardous than for equities. The share of profits in GDP has a firmer anchor than the ratio of new rental levels per square metre to GDP. (New rents refer to space let in the current period – in contrast to old rents which may still be payable under long-term contracts drawn up possibly many years before.) Like the commodity markets, the real estate markets can enter phases of extreme optimism on price (rent) increases continuing over a long period of time, and conversely. Competition and capacity constraints impose limits on potential profits growth. But for new rents on scarce land the sky sometimes appears to be the limit.

The associated bubbles in real estate markets are almost always fuelled by a rapid growth of bank credit. But the banks themselves are not the source of the boom. Rather, their managements unfortunately come to believe the optimistic assessments of rental income growth presented by their clients, perhaps corroborated by poor independent analysis. And sometimes conditions of excess competition in the banking industry encourages general managers there to give their loan officers a freer rein so as to produce performance.

Super-optimism on rental growth is not the only cause of net earnings yields on real estate falling below those in the equity market. 'Inflation scare' is also a possible explanation, especially when the central bank is holding short-term money-market rates at a level which is quite negative in real terms. Earnings from equities may be seen as subject to greater potential erosion by inflation than rental income (for example, corporate management might be slow to adjust profit margins to take account of increasing replacement costs, and taxation may be levied on purely inflationary inventory gains).

This inflation-hedge argument for real estate, however, has to be treated with extreme caution. Real estate values have often proved to be a victim of, rather than safe-haven from, inflation shocks. Inflation erodes the benefit of the rent floor set in most long-term lease arrangements (whereby only upward revisions in rent are possible at stated intervals). And inflation shocks are usually followed eventually by 'recession shock', which is surely negative for the real estate market. Given the natural illiquidity of real estate, investors cannot hope, by adept timing, to get out before the mood of the market swings from inflation anxiety to recession surprise.

Of course, investors in real estate via mutual funds or equity holding (a portfolio of shares in real estate investment companies) can hope to operate more flexibly, as they enjoy the liquidity advantage of the equity market. Indeed the possibility of liquifying real estate investment sets some limit to the size of liquidity premium on equity yields relative to real estate yields (put another way, liquidity considerations alone might not justify the net earnings yield on real estate being well above that on equities).

Residential real estate for owner-occupation, unlike commercial real estate, cannot be bought indirectly in liquid form. Thus the disadvantage of potential illiquidity should be an important factor in the pricing of homes. And illiquidity can at times be severe. An insight into liquidity variation in the residential real estate market can be gained from dividing potential buyers and sellers into different categories, distinguished by the degree of urgency with which they wish to transact, and by whether they are on just one side of the market or both (selling a present home and purchasing a new one). The most urgent sellers are the so-called 'forced sellers', who include mortgage lenders (repossessed property), executors (seeking to realize cash from an estate) and family break-ups. These forced sales are not directly linked to an intended purchase.

Other categories of urgent (not forced) sellers include those seeking to relocate for changed employment, or those whose families have expanded and need more space. These sellers are also on the buy side of the market, in that they are simultaneously seeking to satisfy a new requirement for residential space. Also on the buy side are the so-called 'first-time' buyers – either setting up home for the first time or having moved country. Urgency here, however, is variable, especially if there is a well-functioning rental market. The first-time buyer is by definition not simultaneously a seller.

One type of non-urgent buyer for cash (not simultaneously selling) is the investor. Investors are looking to acquire residential real estate for income and capital gain, not as places to live. Indeed, investor-buyers form the least urgent category of transactors. They may often be outbid by owner-buyers who (unlike themselves) can derive advantage from imputed rental value (the benefit of using the space themselves) and are exempt from tax (under most fiscal codes). Above investor-buyers (in the hierarchy of urgency) are 'consumer-buyers'. The latter would like to move from one house (or apartment) to another, perhaps because their tastes have changed, perhaps because they can afford something better, perhaps because they now wish to 'economize'. Consumer-buyers are also consumer-sellers.

In a recession, the less urgent categories of buyer (excluding here the investor-buyer) and seller tend to withdraw from the market. A prime motive for withdrawal is to delay consumer expenditure. The cost of 'doing up a new home' and removal itself, including transaction expenses, can represent a large share of annual income. When the economic future is particularly uncertain, caution prevails. Likewise first-time buyers become scarcer, as new householders decide to retain liquid balances and continue renting. And anyhow they would find that banks were less ready to lend to them than during boomtime.

The withdrawal of some consumer transactors and first-time buyers means that the volume of turnover shrinks. Properties take longer to sell. Consumer-sellers still in the market become discouraged by the failure of their house to move and some withdraw. Those who stay mostly become resistant to any idea of buying before they sell, not just out of fear lest they fall into an illiquidity trap – unable to 'extract cash' from their unsold previous home – but also because they could ill afford the income loss suffered (payment of interest on a bridging loan or loss of income on other assets sold) at a time of economic hardship.

The reluctance to buy before selling in itself deprives the market of liquidity. Long chains develop, where B's purchase from A is conditional on B's sale to C, which is conditional on D's purchase from C, etc. Any break in the chain (a deal being cancelled) thwarts all transactions. In effect, the normal dealer inventory of houses, in the form of unsold property held by transactors who have purchased first, dwindles. The existence of a rental market helps to check liquidity declines in these circumstances. Once successful

in concluding a contract, sellers can move into rented accommodation whilst negotiating a purchase. Outside investors (the owners
of rented accommodation) replace buyers-before-sellers as the
holders of dealer inventories.

The paucity of information on rentals and yields hinders any
attempt to estimate the extent to which the pricing of residential
real estate allows for the problem of illiquidity. A large amount of
residential real estate is traded as a consumer durable with no
explicit rental value or yield being observable. Even so, the economist, in appraising the general level of the residential real estate
market, should seek to derive implicit trends for yields and rents,
drawing on evidence from the small volume of investment transactions (where outside investors buy residential property already
let or to be let) and new rentals.

Powerful rises in residential real estate markets can stem from
climbing rents or falling yields. A climb in rents may reflect
increased affluence which goes along with a raised demand for
living space (especially in the more desirable locations). A fall in
yields could reflect expectations that implicit rents will continue to
grow rapidly – or that there are a large number of renters who in
the better economic climate would now prefer to become owner-
occupiers. Economists can use their expertise to explore the
bounds of valuation which are consistent with reasonable hypotheses about the future and hope to be able to warn participants of
danger as zones of irrationality are approached.

ECONOMIC BOUNDARIES TO BOND MARKETS

In both the evaluation of equity and real estate markets, considerable reference was made to the yield on bonds. The earnings
yield on equities was compared to bond yields, and in turn real
estate yields were evaluated by comparing them to equity yields.
Now we go one stage further back and ask what anchors can be
found in economic reality for the level of bond yields, and what
role 'psychological factors' might play.

There is now no shortage of computer software which can
translate a 'yield curve' in any given currency into a term structure
of interest rates. As illustration, take one-year dollar interest rates at
3.75 per cent, two-year at 4.25 per cent, three-year at 4.7 per cent,
four-year at 5.06 per cent, and five-year at 5.35 per cent. Then the
implicit one-year rate one year forward is 4.77 per cent, two years

forward 5.67 per cent, three years forward 6.27 per cent and four years forward 6.7 per cent. Rolling over a one-year fixed rate deposit at maturity into a new one-year fixed-rate deposit and so on at the given implicit forward rates until year five would provide the same cumulative sums investing in a fixed-rate bond bought at par with a coupon of 5.35 per cent (where the coupons are reinvested at the above forward rates).

Economists, in their appraisal of bond markets (or other fixed-rates markets, such as swap markets), can examine whether the implicit forward one-year rates appear 'reasonable' year by year. But beyond, say, three years into the future, it is doubtful that their 'probabilistic vision' is powerful enough to make such discreet estimates. A better procedure is to amalgamate forward one-year rates further out than three years into a fixed rate, so that they study a term structure of one-year rates only up to their medium-term horizon, and beyond that they consider a forward multi-year fixed rate.

In assessing the 'reasonableness' of the forward projections built into the fixed-rate markets economists are on more familiar ground than when commenting on the real estate or equity market. No need to do a sounding of real estate brokers as to future rent levels or turn through pages of 'bottom-up' forecasts on the equity market. Rather their database here comes from finance ministries, central banks and offices of economic statistics. Macro-economic projections and monetary analysis, both an essential part of their training, come into full play. Unfortunately, this does not mean that their appraisal can set tight limits for the reasonable level of bond yields in any given currency.

The theory underlying their appraisal is most likely a combination of elements drawn from Wicksell and Fisher (the former a Swedish economist and the latter an American economist in the early part of this century). First, there is the concept of a *natural real rate of interest* at which the economy would be in long-run equilibrium (full employment of resources and inflation at a steady low level). Here domestic investment spending plans would be in balance with the intended amount of savings accumulated by the private sector less the budget deficit.

Second, long-maturity nominal interest rates (including bond yields) should settle at a level equal to the natural real rate plus the prevailing expectation (in the marketplace) of inflation over the long-run. Short maturity rates, however, and money-market rates in particular, can deviate considerably from the natural rate adjusted for inflation expectations. Indeed, there is no automatic mechanism which keeps the two in line with each other. Very short-term money-market rates are determined by the supply and demand of deposits at the central bank. Often the central bank itself pegs the short-term rates, and supplies whatever reserves are needed to the money market each day to hold the rate.

In the medium and long term, however, a persistent deviation between the level of market interest rates and the natural real rate gives rise to disequilibrium – either economic overheating (accelerating inflation) or persistent deflation. If, for example, the central bank pegs the short-term money market rate at well below the natural real rate (plus inflation expectations), the subsequent acceleration of inflation will force the central bank to adjust the peg upwards, possibly to above the natural rate (again adjusted for inflation expectations) for some time so as to cool the economy down.

The natural rate of interest cannot be measured directly. It reveals itself to some degree through the errors of central bankers. Indeed, some monetary economists claim that the lack of knowledge about the natural rate means that central banks should relinquish control of short-term money rates, leaving these free to float, and instead concentrate on reaching a specified target for growth in monetary base (bank reserves plus currency in circulation). Under this latter procedure, the average deviation of rates from their natural level might well be less than under the rate-fixing alternative.

Economists, in evaluating the bond market, have to form a view on the likely course of interest-rate pegging by the central bank over say the next year or two. When is the peg likely to adjusted and by how much? If the central bank is not pegging rates but targeting the growth in monetary base or bank reserves, then economists must estimate what rates would average over the period to be consistent with that target. Either task, of course, is daunting – requiring in effect that economists venture opinions into areas where the central bank itself has no firm opinion. (The Federal Reserve Open Market Committee members have no precise idea of where they will be seeking to peg the 'fed funds rate' six months from now; and if they reverted to targeting non-borrowed reserves, allowing the key overnight rate of float, they would lack conviction about where the rate would average out.)

Economists, in appraising the term structure of rates beyond short maturities, must form a view on the natural real rate of interest for the economy in question and on the likely long-run average rate of inflation. For example, he could compare the two-year forward eight-year interest rate (derived from the term structure of interest rates quoted above) with their estimate of the natural real rate plus their 'guesstimate' of where inflation expectations will have settled by two years from now.

No serious economist can have a high degree of confidence in his/her view about the real natural rate or inflation expectations. Yes, economists can draw on the previous history of real rates (albeit that there is the problem of assessing what were inflation expectations as against actually recorded inflation in past periods). But what can they say about the investment opportunity set two years, five years, or ten years into the future, or about likely shifts in savings behaviour – both by the private and public sectors, and about what will be the balance of influence on the natural real rate? They can at best 'catch on' to hypotheses about shifts in consumer attitudes (to or away from a 'spending mentality'), speculate on how demographic factors (for example, ageing populations) might affect savings behaviour, form critical judgements of medium-term fiscal programmes, and forecast the 'robustness' of investment opportunity, taking account of the development of new technologies and political change.

Furthermore, economists' evaluations of the natural real rate and the corresponding level of bond yields in nominal terms should include an international dimension. Their analysis of yields on the three 'big' international moneys – US dollars, Deutschmarks, and Japanese yen – might well start with the questions being asked in a national context. But then international linkages have to be considered, even though exchange rates between the three currencies are floating and the respective central banks run ostensibly independent monetary policies. In particular, economists should be aware that an 'inflation shock' in the USA might well have a negative impact on German and Japanese inflation prospects.

There is usually a long lag between the original error in monetary policy and inflation shock. Often the exchange rate proves to be an early warning symptom of the error, but is not recognized as such due to other alternative explanations of currency market turbulence. A sudden sharp fall of the dollar against the Deutschmark and Japanese yen could trigger monetary easing by both the Bundesbank and Bank of Japan (out of concern about, say, the negative impact of the currency swings on economic recovery). Only much later might it become clear that the source of the dollar crisis was a big mistake in an inflationary direction of US monetary policy. Thus there is a serious risk of the 'inflation virus' spreading from the USA to Germany and Japan well before it has been diagnosed. If at any time US yields come to include a substantial premium against the risk of inflation shock, it is wholly consistent with rational expectations that some premium, albeit smaller, should form on Japanese and German yields.

The greater the extent of international trade and the smaller the impediment of exchange risk to capital flow, the stronger are the forces bringing natural real rates of return into convergence over long periods of time (new 'shocks', however, can prevent convergence ever being reached). For example, an upward jolt to the real yield on US bonds, even if of wholly US origin (say a big increase in the US budget deficit or a sudden brightening of the outlook for business investment spending), is likely to pull the equilibrium real rate upwards in Japan and Europe. The stimulus to aggregate demand in the latter two areas from increased exports to the USA (where domestic demand is buoyed by the enlarged budget deficit or increased investment spending) would justify a higher real rate.

As investors looked to switch into now higher yielding US bonds, the dollar would rise in the foreign exchange market, a development which could further buoy the export sector in the European and Japanese economies (in that their cost of production would fall in dollar terms). In turn this additional stimulus would underpin the rise of natural real rates of interest in Europe and Japan. But the appreciation of the dollar (and so the additional stimulus) would be limited by, first, investors' aversion to assuming exchange risk (incurred when switching into US bonds from European and Japanese bonds), and second, their awareness that in the very long-run the strong cumulative capital inflow to the USA would put downward pressure on the natural real rate of interest there. The cumulative flow of capital might eventually bring the stock of physical capital in the different countries to a level where their marginal rates of return and so natural real rates of interest were equal. At that stage, the dollar could have fallen back to its initial value (prior to the upward jolt to US yields).

Thus in evaluating bond yields, economists must take a view on the strength of the link between those they are studying and those in foreign centres. In doing so, they might look at this history of the relevant international yield spreads. But they must realize that a change of exchange rate regime can greatly reduce the relevance of history. (For example, a switch from a freely floating to a fixed exchange rate means most likely a higher correlation between bond yields in the two currencies.) Moreover, in applying the theory of international linkages between interest rates they still face the hurdle of converting nominal bond yields quoted in the market into real expected yields (specifically, when they observe a big jump in US Treasury-bond yields, how much of this is due to a rise in the natural real rate of interest and how much to a worsening of inflation expectations). The problem of measuring inflation expectations besets bond market analysis whether undertaken simplistically within a wholly domestic context or thoroughly taking account of international linkages.

Inflation expectations, even with respect to periods far ahead of the present, tend to reflect recent experience of inflation. Economists, in forming their own views about the course of inflation over say the next two to three years, can draw on a combination of monetary and real indicators – for example, monetary growth rates, past history of the income velocity of money, degree of capacity utilization, tightness of labour markets, and commodity prices. Politics – including those surrounding the leadership of the central bank – must be taken into account. The economist realizes, though, that there is a margin of indeterminacy around the future inflation rate – not least where the relationship of demand for money to national income is quite unstable (meaning that key monetary indicators become unreliable).

Economists, having undertaken their evaluations, as described, of the bond market, and having prepared their commentaries accordingly, might well turn to a review of relevant 'psychological influences' in order to narrow the zone of indeterminacy for yields. Two opposing fears – first, a collapse of the real rate of return to investment (on account of a prolonged economic depression or stagnation) and second, run-away inflation – play on bond investors' state of mind. Concern that short-term rates could fall to very low levels as the authorities seek to pump-prime the economy can encourage many investors to play it safe by fixing their rate of return for a number of years into the future. By contrast, when the economy is thriving and the uppermost fear is that the central bank could be tolerating some overheating, then the 'play-safe' strategy is to move into the money market.

On top of the final investors, the evaluator should consider a tier of financial intermediaries who 'play the yield curve' by borrowing at short maturities and buying at the intermediates. So long as the bond market is steady or rising they have no loss to offset against their income gain (equal to medium-term rates less short-term rates multiplied by the amount involved). By the time loss hits, the senior officials involved in running the portfolio described might already have moved on to new responsibilities and taken the credit for good intervening profits. In any case, losses from the yield curve strategy tend to be realized when private demand for credit from banks is running strongly, and so the adverse outcome is lost in the overall results.

Some retail investors can be put in the same category as the bank traders. They move into bonds when the yield curve is highly positive sloping – not out of concern that short-term money rates are to fall still further but driven, rather, by the higher income which can be earned (from lengthening the maturity of their invest-ment) and hopeful that they can get out of their positions before the music stops. Collectively they cannot.

Economists, in their review of psychological factors, should recognize that occasionally geography appears to have a strong influence on 'state of mind'. Then investors on one side of the currency frontier have a view which differs significantly from that held by investors on the other. For example, in autumn 1995 many German investors were supposed to be anxious about the possi-bility of the Deutschmark being replaced, as early as 1999, by a new European money which would be subject to considerably greater inflation risk. By contrast, investors outside Germany were fairly confident that monetary union would be delayed (beyond 1999) or would occur only in a form which meant the new money would be as good as the Deutschmark. Such differences in 'national psychology' can at times be the source of a large swing in exchange rates and a seemingly obvious misalignment of bond yields from an international perspective.

A particular bond market will usually be most influenced by the national viewpoint of its domestic constituency. Thus, if US investors and commentators tend to be more pessimistic than foreigners about the long-run inflation outlook in the US economy, then yields on dollar bonds are likely to settle at a level which seems quite generous as seen from the outside. This was indeed the state of affairs in the US bond market during the years 1983–5 when dollar yields remained well into double digits. In conse-quence the dollar came under strong upward pressure in the foreign exchange market. As the dollar soared against the Deutschmark, and later also against the yen, many foreign investors were scared by the possibility of a big corrective fall in the future from taking advantage of the high real yields on US bonds (in terms of US purchasing power). And many US investors were already sufficiently stimulated by potential gains on foreign currencies (as these reached exceptionally cheap levels against the dollar) into undertaking unusually large portfolio shifts out of their home currency (the US dollar).

Of course, foreigners could protect themselves against exchange loss by adopting hedge strategies – for example, switching their operations to the Treasury bond futures market or borrowing floating rate dollars to invest in the cash bond market. But these hedge strategies would have involved the incurring of substantial transaction costs (including the embarrassment of reporting possibly large short-term losses on futures positions) if continued over a lengthy period and there was little reason to anticipate instant success. Moreover, in adopting a futures of borrow-and-invest strategy, they would not gain at all from money-market rates (say for three- and six-month maturities) being at what they considered to be well above the natural rate. After all, the setting of short-term rates is dominated also by 'resident' rather than foreign expectations. The central bank is concerned foremost with inflation expectations held domestically.

Further examples of divergent expectations between domestic and foreign investors affecting the key Deutschmark–US dollar exchange rate can be found during summer 1993 and autumn 1995. In the first case (summer 1993), German investors – and the Bundesbank – were sceptical of claims that the natural real rate had fallen below the 'historical average' of 4 per cent, even though the economy was in sharp recession. But US investors, conditioned by evaporating interest income at home (where money rates were at 3 per cent, real short-term rates at zero, and real long bond yields at below 3 per cent) viewed German rates as abnormally high. Some, especially the so-called 'hedge-funds', plunged into the Bund futures market and thereby did not take any currency position. But many others bought Deutschmark bonds outright. Their operations helped to explain why European currencies remained remarkably firm against the dollar, despite the US economy being in a favourable cyclical position relative to Europe.

In the second case (autumn 1995), US Treasury-bond yields fell to below 6 per cent at ten-year maturities, even though the US economy was operating at full stretch as US domestic investors became euphoric about inflation being dead and 'revolutionary' budget tightening in prospect. Foreign investors were sceptical – giving more weight to the hypothesis that the surprise easing of inflation pressure in summer 1995 stemmed from coincidental factors such as the Mexico shock and an inventory sub-cycle rather than from a new-found super-competence of the Federal Reserve. And if prospective budget balances are so important for the bond market, why were Japanese bond yields the lowest in the world when Japan's budget deficit was one of the largest? Anyhow, in 1996 US budgetary policy might actually be reflationary, never mind the 'fiscal revolution' underway. Thus foreign investors, seeing little value in the US T-bond market and the equity market (which was buoyed by the low US T-bond yields) could only be tempted to hold onto their outstanding positions in US assets by the dollar being at an obviously cheap level against the number two international money, the Deutschmark.

Examples of divergence in view between domestic and foreign investors are not confined to the US and German bond markets. In spring and summer 1993, when the yen was soaring against the DM and dollar, Japanese and foreign viewpoints with respect to the yen bond market were quite different. Japanese investors, influenced by the 'cautiousness' of the Bank of Japan under Governor Mieno (who had directed monetary policy towards the bursting of the 'bubble economy' in 1989/90, and remained highly alert to the risk of a new bubble emerging), were still concerned about the risk of inflation. By contrast, foreign investors were readier to accept the view that the post-bubble Japanese economy was in a highly deflationary situation and that Governor Mieno was a general fighting the last war. The foreigners were influenced by commentaries drawing an analogy between the Japanese economy in the aftermath of the Tokyo equity market crash (1990-1) and the US economy in the years following the Great Crash of October 1929.

The corollary of the mismatch in views between Japan and the outside world as to the existence or extent of price deflation was that the yen during spring and summer 1993 daily reached nearer to the sky instead of showing the weakness typical of a depressed economy. Foreign investors viewed yields on Japanese government bonds (as in the first half of 1993) at nominal yields barely

100 basis points below US yields (at ten-year maturities) despite a much wider difference in inflation outlook between the two countries (3 per cent p.a. in the USA as against 0 per cent in Japan) as way above the natural rate of interest. And money-market rates in the USA were at virtually the same level as in Japan. Even though the yen was most probably overshooting its long-run 'sustainable' level (adjusted through time to take account of zero or negative inflation in Japan compared to positive inflation elsewhere), foreign investors could justify holding on to their yen assets in view of potential large capital gains on bond holdings as market interest rates fell towards the natural rate, and of a running real interest income gain.

How can we explain the occasionally yawning gaps which open between domestic and foreign perceptions of the same economic reality? Sometimes we have to look no further than the story of the emperor's new clothes. The 'in set' of analysts, journalist-commentators, and senior officials (central bankers in particular) in the home country of the asset in question can sometimes mutually reinforce each other's respect for a fashionable hypothesis about the long-run which normally would be treated with considerable scepticism. Investors in foreign centres are less likely to be 'taken in' by the fashionable yet highly speculative hypothesis. They are not in general accessing the identical media (albeit that there is significant overlap). They may well have learnt from experience that by the time they 'catch on' to the latest fashionable view, the scope for making profit has already vanished. Other times, the yawning gap can reflect a staid domestic consensus. Investors and analysts on the outside prove to be more flexible in altering their perceptions as conditions change.

2

SO WHAT IS NEW?

'The news' is the biggest day-by-day influence on market prices. Yet most news items are ephemeral – either they are snuffed out by counter-evidence or they join as indistinguishable particles a 'trend story' which transcends daily happenings. The exceptions are the dramatic discontinuities which enter the history books – such as the closing of the US gold window in August 1971 or the opening of the Berlin Wall (November 1989).

Short-term traders – whether in the futures pits, dealing rooms, or the privacy of their own homes and offices – are rapacious consumers of the news. Flashes across their Reuters or Telerate screens are like the turnings of the roulette wheel in determining the outcome for the players. The dealers who are striving to make a continuous market cannot be out of touch with the latest happenings or their quotes would be an invitation to huge loss-making business coming their way.

Marcel Proust could have written the same about today's traders as he did about Bloch, his speculator on the Paris Bourse, during the First World War. 'In stock exchange circles, every monarch who is ill, whether it be Edward VII or Wilhelm II, is dead, every town which is about to be besieged has already been captured.' Traders are concerned not just with news, but with 'embryo-news'. They cannot afford to haughtily dismiss all stories until they reach the 'Rolls-Royce' standards of verification demanded by 'quality' newspaper editors.

Economists in their role as 'valuers' – whether of bonds, equities, currency, or real estate – have less reason than the traders to be concerned with day-by-day news reports. They can absorb the news with the aid of a time-filter which reduces their exposure to the flashes which contribute to the 'white noise' in price movement. But economists should not shut themselves off from the flow of news. It has been said that the successful writer should be curious enough to look out from the quiet of his/her study at the street scene below but not so curious as to be drawn to join the crowd below. And so it is with 'market valuers' – they must be students of the news media and up to date with what is being considered there, but they must not become immersed.

Economists are both consumers and critics of the news media. As consumers, they are looking for insights into 'The Castle' (the corridors of power) – who are the people making policy, what are they like, what are they now working on? Like traders, they rely on the media for information of new happenings. They are readers of 'interpretative pieces' where journalists try to get behind the news and find out what is really happening. They could be keen readers of 'slice of life pieces', where the journalist interviews Mr Jo on the farm or Mr Smith the entrepreneur deciding in the light of current conditions whether to invest. And sometimes futuristic articles in the newspaper can be a prompt to their own imagination in the drawing up of future possible scenarios.

As media critics, economists question whether journalists have 'got the stories right'. Who were the likely sources of information and is there a bias? Are there some stories about to break on the horizon which are getting insufficient attention from newspaper editors? Did the journalists fail to get the punch questions through when interviewing the Finance Minister? Do the editorialists and commentators have particular hang-ups?

NEWS EDITORS ARE NOT SPECULATORS

The economist, as market-valuer, and the news editor have quite different tasks. Valuers should be constantly seeking to sharpen their probabilistic vision – increasing their power to imagine likely future scenarios and assess outlying risk factors of significance. By contrast, news editors are firmly focused on the present – 'discovering' the real situation. Yes, the economist-valuers (including the many investors who perform this role for themselves) may be an important sub-segment of demand for the particular news service or newspaper. But mainstream media publications (including high-circulation financial newspapers) can survive only by marketing a 'package deal', not ideal for any segment but useful enough to be worth purchasing.

In the 'package deal', pieces speculating about the future are produced irregularly at editorial whim and are generally quite superficial. In the days, weeks, and months before dramatic events in history, it is not in the newspapers that you will find lucid accounts setting out the shifting probability of likely scenarios ahead. Turn to the newspapers, for example, in the weeks before any major currency 'event' – whether the dollar coming off gold in 1971, the floating of the mark–dollar rate in March 1973, the announcement of monetary union between East and West Germany in February 1990, the shake-ups of the ERM in autumn 1992 and summer 1993 – and you will find no speculative articles on how the currency map might change and what the medium-term economic implications would be.

Ahead of great political events there is the same lack of speculation about possible scenarios stretching into the medium term. Perhaps most dramatic is newspaper coverage ahead of the two world wars. During the fateful days of July 1914 and of August 1939, you will not find in the newspapers a considered article day-by-day – or on any day – setting out the editor's view (based on the collective judgement of his defence, foreign, and political editors) about the probability of war. By contrast, ahead of a general election or referendum, journalists may take a stab at outlining post-poll scenarios. The publication date for these, however, is usually just before polling day – not much use for investment appraisal in the weeks and months before. And the speculative writing does not stretch far into the future.

The Canadian general election of 25 October 1993 provides a good example of boundaries to speculation about the future in the newspapers. The election presented two large uncertainties for investors (in their approach to the Canadian dollar). First, what was the nature of the next government which was likely to emerge, and how would its economic policies differ from that of its predecessor? Second, what would be the significance of the Quebec nationalists, fighting a general election at the Federal level for the first time, winning a large number of seats, in that their aim was ultimately the break-up of Canada?

On the first question, the press did report opinion poll evidence (intermittently in the foreign press, regularly in the Canadian press). Thus investors could be fully aware, week-by-week, of the collapsing support for the governing Conservative Party. But a glance through the major titles read in European marketplaces – *Financial Times*,

Wall Street Journal, International Herald Tribune, Neue Zücher Zeitung, Handelsblatt, Frankfurter Algemeine – carried no serious comment on economic policies likely to be followed by a Liberal government (the Liberals and Conservatives entered the campaign each with 35 per cent poll ratings; by the last week of the campaign the Liberals were at 43 per cent, the Conservatives at 18 per cent). Only immediately following the Liberal win (a landslide victory in which Conservative representation was cut to only two seats) were potential candidates for the post of Finance Minister discussed and the 'orthodox' credentials of the most likely choice highlighted.

During the campaign there was some coverage in the newspapers of the prospect of Governor Crow, the head of the Bank of Canada, being reappointed by a liberal government – his present term expiring in January 1994. Mr Crow was widely seen as a staunch defender and author of the low inflation policy, and some investors might have been concerned that his dismissal would signify a turn towards 'currency populism' by a Liberal government. What was totally missing in the press articles, however, was any discussion on evidence as to whether Mr Crow's reputation was justified. Might there not be potential replacements on the Canadian monetary scene who would inspire confidence in their own expertise and also commitment to the aim of low inflation?

On the Quebec issue, newspaper readers were informed that provincial elections to be held by autumn 1994 would be crucial. A victory of the Parti Quebecois (PQ) (the provincial arm of the Quebec nationalist movement) at these elections over the incumbent Liberal government would clear the way for a referendum on independence to be held in Quebec during 1995. But readers (of the newspapers listed above) were not given any insight as to whether a PQ victory in 1994 was likely in the event of the Bloc Quebecois (the Federal Party linked to the PQ) performing well at the general elections. Or could a good performance by the BQ reflect a protest vote (indicating Quebeckers' anger at the failure of recent constitutional initiatives which would have given Quebec a special status in the Canadian Federation) with differing forces likely to be influential in a provincial poll?

And there was no enlightenment in the international news media (in autumn 1993) about what an independent Quebec would mean for the Canadian financial markets. Did the BQ and their PQ allies have a clear programme for the relationship between Quebec and the rest of Canada? The BQ leader made references to a monetary and economic union between the two successor states on the 'Maastricht model'. But could a long-term union be negotiated, or would there be a temporary union as a mere stepping stone to a separate currency for Quebec? If the Canadian dollar were trans- formed into a Quebec–Canadian dollar, for which the monetary authority was an independent central bank on which both Quebec and Canada had representation, what would be the implication for the exchange rate? How would currency divorce between Canada and Quebec affect the value of the Canadian dollar?

News editors outside Canada could justify the lack of coverage of these issues by pointing to micro-economic considerations. More extensive coverage of Canadian futuristic issues would have been at the expense of other news stories or feature articles. Some US and European editors see Canada as a 'boring story' (in the same way as Belgium). To have done a quality piece on the Canadian dollar seeking to answer the questions posed would have demanded a considerable budget. And even then, the economic journalist's final product might not have carried great conviction with those readers strongly interested in Canada. Meanwhile, with perhaps only a handful of skilled economic journalists on his staff, the editor would have lost the chance to produce some other stories.

The alternative would have been to commission a series of arti- cles from a Canadian politico-economic expert, subject to consid- erable editorial intervention. But such 'freelance input' is widely frowned on by newspaper editors – direction is difficult and internal rivalries can be inflamed (why was the foreign editor who normally covers Canada not asked to do the piece?). And potential contributors are wary of their articles never seeing the light of day.

Some specialist news and information services for financial markets – largely screen-based – are not subject to the same 'opportunity cost' considerations as the newspapers. And, indeed, screen-based commentaries are an essential addition to the econ- omist's information base. Reuters or Telerate for example can carry much fuller stories on many events of key market interest than can even a financial newspaper. Futuristic comment, however, is in even shorter and poorer supply on the screen than off. Screen service editors do not have budgets for commissioning wide- ranging well-researched pieces speculating on possible long-term futures. The ideal medium for such a piece, anyhow, is not a screen-service whose audience is mainly market traders and whose output is obliterated (wiped off the screen) after at most 24 hours.

In principle, news editors in Canada should have been in a different situation from their counterparts outside. Canadians would surely not be bored with their own future. The opportunity cost in the form of squeezed-out alternative stories should have been less (than in the case of the foreign press). Investors in Europe or Japan, for example, with a keen interest in the future of the Canadian dollar might have turned for enlightenment to the Canadian media. But even here they would have been disappointed. The uncertainties were presumably too great for editors to believe that a well-researched (asking a variety of experts for their views), high budget, futuristic story about a possible nationalist threat to the Canadian dollar in two years' time would carry conviction amongst their readership or improve their circulation.

GAINING ENTRY TO THE CASTLE

Whereas news media editors and economists have markedly different levels of enthusiasm for speculation about the medium and long term they are both keen to find out what is really going on inside the Castle of Power. Usually the editor is in the position of producer of such information, and the economist as consumer – but as we shall see the roles are sometimes reversed. As producer, the editor is sometimes passive. He/she simply relays official announcements and excerpts from speeches.

In active mode, the editor could set up interviews with key officials (including politicians) inside the Castle. 'The interview', though an important technique for gaining entry, has severe limits. The key official might not agree to the interview or he might cite a strict time limit. The interviewer might not have enough command of his subject to be able to cross-examine the official effectively. On the other hand, if a specialist interviewer becomes too technical or aggressive, he/she risks losing the interest and sympathy of an audience (readers or listeners) – and might well lose the chance of the same official or other key officials agreeing to be interviewed by him/her in the future.

The press conference is perhaps even a more precarious route into the Castle than the direct interview. The official taking the conference has virtually complete discretion as regards who to take questions from and whether to permit a follow-up question. The investigative journalist at a news conference is out of place – sure to be unpopular with his/her fellows for 'hogging the floor' and in general unsuccessful in getting to his/her end. (English-speaking journalists complain that they are at a disadvantage at Bundesbank press conferences because in German the verb comes at the end of the sentence, which gives them insufficient time to formulate a follow-up question!)

If the only ways into the Castle were indeed guided tours in the form of press briefings, conferences, polite staged interviews to friendly journalists, speeches, and official communiqués, then investors would be largely in the dark about what was 'really going on' in the policy-making process. None the less, there would be a strong demand for such news items, such as when Soviet citizens lined the streets to buy *Pravda*. But the market would be trading on informed misinformation. Some officials in the Castle might regard themselves as liberal and benign, following policies of full disclosure. But reality is likely to be otherwise.

The Bundesbank is a good example of a public agency with huge power, where accountability is limited strictly to the channels listed above. Bundesbank officials follow an open disclosure policy of frequent speeches, comprehensive monthly reports setting out their collective assessment of the economic and financial background to policy and justification for new steps taken, regular press conferences, and 'availability' for newspaper and radio interviews.

But meetings of the policy-making council of the Bundesbank occur in strict secrecy. Only concisely edited minutes of these meetings are taken. Thirty years must elapse before the minutes become available to the public. Bundesbank council members do not have to cope with gruelling questions from any parliamentary body. No Freedom of Information Act applies whereby academic critics and economic journalists could sift through the record – either recent or further distant – and examine Bundesbank efficiency in setting monetary policy.

If, by contrast, there were full disclosure of Bundesbank policy-making, then both economic journalists and market economists could investigate such questions as how did the Bundesbank fail to raise its key lending rates for almost a year following the announcement of monetary union between East and West Germany in February 1990. Had such action been taken, this might have saved the West German economy from a spell of serious overheating and a subsequent recession.

The interests of economic journalists and market economists in pursuing such a story might well diverge. Journalists could see themselves as fulfilling the highest calling of their profession – the defence of a liberal order by exposing the incompetence of the authorities and thereby making these accountable. The threat of accountability should improve the standard of performance of the various government agencies, including the central bank. Market economists are interested in predicting how a given set of public officials – for example, the monetary policy-making committee at the central bank – might act in the future. Sifting through the record of past decisions and how these were made might improve their predictive power. Of course, journalists, in satisfying their own calling, can produce articles which are of considerable interest to market economists.

In democratic countries where there is no tradition of open government – that is, in particular, freedom of information legislation – the ways into the Castle for the journalist, other than on official excursions as already described, are largely blocked, except for two possibilities. The first involves joining in searches undertaken by the legislative branch of government (parliamentary or legislative committees demanding information from the executive branch). The second way is the obtaining of leaks – disenchanted bureaucrats or Cabinet Ministers disclosing information which is meant to be secret.

Market economists in their pursuit of 'fair value' can find other routes into the Castle. They can make direct contact with officials in the Castle, and in private conversation these are often more forthcoming than in interviews with the Press. Certainly it would be rare for any inside information to be slipped their way, but the economist can gain a sense of the personalities involved, 'what makes them tick', and how they might act in future situations.

For example, economists might discover from their visits to the Federal Reserve in Washington that there are two or three favourite cyclical indicators followed by senior policy-making officials. They might also sense that the Chairman (of the Federal Reserve) has a 'hang-up' about the budget deficit – meaning that he/she considers changes in the long-run stance of fiscal policy as an important factor when determining the optimum monetary course to follow. Similarly the economist who makes a journey every six months to the Bundesbank, meeting a range of high-up officials there, could form a view on their likely range of responses to new problems as they arise and their commitment to any particular theoretical approach.

Some market economists seek to gain a reputation for having the inside story (including some psychological 'titbits' such as the Federal Reserve Chairman being anxious to maintain his/her self-respect as a top-rate academic economist and so being influenced strongly by the two academic members of the key policy-making council – not going against their opinion if he/she has no intellectually respectable counter-case to make), developing a network of contacts in Washington, Frankfurt, and Tokyo say, who are near to or at the centre of key policy-making decisions. What do the senior officials gain from entering into the dialogue? The explanations are diverse but may be no more complicated than enjoyment of conversations free of internal political rivalries with a stimulating economist who might have some insights into market behaviour which could not be gained in the central bank's ivory tower. Most central banks have a policy of being open to market experts coming in for discussions on a similar basis to a publicly quoted corporation being ready to talk to equity analysts. Closing the doors to market commentators might well leave the currency more exposed to floating rumours about the policy agenda which have no basis in fact.

We must, however, maintain two reservations about how reliable a route the private expert can find into the Castle. First experts must not only exercise some charm, but hide critical intent. If they started to ask brutal questions towards exploring the extent of incompetence they would find the door slammed shut in their faces. Second, if they eventually get to the end of the path, would their efforts have been worth while? Remember poor Josef K in Kafka's *The Trial* who having made strenuous efforts to find out who are his judges and what is in their volumes of notes eventually obtains his objective by seducing the wife of the Court Usher. K takes the old dog-eared volumes. The cover of one is almost completely split down the middle. The two halves are held together by mere threads. 'How dirty everything is here,' says K, shaking his head. He opens the first of them and finds an indecent picture. K glances at the second book – a novel entitled *How Crete was Plagued by her Husband*. K says, 'These are the law books that are studied here. These are the men who are supposed to sit in judgement on me.'

Economists advising investors on market strategy might well do better operating outside the Castle, studying forces which are larger than the policy-makers, rather than exploring within. An example illustrates the point. The economist who is skilled in monetary analysis might form a view that the Federal Reserve is making a big error in monetary policy – for example, being lulled by some weakness in presently available US economic indicators into underestimating inflation risks. The economist might point to a bigger picture of the economy operating virtually at full stretch despite the latest blip, and argue that a still rapid money supply and credit growth herald inflation danger which is maybe only six months away.

If the economist's suspicions are correct, then an 'inflation shock' will eventually bring a big rise in interest rates. He/she would caution clients about the overvaluation of bond and equity markets. His/her advice may be of less immediate relevance to market movements than the newsletter from economist B summarizing the latest findings in Washington as to whether a majority might be forming on the Federal Reserve's Open Market Committee in favour of a slight cut in the key overnight interest rate (Fed funds rate). But for investors keen to profit from the next big move, economist A's warnings are likely to carry more weight.

In keeping his distance from the Castle, economist A should not shut his/her eyes and ears to information about what is going on there. Rather, it is a question of emphasis. His/her hypothesis (in the example above) about inflation error is sturdier if he/she has some knowledge of the Federal Reserve's present method of reaching key decisions on monetary policy. Economist A should have an answer to the question of how so many skilled people on the Federal Reserve Open Market Committee (FOMC) could be making a major error in policy. He/she should also seek to assess how quickly they would change course as the error reveals itself. Nor can the economist ignore the fact of life that a travel tale about his/her most recent visit inside the Castle is an easy way of entertaining clients – and the traders or salesmen with whom he/she works.

If on his travels the economist gains a working knowledge of 'Castle-speak', he/she could find himself/herself in a good position to speculate on possible shifts in government policy already underway but not yet declared. Most dramatically, in a currency crisis all market participants realize that official statements of support are automatic, but may lack total substance. The trained crisis-analyst looks for what is not said.

For example, in the run-up to the ERM shake-up of 31 July 1993 (when the band of permitted fluctuation for the key FF/DM rate was widened to 15 per cent from 2.25 per cent), the French Prime Minister threatened to resign 'if the parity is changed' (but, of course, the parity could remain unchanged, and an effective deval-uation occur via a widening of the bands). From the Chancellor's office in Bonn came the statement 'we want France to stay in ERM' (but within what band and at what price?). And then from M. Chirac, the head of the Gaullist Party (the bigger partner in the French Coalition government), 'I am behind the policies to defend the franc' (but in terms of what, and did he mean the external or internal value of the currency? – important reservations given reports earlier in the crisis that he was pressing the government to change policy and reflate unilaterally).

Note that 'translations' of official statements are not generally to be found in the media. Financial journalists and their news editors assume in general that market-participants make their own assess-ments of the official spoken word, and, indeed, at certain stages might disregard them altogether. It would be insulting to readers and wasteful of space on the front page to carry a warning of likely official intent to mislead. Moreover, the journalist cannot usually underline the possible guile in official statements without appear-ing to enter the policy debate – an entry which is restricted to the editorial page in the high-quality financial press.

ECONOMISTS VERSUS JOURNALISTS

Enough has been said to realize that the economist who simply passed on a distillation of comments from his daily reading of the news media would have grave shortcomings as an investment adviser. Clients are looking to the economist to appraise the general level of prices in a market, and information coming from the press is only one element in the appraisal. That is not to belittle the importance of the information. The economist who is able to scan the main stories each morning in the German, US, French, Swiss, and Japanese financial press, and to speed through the screen-based reports for each of the major markets, is off to a good start. But information must also be drawn from other sources – in particular the vast array of financial and economic data released by national and supranational official statistics offices.

Beyond information gathering, the market economist must func-tion as a scenario builder. In our previous example of the Canadian general election of autumn 1993, the economist-analyst of the Canadian markets should have been reviewing scenarios of the political outlook stretching through and beyond a possible referendum on Quebec's independence two years ahead – well before newspaper editors did this in a limited fashion several days ahead of the poll. Canada provides a further case-study just two years later (autumn 1995) for the difference between the financial or economic journalist on the one hand and the market economist on the other. After the victory of the PQ (Quebec nationalists) in the provincial elections (autumn 1994) it was virtually certain that a referendum on independence would be held within a year. Well before the eventual date (30 October 1995) was fixed (for the referendum) the market economist should have developed scenarios from answers to a range of speculative questions.

For example, if indeed the nationalists won the referendum (in which the Quebeckers were asked to approve a declaration of sovereignty 'linked' to the Quebec government committing itself first to negotiate a new economic and political association with the rest of Canada), how would the Federal government respond? Would Ottawa call a nation-wide referendum in which citizens were asked whether they wished to give it (the Federal government) a mandate to negotiate a political and economic union with Quebec, subject to a prior understanding with the provincial governments and constitutional experts as to the minimum requirements for approval (a 'yes' majority overall and in at least two-thirds of the provinces)? In the perhaps likely event of the answer in the referendum being 'no', would the Federal government then hold its own referendum in Quebec, asking a straight question 'do you want to separate from Canada?', in place of the confusing one originally posed by the Quebec nationalists?

In spelling out that monetary and economic union was a fantasy, and pointing to the interim heavy costs of political uncertainty, could the Federal government hope to win this subsequent referendum? Or could the Quebec government prevent it being held? If indeed Quebec proceeded to full independence with no economic and monetary union with the rest of Canada and no immediate or early entry to the North American Free Trade Area, what would be the economic and political outlook for Quebec and the rest of Canada? What would be the implications for the Canadian dollar, bond and equity markets? In particular, would any agreement between Quebec and the rest of Canada about dividing the burden of outstanding Federal government debt at the point of separation mean that its credit risk would increase substantially? (The big credit-rating agencies, who were presumably ready to put Canada on alert for a potential downgrade if the referendum went in favour of separation, published no treatises on the risks ahead of the referendum.) Could an economic boom occur in the rest of Canada as skilled labour and capital fled westwards (into Ontario and the Western provinces) from Quebec?

The range of illustrative questions posed above is just a sub-set of the total which the market economist should have considered in his scenario-mapping ahead of the Quebec referendum on independence. From the sheer number of questions and the highly speculative content of the answers we can understand why newspaper editors did not see it as their role to compete with the market economist in the exercise. (In fact, the *Financial Times* in its 'Global Investor' column of Monday, 30 October 1995, highlighted a few of the questions relevant to determining the course of the Canadian markets should there be a yes vote in the referendum to be held that day.) We can also understand why so few market analysts attempted to exercise fully their probabilistic vision. In the event, the nationalists failed by a tiny margin to win the referendum. But the tightness of the result confirmed how real the threat had been and how justified market economists, if not economic journalists, would have been in putting effort into scenario-building during the months before.

Even so, economic journalists and market economists overlap in their function. And the extent of their common interest draws them into communication. Journalists swap 'inside stories' and other people's comments for insights from market economists and ideas for articles. Sometimes there is a wider deal, usually implicit rather than explicit. The market economist gives a rundown on how he/she analyses a given market or economic 'situation' to the journalist, who in return 'endeavors' to mention the economist's name as the source of comment. The economist cannot be expected to get a mention every time he/she passes comment to the journalist writing a column. If unlucky this time, the economist would expect 'compensation' (an especially good quote) in a future article. Thus there is a simple exchange of information and analysis for self-advertisement.

Occasionally the specialist economic journalist strays into the area of market strategy – writing a piece which analyses long-run prospects and risks for a market and even giving some investment advice. Sometimes a market economist might write a general economics piece with no investment implications for the editorial page in the financial press. But these cross-overs of function are limited by the micro-economics of reward. The market economist's financial reward in the long-run is related to his/her reputation for making good calls on market direction (alerting investors to situations of substantial valuation or overvaluation for a particular asset class). Elegant provocative articles can bolster and promote a reputation as a good market economist, but they cannot make it.

By contrast, the economic editorialist 'lives' largely by writing skill. To be successful, he/she must become a master at writing 750- to 1,000-word articles with catchy beginnings and ends which are readily comprehensible and of interest to a wide readership (not just five key client fund managers). He/she must have an ear for gossip (especially from inside the Castle). Even highly serious readers of a taxing editorial welcome a midway breather. Economic journalists know that an easy 'high-brow' story which excites human interest is conflict between key officials. A difference in view between Federal Reserve Chairman Alan Greenspan and Deputy Chairman Alan Blinder about whether or how far monetary policy should be eased made front-page news off and on through-out 1995. Yet insiders insist that the difference was totally exaggerated. But the image of the two 'Alans' in conflict – the Chairman pitted against his professorial Deputy from Princeton University – was too good to suppress, even if not wholly factual. The technique of highlighting a conflict of views and, between well-known personalities, extends also to the 'hard core' section of the economics editorial.

Economics editorialists who make strong personal pronounce-ments on the optimum policy (in contrast to passing on the opinion of well-known economists) or the best investment strategy (rather than relaying the experts' views) are following a dangerous road to furthering their own reputation. They will 'turn off' readers who disagree with the policy and, if indeed it proves wrong, their own reputations will suffer (for example in the UK, economic editorialists who supported the government's decision in autumn 1990 to put the pound into the European fixed-exchange rate system (the ERM) lost the respect of their readership in the débâcle which ensued). The editorialist, unlike the market economist, does not enjoy the flexibility of opinion expression which frequent and sometimes direct communication allows. The strategist will doubtless on occa-sion make a faulty analysis of the market outlook – but can correct this in a continuous fashion in the course of regular discussions with clients. He/she is not the hostage of one written piece.

NEWS AS MARKET CATALYST

The interest of market-participants, including market economists, in news reports does not just stem from their possible information content. A seemingly trivial item of news can sometimes act as a catalyst to a big change in market prices. Analysts must seek to develop a sense for recognizing periods of high risk in the market-place when an avalanche might occur. They should be on guard for certain types of normally innocuous information which could set the process off.

Let us look at some historical examples of the market catalysts. One of the oldest is the Wall Street Crash of October 1929. The US historian Jude Warniski has sought to explain the exact timing of the Crash in terms of a news report about US Senate action the day before which only hit the inside pages of the daily press. Specifically, forces in the Senate resisting an increase in the tariff on carbides were defeated. Warniski suggests that the defeat was the writing on the wall for world trade. Only nine months later the Hawley–Smoot tariff bill made its way through Congress and was signed into law by President Hoover. The tariff ushered in the disastrous trade wars of the 1930s.

Many contemporary analysts saw the trigger to the next Great Crash in October 1987 as the failure of the Bundesbank at two successive bi-weekly Council Meetings to cut its discount rate, despite evident pressure from the US Administration to do so. Whereas the US economy had clearly emerged from the growth recession of 1985–6, the German economy was still sluggish. 'Tight' German money was seen as contributing to the weakness of the dollar, which was in turn undermining the US bond market. And equity yields were already at 'dangerously' low levels relative to bond yields.

Currency 'crashes' have occurred both under fixed and floating exchange rate regimes. One of the big floating rate crashes was that of the Deutschmark against the US dollar in spring 1991. In just six weeks the Deutschmark fell by around 20 per cent against the dollar. The catalyst was a remark in a speech by Otto Pöhl, President of the Bundesbank, to the effect that German Monetary Union (1 July 1990) had been a disaster. The comment was taken out of context from a lengthy speech on European Monetary Union (EMU). But the confession by the Bundesbank President of a ghastly mistake in German monetary management (albeit that Bonn, not the Bundesbank, was the culprit) touched many raw nerves.

The Deutschmark crash of spring 1991 provides some useful insights into the role played by the 'catalytic event'. Already before Pöhl spoke, many market-participants had registered questions in the pre-decision stage of their consciousness about whether Germany's reputation for excellent monetary management was any longer deserved. Meanwhile, talk of a new *Pax Americana* following the victory of the US-led coalition against Iraq made some investors feel more positive towards the dollar. Bullish sentiment was also stirred by evidence of the US economy emerging from recession. Pöhl's remarks were enough to trigger decisive action by many of the 'troubled' investors. Yes, they concluded, the time had come to lighten the weight of Deutschmarks in their portfolios. The German currency no longer deserved a premium rating for monetary excellence. Other market-participants, alarmed by the new fall of the Deutschmark, came to feel that their own doubts about German monetary management were justified. They gained confidence in their own view by seeing that others share it – the demonstration coming from the Deutschmark's slide.

We can generalize the operation of the catalyst in the above example. A catalyst depends on there already having been a shift in investors' confidence in the overall valuation of a market, but not yet of sufficient extent to have triggered significant portfolio action. The implicit assumption is that investors do not change the desired weights of different assets in their portfolios continuously in response to each small change in their perception of the future. Rather, the shift in perception must be of sufficient force to hit a trigger point that swings investors into action. Moreover, the investors' perceptions of the future, and the degree of confidence they have in the probability weights attached to future possible scenarios, are influenced by the 'group'. If market movements indicate that other investors are sharing their concerns, and forming similar views, then they are more confident than if they were standing alone. Even investors of unusual boldness begin to question their own analyses if the market is stampeding in a direction opposite to what they predict (have they omitted to consider one key scenario?).

'Catalytic' events can take a number of forms. A colourful news item can help stabilize a shift in investor perception. Pöhl's warning on unification is such an example. A big corporation going into bankruptcy might be the catalyst which drives investors into action as they respond to a growing likelihood that the US economy has

41

slipped into recession. A sudden cancelling of a meeting by the German Finance Minister with his French counterpart turns investor unease about deteriorating Franco-German relations into hedging action – get out of the French franc now in case the franc is soon floated. A shock economic statistic can be the final straw which causes investors to switch their central scenario. For example, a sudden widening of the monthly US trade deficit to $15 bn from $10 bn, or a sudden jump in the monthly employment report, might bring a big change in market prices – much more than could be justified strictly in terms of the significance of one piece of monthly data.

Sometimes a clumsy statement by a key official can send investors rushing for the exit if their worst fears seem to be confirmed. Thus in spring 1995 a report in a Japanese news service that a Federal Reserve Governor (also a member of the FOMC) had said the yen was not yet at a critical (high) level sent the dollar plummeting – a fall which ended with the yen/dollar rate below 80 in April 1995 compared to 100 at the start of that year. The Governor's remarks confirmed the worst suspicions of Japanese investors that the Federal Reserve was in league with the US Administration in seeking to push the dollar down (via loose monetary policy) as a way of putting maximum pressure on Tokyo to reach a deal on measures to lower barriers to US imports.

Sometimes the catalyst can be a shift in market-price itself. Over a period of time many investors may have moved into a 'pre-decision' stage of doubt about the basis of present market levels. For example, during several months many investors may have become less sure of a consensus hypothesis that US economic recovery will remain slow and inflation 'dead' – but not doubtful enough to have altered their central scenario or to have lightened up on their holding of US Treasury-bonds.

Then, over a period of several days only, a sharp set-back takes place in the US Treasury bond market for no apparent immediate cause. Perhaps there was initially a big sell order from a weighty institutional investor. Then several stop-loss orders are triggered in the futures pits, the technical picture begins to look bad, and this triggers short-term traders into action. Longer-term investors, already in an unconfident mood, are not disposed to come in and buy, even though prices are below previously perceived equilibrium levels. In effect, the structure of Treasury bond prices over the summer months had become like Humpty Dumpty – once knocked over by whatever chance event there would be no bounce-back. Investors perceiving the lack of bounce-back obtain confirmation that many others in the marketplace share their lack of confidence in the consensus central scenario. They become emboldened in their own doubt. Some shift their central case and act. The initial price decline develops into a slide.

If, in the above example, the initial price decline in the Treasury-bond market had been readily attributable to a specific news event which carried no new information relevant to investors' chief concern (was inflation really dead?), it might not have acted as a catalyst to a further slide, even though the risk of avalanche was already substantial. An illustration of how a price move based on specific non-related news might fail to be a market catalyst can be drawn from an episode in early autumn 1993. The dollar rose abruptly on news of President Yeltsin's showdown with Parliament, raising the prospect of a civil war in Russia. Investors could not deduce from the sudden swing in the exchange rate that many other market-participants shared their view about the dollar being undervalued and that some of these had at last gathered the courage to act. Indeed when President Yeltsin successfully asserted his authority, the dollar fell back to its previous level against the mark. Market commentators who had heralded the dollar's rise as the catalyst to an immediate big rally were proved wrong, even though they were right in detecting a 'ripe mood' amongst investors for such a move (which occurred eventually in winter 1993/4).

OVERPRODUCTION OF NEWS

Some critics point to 'market failure' in information use leading to an excess production of certain types of news and excess invest-ment in its instant transmission across the globe. Yet wide areas of news production are no more advanced than they were fifty to seventy-five years ago.

For example, a wide array of economic indicators are now broad-cast across screen-based information networks in dealing rooms throughout the world within instants of their release. Yet the data is no more reliable and in many cases less so than decades ago. The lag between a change in economic reality and its reflection in data is at best several months. What difference does it make to economic well-being that the data, much of which will be subsequently revised, is available within instants rather than hours of its release? Indeed, the huge investments in instant information communication could be seen as a cost of market functioning rather than a benefit. Individual dealers couldn't survive as active market-makers if they did not have access to the latest in information technology (otherwise they would find themselves leaning against the wind at huge expense in the seconds following release time, as those 'in the know' took advantage of stale quotations).

Huge investment in instant news communication has made it more difficult for 'insiders' to gain from macro-economic or political information. Once upon a time the US brokerage with a messenger at the door of the Department of Commerce in Washington could make some profit from releases at the expense of less well-placed investors – the counterpart of the agricultural commodities trader in Kansas City being at an advantage to the New York speculator in knowing current weather in the most important crop-producing area. And outsiders would have to include in their dealing costs some allowance for a running loss to insiders. But these inside profits now eliminated surely pale in comparison with the investment in instant news transmission.

None of this means that free-functioning markets are wasteful. Rather, the simple hypothesis is being made that instant communication of information and instant comment are costly but inescapable trappings of international financial markets. Investment in communication occurs up to the point at which no trader can expect to make profit from having the information sooner than another. The trader might still hope to gain if the economist sitting near to his/her desk can come to a snap and well-considered judgement about the significance of the data for market prices sooner than competitors in other organizations. If he/she does not have immediate privileged access to a sound economic viewpoint, and is not skilled in data analysis, the trader might hope that his/her knee-jerk reactions to new information (measured by changes in his/her two-way price quotation) will at least avoid loss on average around data release time.

We can describe a market equilibrium in which traders able to take quick well-informed views, and with a good sense of how far to back these by action, tend to make profit from the 'release process' even taking account of input costs (including technology and cost of advice). Another group of traders, with less good advice or none to hand, tends to break even or perhaps make modest loss in the immediate aftermath of new information, but with the total drain being less than the cost of enhancing the information technology used and improving their economic input.

A third group of traders simply withdraws from the market around data-release time (or when other important pieces of information are broadcast) until a new equilibrium is reached. The last option, however, is not available to any trader or trading house with the ambition of being seen as a serious market-maker, who by definition must maintain a two-way price at all times through the trading day. And often large fund-managers prefer to deal in the immediate aftermath of important data releases, because the risk of being proved wrong 'with a bang' has lessened. A dealer not available to quote with commitment then would not be in the running for fund management and many other types of business.

Dealers, in judging how to adjust their quotes in the light of new information, or on how to position themselves ahead of the scheduled release of key data, must assess what is already discounted in the market. They might quickly conclude that US GDP data just released is quite positive evidence for the 'recovery story'. But is it more or less positive than what was already built into market expectations? In the case of economic data releases several screen-based news services give so-called 'consensus' estimates several days in advance. These are simple averages of estimates supplied by a sample of economists at various banks and brokerage houses. They are sometimes far from reliable guides to what average expectations are of the major players, as illustrated by the failure of a big gap between the released data and the so-called consensus to trigger any significant market response.

For some types of political information, an advance consensus can be identified. The most important example is elections. In the weeks and days ahead of the election, a daily or weekly average of opinion polls can serve as an indicator of average expectation in the marketplace as to the result. Given the likelihood of wide fluctuation in popular mood during the election campaign, it is the polls on the eve of voting which carry most weight. The dealer (or speculator) taking a position ahead of the election must first assess whether the market accepts the latest 'average of polls' as the best predictor of the result, or if there is a consensus view that a bias exists. Second, the dealer must estimate the market significance of the potential political change.

Take the example of Switzerland's referendum in December 1992 about whether to join the proposed European Economic Area (a union of the EC and EFTA countries). In the days ahead of the referendum, polls suggested that opinion was about evenly split, meaning that the outcome was unpredictable. The consensus view according to market reports (summarized on screen-based services) was that a rejection of the EEA would spell economic isolation for Switzerland and that its growth prospects would suffer over the long-run. That could be bad news for the Swiss franc.

But when the result came, a 'no' to the EEA, the Swiss franc rose sharply. Clearly the dominant view amongst short-term traders in the Swiss franc was different from the media consensus – they saw a rejection as positive (for the currency). Important arguments in favour of that conclusion were the threat to bank secrecy in Switzerland from EEA membership, meaning the franc could lose some of its safe-haven status, plus the burden of huge transfers to the EC budget which the Swiss economy might eventually have had to bear.

A more dramatic example of markets failing to respond as widely expected to a particular result of a referendum which was too close to call in the days before comes from the Canadian dollar in autumn 1995. The modest fall of the Canadian dollar in the days before the 30 October referendum on Quebec independence, despite opinion polls swinging from the prediction of a clear win for the pro-unity slide to a razor-edge win for the separatists (statistically insignificant), suggested that market-participants did not believe the polls (some respondents saying 'yes' to the pollster might be less bold when it came to the secrecy of the polling booth).

Another type of political information to hit markets is a change in central bank leadership. As illustration, in late 1993 the Canadian dollar came under some downward pressure on speculation that the new Liberal government would sack the Governor of the Central Bank, John Crow, who had been the architect of the tough anti-inflation policy followed in recent years, but who had antagonized several key Liberal politicians when in opposition. A survey of economists and dealers taken in mid-December showed that his chances of being reappointed (in January 1994) were rated at around 50 per cent.

When the announcement came on 22 December 1993 that Mr Crow had resigned and been replaced by his deputy, Gordon Thiessen, the Canadian dollar rose immediately by almost 1 per cent. Clearly the prevailing view in the Press that any change would undermine confidence in the currency was wrong. The reaffirmation of unchanged aims for monetary policy by the new governor and Finance Minister at a joint press conference, plus Thiessen's own reputation as an anti-inflation hawk, did the trick.

The behaviour of the Canadian dollar described could have been due to fears before the announcement that a bigger change in policy leadership was in store – for example, the appointment of an academic monetary economist less renowned for anti-inflation dogma. The eclipsing of that possibility was worth more to the Canadian dollar on the upside than any slight risk from the promotion of the Deputy Governor on the downside.

Hardened by long experience of market prices sometimes not responding to news as they were meant to, many dealers and short-term traders are understandably reluctant to pre-empt outsiders (who are slower acting) by taking large positions. Rather, they prefer to take their cue from early evidence of market response – following the trend rather than leading it. Hence we have the occasionally observed phenomenon of transitory market-price paralysis in response to dramatic political events. One of the most striking examples of this phenomenon was the response of currency markets to the German invasion of Czechoslovakia in March 1939. It was not until two days following the entry of German troops into the truncated Czechoslovakia that a wave of capital outflow from Europe to the USA became evident, and the Swiss franc, as the currency of a small neutral country now itself under threat, fell sharply.

How can we explain the lack of an immediate rise in the value of the dollar as a knee-jerk reaction to the invasion? Perhaps traders assumed at first that the news, albeit dramatic, was already discounted. Had not a German invasion been inevitable for several months? The initial euphoric response of markets to the sell-out of Czechoslovakia at Munich the previous October (when Britain and France had prevailed on the Czechoslovak government to cede the Sudetenland to Germany in order to buy 'peace with honour') had long since given way to a new sober mood. And truncated Czechoslovakia had already become an economic satellite and puppet of the Third Reich. Did the entry of troops really add to German power? And the absence of immediate strong protest from the Western powers suggested they were sticking with the policy of appeasement. Market paralysis was broken by direct evidence that investors had indeed decided to flee Europe and by the eventual reaction of the British government which suggested that the policy of appeasement was being discarded. The risk of early war between Britain and France on the one hand and Germany on the other had increased sharply.

A less dramatic contemporary example of market paralysis in the face of a political shock is the immediate aftermath of the Russian elections in December 1993. The emergence of the ultranationalist 'Liberal Democrats' as the largest party had not been predicted and could have serious implication for future security, not just of the ex-satellite nations of the Soviet Union. In principle, a new, albeit far-distant threat to international peace from Russia should have added a safety premium to the valuation of the dollar. But dealers and short-term traders were reluctant to pre-empt market movement in this case. Many had lost vast sums during the previous Russian domestic political crisis of September 1993, when President Yeltsin confronted the Parliament (a sharp rise of the dollar was reversed when forces loyal to Yeltsin took control of the Parliament building). Many had concluded it was safest not to respond to Russian events except as driven to do so by a flow of customer orders (in the case of market-makers).

A delayed reaction to the Russian election outcome was evident in the marketplace after two to three days. The dollar rose and German bonds were sold. The catalyst to the price change was a news service reporting a comment by the ultranationalist leader Zhirinovsky that he would use nuclear arms against Germany (once he became President – the next Presidential election being due by 1996) if that country continued to meddle in Russia's affairs.

It seemed as if many market traders had come round to the view that with the Cold War over, Russia was just another large Third World country and events there were no longer of great global significance. The paucity of coverage in the international press about how the Soviet Union was unscrambling suggested that many newspaper editors were of the same view – or at least believed that interest amongst their general readership in the process was quite limited. The reader of the Western Press had as little information about life in the Successor States of the Soviet Empire in the years following its dissolution as about existence in the Successor States of the Austria-Hungarian Empires in the years following the First World War.

3

WHERE THE LONG-RUN AND SHORT-RUN MEET

Perhaps Joseph was the first long-term speculator. He interpreted Pharaoh's dream of seven fat cows being eaten up by seven lean cows to mean that Egypt would enjoy seven years of plentiful harvests followed by seven years of famine. Accordingly he advised Pharaoh to build warehouses and store grain in the years of plenty. Joseph was put in charge of the enterprise.

Economists cannot expect to enjoy the divine insight of Joseph. Even so the biblical story is a beacon. The economist or investor should not ignore the power of the dream, sometimes recounted by contemporary artists, to unlock the mysteries of the future. The much-quoted tawdry truism – 'in the long-run we are all dead'– is not a serious competitor to Joseph's dream. Keynes, who popularized the truism, viewed financial markets as casinos, where the long-run has hardly any bearing.

It is too simplistic to dismiss markets as myopic even if the evidence of huge resources devoted to 'sports like' commentary about immediate happenings makes a strong case for the prosecution. But there are strong counter-arguments. Less is known about the long-run than short-run, so it is hardly surprising that the short-run receives a larger weight in the valuation process. Yet there are many examples of assets for which the long-run economic and political outlook are crucial determinants of price. And occasionally, especially during episodes which are subsequently described as bubbles, market error seems to be attributable to an excessive and uncritical focus on a dubious hypothesis about the long-run rather than to myopia.

FRAGILE LONG-RUN PERCEPTIONS

Most investors or economists if asked for their central case long-run macro-economic view would express this in terms of a specific prediction say for year one, year two, and year three, followed by a trend forecast in which individual years are not differentiated. For example, the economist might predict US growth at 2.5 per cent this year, 3.5 per cent next year, and 3 per cent per annum thereafter. Real earnings growth (for corporations) seen from an early stage in a business cycle upswing might be put at 20 per cent, 10 per cent, and then 3 per cent p.a. (in line with GDP).

An example of investment action based on a long-run view would be of portfolio managers deciding to underweight or over-weight a particular asset class in their portfolios out of a disagreement with the implicit market view on the macro-economic path from year two onwards. Of course they would hope not to have to wait for the arrival of the long-run to make their profit from long-term speculation. It would be much better if the predominant market view came round to their own, say within six months.

As an illustration, take equity market valuations as at end-1993. The German market stood out then as the most highly valued (excluding Japan) on the basis of conventional criteria. Even assuming 50 per cent earnings growth over the next twelve months, as shown by surveys of analysts to be the average expectations for 1994, the prospective earnings yield would climb to only 4.5 per cent compared to a present real yield on bonds of 3 per cent. But many analysts were talking about another 50 per cent cumulative growth of earnings over the subsequent two years (1995–6) as the German economic recovery moved into higher gear and big corporations shook off excess fat.

Corporate restructuring was the buzz-word, with US experience through 1990–3 taken as the example. Long-term speculative investors might have dared to take a position against the consensus – not because they disagreed with the likelihood of a profits rebound in 1994, but out of scepticism concerning the growth rates estimates (for earnings) with respect to both 1994 and 1995–6. If, indeed, profits growth recorded in 1994 were somewhat disappointing, then the consensus view about 1995–6 would change.

It is the operation of such investors that makes market prices sensitive to long-term views. But rarely are shifts in the 'average' perception of the long term the dominant influence on changes in market prices measured over periods of, say, one week or one month. Investors act (underweighting or overweighting a particular asset class relative to a neutral position in their portfolio) on the basis of a long-term hypothesis usually only when their valuations based on fundamentals are far away from current market levels. There is a wide band within which the market-price can move under short-term trading influences without much long-term investor action being triggered. The area within that band could be called a speculative desert with respect to long-run views.

We must admit that even in the new bold age of rational expectations views about the long-run are sensitive to short-term price behaviour. The long-term investor who believes that the equity market has taken off into a fantasy world needs strong 'independence of mind' to maintain that position if the raging bull market continues. He or she might be persuaded by the bull-run to question his/her own previous analysis and rationalize what is occurring in the marketplace.

It would be wrong to criticize all conversions of view undergone by analysts of the long-term future. Sometimes the market acts as a jolt to a constructive remodelling of reality. For example as the dollar continued to rise inexorably through 1983 and 1984, many economists (and investors) came to put much greater weight than previously on the importance of capital flow analysis in the understanding of exchange rate determination. Correspondingly their emphasis on the current account of the balance of payments (and on the contemporary huge US current account deficit) diminished. They also woke up to the importance of Japan's huge savings surplus in international capital markets. These new considerations could justify the dollar being at a level well above the equilibrium range consistent with 'conventional wisdom'.

Thus it would be wrong to characterize at least the early stages of the great dollar bull-run of 1982–5 as a bubble where long-run investors decided simply to join the party and ignore any concept of equilibrium value. Rather, long-run investors changed their view in a rational manner, albeit that the trigger to change was the behaviour of the market-price. The experience illustrates that 'market runs' are not in themselves evidence of 'inefficiency' – as some economists have maintained. This does not mean that the dollar bull-run remained a wholly rational phenomenon – the possibility of a bubble finally emerging in late 1984 and early 1985 is one to which we return.

Coming to a bubble verdict with respect to any particular episode of market history is extremely difficult, even with the benefit of considerable hindsight and accumulated evidence from market-participants. Yes historians may strongly suspect a bubble, but they might well fail to find proof 'beyond reasonable doubt'. For example, still in late 1995 it was not possible to conclude that the great bull-run in US bonds from fourth-quarter 1992 to third-quarter 1993 ended in a bubble rather than remaining well founded on a continuing rational adaptation of long-term views about inflation, albeit triggered in part by the contemporary strength of the (bond) market. The case for a bubble verdict turns on piecing together much of the accompanying market commentary. There was no new insight into the inflationary process to justify the view that long-run risks had decreased. Why could central bankers not make mistakes in an inflationary direction in the future? Much of the bullish commentary on bonds seemed to ignore the monetary roots of inflation and instead emphasize a variety of real factors (competition from the developing countries, slack product and labour markets globally).

It is indeed in the bond markets that long-term speculation can be most explicitly monitored. From a yield curve stretching from say, one-year to ten-year maturities, a term structure of one-year interest rates can be calculated with the aid of a computer (see Chapter 1, pp. 16–17). For example, in midsummer 1993, the dollar swap yield curve stretched from 3.81 per cent at one-year to 6.1 per cent at ten-year maturities. That was consistent with a term structure of one-year rates rising from 3.81 (now), to 4.81 in August 1994, and then successively to 5.72 per cent (August 1995), 6.32 per cent, 6.75 per cent, 6.83 per cent, 7.06 per cent, 7.17 per cent, 7.5 per cent, 7.9 per cent (August 2002).

A long-term speculator might have taken the view that the implicit one-year rates for the period 1998–2002 were far below what would probably be quoted spot at the time. Perhaps he/she did not share the optimism prevalent in the marketplace about inflation being dead and was more impressed than most by the hypothesis of a capital shortage lying ahead (unusually extensive investment opportunities coupled with shrinking personal savings as populations aged). In acting on this view the long-run speculator could underweight fixed-rate bonds with a maturity of say ten years – but in doing so would also be taking a view on rates from 1993 to 1998 (standing to lose if these were to stay at 4 per cent right through 1994–6 before rising sharply in say the second half of 1997).

A more precise strategy would be to combine positions in two swaps – the first as a fixed-rate receiver for five years, the second as a fixed-rate payer for ten years (he/she is a floating rate payer on the first swap and receiver on the second). If, indeed, the implicit term structure of one-year rates from 1998 to 2002 were to rise sharply in 1994, then the two swaps could be closed out and substantial profit realized – well before the arrival of the time period which is the subject of speculation.

Note that the existence of long-maturity fixed-rate markets and a smooth series of implicit one-year rates (in the term structure) are themselves no proof of a substantial body of long-term speculators. In principle, the main players in the, say, ten-year bond market could be speculators taking a geared position on where one-year interest rates will be one year from now (ten-year bond prices should change much more in price than a two-year bond in response to any interest rate shock, although the actual gearing factor is unpredictable). Arbitragers could smooth out the term structure of one-year rates without having any strong view about actual levels (for example, an implicit one-year rate of 4 per cent in 1996, 11 per cent in 1997, and 7 per cent in 1998, would be an invitation to swap market arbitrageurs to 'play' in this area).

Less active, but quantitatively much more important, as partic
ipants in the fixed-rate markets (than those mentioned so far) are investors and borrowers looking to reduce the potential volatility of their assets or liabilities including accumulated interest at a horizon date several years into the future. If their entire portfolio were in the form of short-maturity deposits or loans, the amount of accumulated interest would be quite uncertain, even after adjusting for inflation. Indeed, assuming that inflation uncertainty is fairly modest but non-zero, a mixed portfolio including both fixed and floating-rate instruments should be lower risk in terms of terminal value (in constant purchasing power), than 100 per cent floating or fixed-rate. The lower inflation uncertainty is, the higher should be the proportion of the portfolio (either of assets or liabilities) in fixed-rate rather than floating-rate for decision-makers concerned with minimizing risk at a horizon date several years into the future.

INFLATION PROJECTIONS – REAL OR IMAGINARY?

We do not know what proportion of investors and borrowers in the fixed-rate markets are acting (at least in part) on the basis of long-run projections of inflation and of inflation risk. But the marked variations through time in the popularity of fixed-rate instruments and the abundance of market commentaries which advocate long-run position-taking based on an inflation view suggest that the proportion is substantial. Yet how firm are the foundations for taking any long-run view on inflation?

In practice, inflation expectations are highly sensitive to present and recent experience. At a time when inflation is very low, say 1–2 per cent, long-run inflation expectations are also subdued. In the high inflation years of the 1970s, long-term inflation expectations rose sharply. The 14–15 per cent yields on ten-year Treasury bonds in the early 1980s reflected expectations of inflation staying at the high levels of the recent past. The Treasury bond market totally failed to anticipate the dramatic decline in inflation during the following decade. The low and declining inflation during the first half of the 1990s convinced many market-participants that inflation would remain very low for a long time to come.

The observed dependence of long-term inflation expectations on present and recent inflation performance could well be consistent with so-called 'rational expectations'. When inflation is high, market-participants have grounds for being sceptical of the competence of the monetary authorities. If they could make such a mistake in policy to get us into the present mess, how can we be confident about their ability to steer a low inflation course in the future? And even if the central bank is committed to the long-term goal of low inflation or price stability the optimum path to that state from the present situation of high inflation is surely gradual. There is a trade-off between speed in reaching the goal and economic output loss (the relationship, however, is complex: very gradual policy could mean a bigger cumulative loss of output than a sharp counter-inflation therapy in that continuing high inflation damages economic efficiency). A mistake in the direction of high inflation takes a long time to reverse.

Conversely when inflation is low – and has been for some considerable time – the competence of the monetary authorities tends to be held in high esteem. Market-participants have a raised level of confidence in the central bank's ability to avoid inflation mistakes in the future. The critic might say, however, that the confidence level rises too far. Central bankers tend to become smug, exaggerating their role in bringing about the present low inflation, and investors tend to exaggerate the safety brakes which would operate against any incipient inflation.

Examples of smugness include the Federal Reserve Open Market Committee (FOMC) congratulating itself in autumn 1993 that the directive which it gave to the New York desk to be on the alert for a decision to tighten, but which was never acted on, was responsible for the smothering of some mild inflation pressure spotted in the early months of the year! In similar vein were those bond analysts and economists who argued that the bond market was now so sensitive to any risk of inflation turning up that the Federal Reserve could not 'get away' with running an inflationary policy for any significant period of time.

What neither the FOMC (according to the minutes of its meetings) nor bond analysts admitted in their commentaries was the scope for a major mistake in monetary policy to go undetected for so long that by the time it was perceived (whether in the marketplace or within the Federal Reserve), a new period of high inflation could already be on its way. After all, the Federal Reserve, on its own Chairman's admission, was operating without any reliable compass. The old stable relationship between the key M2 aggregate, inflation, and national income, had broken down. (The crisis of the savings and loan institutions and technological change were two important factors in the breakdown.) Booming sales of bond and equity mutual funds promoted by the banks themselves had a corollary in sluggish growth of deposits and money-market funds.

Low M2 growth did not mean low inflation and growth ahead. And making the attainment of a target for M2 growth the overriding priority of Federal Reserve operations in the market for reserves (the Federal Funds market) might have destabilized the economy (if the target were set well above or below the unknown demand for real money balances which make up M2). With no satisfactory intermediate target for policy (in the form of M2 or some other monetary aggregate), the Federal Reserve had reverted to a highly discretionary management of short-term interest rates towards achieving the unchanged ultimate goal of price stability and low unemployment. Infrequent decisions to change the peg for the key overnight rate were based on a wide range of indicators, mainly cyclical, and a large element of judgement.

None of the so-called composite or diffusion leading indicators of inflation have been shown to have forecasting power much beyond two quarters. Yet the lag between a mistake in monetary policy and its revelation in the economic aggregates (inflation and growth) can be as much as eighteen to thirty-six months. By the time the leading indicator flashes yellow, the central bank may have been pursuing an inflationary policy for two years. And a yellow light might provoke only a gradualist response from the interest rate 'fixers'. A commodity price boom is an example of a 'shock' which might stem from a long period of monetary ease and exacerbate the inflation problem as it emerges. Very quickly, the well-intentioned central bank, despite all its anti-inflation rhetoric, finds itself in the high-inflation scenario.

Could the bond market act as an early safety-brake against inflation if participants wake up to the dangers sooner than the central bank? Not if the difference in wake-up time between market-participants and central bank officials is a matter of weeks or at most one quarter (as is probable). Certainly central bankers would be jolted into action (earlier tightening) by a crisis of confidence in the bond market. Even if they disagree with the market's pessimism (on inflation) they cannot ignore it, because a sharp rise in bond yields (and the likely accompanying steep drop in equity prices) is damaging to macro-economic prospects. They could defend a pre-emptive rise in money rates – against their own 'better' judgement – by their power to bring a rally in the capital markets and in business confidence.

In practice the consensus perception of inflation and inflation risks found in the marketplace, with respect to the next two to three years, is broadly similar to that in the policy-making committee of the central bank. Beyond say, a three-year horizon, an important divergence opens up. Central bankers do not form expectations of inflation for the long-run. They must at least pretend to the world at large that they have confidence in their own ability to meet their stated goal of low or zero inflation. Market-participants, however, must first form a view on the central bankers – not just those in positions of power today but also their successors – and second, on the framework of control within which they (the central bankers) will be operating. In principle, full accountability of the monetary authorities (via disclosure of proceedings at meetings, congressional cross-examination, freedom of information access by the press and academics) should increase public confidence, compared to a framework where individual responsibility for mistakes and even collective admission of error are unheard-of concepts.

The absence of a well-behaved intermediate target for monetary policy is a factor biasing long-run inflation expectations upwards. If, indeed, a stable relationship could be demonstrated both in the medium and long-run between a key monetary aggregate and inflation then the central bank could strenuously defend a policy of meeting a given target for this aggregate year by year and be waylaid by a wide range of populist short-term considerations. If that meant sometimes raising rates barely one year into a business recovery, so be it. By contrast, central bankers are likely to get short shrift from the national legislature and public opinion for raising rates at such a time simply on their hunch that policy may already be creating an inflation problem two years hence, but with no reliable indicator of rising inflation to which they can point.

A stable relationship between a key monetary aggregate and inflation is a public good. Stability means that the aggregate can function well as an intermediate target variable for monetary policy. The central bank, by striving to reach the target, rather than acting in a more discretionary fashion, increases its chances of attaining the ultimate aim of price stability and low unemployment. If it were possible to stabilize the relationship between an intermediate target variable and inflation at the cost of imposing a 'structure' on the monetary system, policy-makers should seriously study the relevant cost–benefit analysis. The oldest proposal in this view is 100 per cent reserve banking (put forward by Professor Simons at the University of Chicago in the 1930s). A more realistic modern version is the proposal for 'substantial' reserve requirements on a wide range of bank deposits, such that the demand for reserves at the central bank has a stable relationship to national income. And the supply of reserves is in principle wholly under the control of the central bank. Yes, such a system may impose a tax on money and lead to its sub-optimal use. Yes, domestic financial centres might lose business to foreign centres. But these could be costs worth paying.

In Europe, the Bundesbank has defended its relatively high reserve requirements and its obstacles placed in the way of certain financial innovations as necessary towards safeguarding the position of M3 as a safe target for policy. Better to have the prize of a well-behaved intermediate target and sound money than the latest in financial wizardry and a slightly larger financial centre. And, indeed, the attributes of a well-behaved intermediate target together with so-called central bank independence are frequently mentioned as important to the Deutschmark's hard status (equivalently to investors' confidence in low inflation being maintained in the long-run for the German economy). Many commentators argue that the low degree of political pressure on the Bundesbank leaves it freer than foreign counterparts to raise rates well before the inflation symptoms appear.

Unification of the two Germanies, however, disturbed the relationship between M3, inflation, and national income. So-called 'independence' did not guard against the Bundesbank itself making a major inflation error (see Chapter 2, p. 41). The optimists on the DM preserving its 'hard status' pointed to the probability (or hope?) that once the unification boom-and-bust was over, and once the ERM 'constraints' were no more, low and stable inflation could be expected over the long-run. The pessimists pointed to the huge budget deficit (as high as 7–8 per cent of GDP) in 1993/4 on the widest definitions, including for example the railways and *Treuhandstelle*) and how this could destabilize the relationship between M3 and inflation, meaning a new mistake in the direction of inflation could be made.

HYPEROPIA – A BUBBLE PHENOMENON

We can see from the above examples that the normal 'state of mind' with respect to the long-run inflation prospects should be one of deep uncertainty. Yet experience in the US Treasury bond market suggests that almost violent changes in the prevailing view about long-run inflation can occur in response to a fairly light-weight dossier of new evidence. Thus, little over a year on from the peak of the US Treasury bond market boom in summer 1993, the barometer of inflation expectations had swung from virtually dead calm to a storm reading. The strong expansion in the US economy during 1994 had gone along with a rapid rise in wholesale prices. From summer 1993 to autumn 1994 the rise in Treasury bond yields (at ten-year maturities) was no less than 275 basis points (from 5.25 to 8 per cent). A year later (autumn 1995), inflation expectations had fallen back sharply, as reflected in ten-year T-bond yields, down by 200 basis points to 6 per cent. The feared acceleration of inflation in 1995 had failed to happen. The hypothesis that inflation was dead had earned new credibility.

It was more difficult to argue the case that the Treasury bond market was 'bubbling' in autumn 1995 than in summer 1993. The advocates of the 'inflation is dead' hypothesis could point to the apparent success of the Federal Reserve, by its timely monetary tightening in 1994, in pre-empting an outbreak of inflation as justification for a raised level of confidence in the monetary authorities' determination and ability to pursue price stability. Moreover, ten-year yields in autumn 1995 were still 75 basis points higher than two years earlier, and that was despite a fiscal revolution under way since the Republicans obtained control of Congress in November 1994. Indeed, bullish Treasury bond market commentaries in autumn 1995 made much of the fiscal policy outlook in justifying still lower yields. None the less, the possibility that a bubble verdict could eventually be sustained against the Treasury bond market of autumn 1995 could not be ruled out.

Probably the prosecution (arguing the bubble case) would concentrate on two issues. First, had a state of euphoria developed in the marketplace about the budget outlook? After all, the change in fiscal policy likely to take place during 1996–7 was quite modest (0.25–0.5 per cent of GDP tightening in total). Indeed, fiscal policy might even prove to be expansionary in 1996 (if a capital gains tax cut stimulated consumer spending). And beyond 1997, who could be certain about how a new Congress and Administration might proceed on fiscal policy? Moreover, changes in the fiscal balance could be dwarfed by other factors in determining the overall balance between savings and investment in the US economy. The extent of new investment opportunity (related in particular to progress in information technology) and private savings behaviour could be much more important influences than modest and questionable changes in fiscal policy on the equilibrium level of interest rates.

Second, the 'inflation is dead' advocates continued (as in summer 1993) to rely heavily on observations about 'real' rather than monetary factors. A popular argument of the inflation optimists involved pressure from global competition. The advanced industrialized countries were now facing unprecedented competition from the developing countries. Any attempt by US corporations to raise their profit margins would invite huge gains in market share for foreign low-cost producers exporting to the USA. Similarly, upward pressure on wages could not develop because US business would simply shift more production abroad, and import competition would increase.

But inflation is predominantly a monetary rather than a real phenomenon. Yes, we can point to historic episodes of real shocks (usually a sudden shortage in supply of some key commodities) leading the inflationary process. But the continuation requires ratification by the central bank. And in the opposite direction, a big increase in supply could bring a temporary fall in the price level, but this does not mean a steadily declining price level unless monetary policy shifts in that direction. In any case increased competition from the developing countries was no sudden shock but the continuation of a long-term trend.

In the long-run increased exports to the advanced industrialized countries from the developing countries would be matched by increased imports (of high technology products and services). Global competition could not depress final demand. Its impact should be seen on relative prices within the advanced industrialized countries rather than on their general price level (or inflation rate). Specifically, the wage rate of highly skilled labour should increase relative to that of low skilled (the latter being in close competition with imports from cheap labour 'countries'), and the relative price of standard-type manufactured imports should fall.

A less simplistic argument put forward by the 'inflation is dead' advocates involved a learning process. Just as the hyperinflation of 1922–3 turned subsequent generations of Germans against inflation (and ready to accept tough monetary policy without criticism) so the great inflation of the 1970s has changed the popular mood throughout the industrialized countries and made it politically easier for central banks to administer hard medicine. Certainly the political tolerance of high unemployment apparently increased in some countries (Britain and France in particular) through the 1980s and early 1990s. But some reservations were still in order.

First, even in Germany, the reputed anti-inflation zeal embedded in public opinion (stemming from the Weimar years) did not stand in the way of big inflation errors (albeit less severe than in many other European countries) – for example, in the late 1960s and early 1970s, and again in the early 1990s. Second, it is far from clear that the inflation errors committed by the monetary authorities in the 1970s were ever generally popular. Neither the mistakes nor the slowness to take corrective action were dictated by a popular outcry for inflation. Third, even in autumn 1995, the skies above the US economy were not free of inflation clouds. The economy was operating at full stretch and only one or two quarters of above-trend growth could bring new evidence of inflation pressure, perhaps this time from the labour market. A roaring equity market, a weak dollar against the Deutschmark (the number two international money) and still rapid credit growth, hardly suggested that US monetary conditions were tight. Asset price inflation might be a forerunner of more general inflation.

In sum, the great confidence in the marketplace about the long-run proposition that inflation would remain low was not founded in a compelling economic thesis. And, indeed, we find over and over again that bubbles in financial markets are accompanied by the music of a strong long-run hypothesis which seems to by-pass the normal 'checks and balances' of rational scepticism. Perhaps the oldest example of this phenomenon in modern financial history is the collapse of the French franc in the period 1923–4 (which was followed by a remarkable rebound as the French franc became the strongest European currency in the second half of the 1920s). The long-run hypothesis which 'took hold' was that the falling French birthright spelt a progressive weakening of France's economy especially in relation to Germany's.

Then there was the euphoria of Wall Street in the late 1920s. The dominant view in the US equity market was that rapid technological progress promised decades of prosperity. Irving Fisher's notorious opinions expressed on the eve of the Great Crash seeking to justify the high level of the US equity market in terms of long-run prospects should always stand as a warning to economists tempted to write rationalizations at times of bubble. In late September 1929, the Yale professor expressed the view that stocks had reached what looked like a 'permanently high plateau'. Even as late as 21 October, when a major break in the market occurred, the professor dismissed the decline as a 'shaking out of the lunatic fringe that attempts to speculate on margin'. The market had yet to reflect the beneficial effects of prohibition which made the American worker 'more productive and dependable'.

In the post-war years, the sterling bubble of 1980–1 and the dollar bubble of 1984–5 stand out as cases where a long-run hypothesis took hold in the marketplace. When sterling reached a level some 40 per cent above common measures of purchasing power parity in winter 1980–1, the accompanying music was oil prices continuing to rise year by year from the then level of $40 per barrel. The pound as a petro-currency (the UK economy having become a large net exporter of oil) was the new gold money. Some commentators went further. Given the ever-present danger of new energy shocks, the pound merited a premium rating as a 'bad news' good whose inclusion in portfolios provided insurance against loss in the event of energy crisis. The pound was resistant to scepticism expressed by a small minority of economists (including Milton Friedman) about the long-run ability of the OPEC cartel to 'rig the oil market' and to their forecasts of an eventual crash in oil prices.

In the case of the US dollar, which peaked at almost DM/$ 3.50 in early 1985, the music was the decades of dynamism which lay ahead for the US economy under the supply-side policies of the new Reagan Administration (so-called Reaganomics). Rapid recovery through 1983 and 1984 from the recession of 1981–2 provided near-term support for the optimistic view. Another theme in the same piece of music was extreme pessimism about the long-run economic and political outlook for Europe (so-called 'euro-pessimism'). The European economies were pulling out of recession only at a slow pace. Euro-sclerosis was widely diagnosed. Articles both in popular business magazines and in learned journals argued that Europe was lagging behind North America and Japan in the key industries of the future.

Sceptics on the long-run hypotheses of US dynamism and Euro-sclerosis argued that their proponents were confusing cyclical and secular phenomena. The sharp upturn of the US economy in the period 1983–4 could be explained by the combination of tax cuts, a big increase in defence spending, and a powerful easing in monetary policy. Indeed, subsequent data showed that the US economy had already slipped into growth recession (economic growth below the rate required to keep unemployment from rising) when the US dollar was making its final run-up during the first quarter of 1995.

Not all bubbles are accompanied by loud music in the form of a strong hypothesis about the long-run. But even then, soft music can usually be detected. For example, the great bubble in the Japanese equity and land markets of the late 1980s was not driven by any widespread belief that earnings growth in Japan would far outstrip that elsewhere in the long-run or that the Japanese economy would be the dynamic growth centre of the world economy. Long-run justifications for the sky-high prices of Japanese assets were drawn from demographic trends and from high marks awarded to Japanese management ability.

The ageing population in Japan was seen as putting upward pressure on the savings rate, as the bulge of employees in their forties and fifties built up capital ahead of their retirement. In turn, the high savings rate meant that interest rates, bond yields, and equity yields, would be low in Japan compared to other advanced industrialized nations. The corollary of low yields in Japan was a huge stream of capital exports in the search for higher returns abroad. Japanese corporations, given their low cost of capital, could simply manufacture gain for their shareholders by buying foreign corporations whose shares had much lower price–earnings ratios. This arbitrage depended on an earnings stream of foreign source (for example, the USA) being valued more highly once it came under Japanese corporate ownership, perhaps on account of a premium-rating for Japanese management ability.

The demographic hypothesis was certainly intellectually respectable. Both the OECD and IMF contemporaneously published research into the links between ageing population, savings rates, and capital flows. But the demographic trends had been discovered well before the late 1980s. The demographic factor was as much a valid factor in long-run investment appraisal in 1983, 1986, or 1990, yet the swing in equity market valuations was ginormous! There were grounds for serious doubt. In particular, how long would the large savings surpluses last? For example, some economists argued that already by the late 1990s the savings surplus would be shrinking, as the bulging population of retirees dipped into their savings. Others argued in reply that even retirees would have powerful incentives to save – uncertainty as to future medical bills, doubts as to whether state retirement benefits would be maintained, and the provision of legacies to their children. Meanwhile the stagnation and subsequent gradual decline in the size of the labour force would put downward pressure on the industrial demand for capital, thereby bolstering the net savings surplus.

Even if the surplus of savings were to prove of long duration, did it justify much lower bond and equity yields in Japan than else-where? Was aversion to exchange risk amongst Japanese investors (and also amongst potential foreign borrowers of yen) so great that yen yields would have to be far below those in, say, dollars and Deutschmarks to generate net capital exports sufficient to absorb the savings surplus? Suppose expected real interest rates and bond yields were only one percentage point lower in Japan than the US. Did that small differential justify P/E ratios in Tokyo of 60 as opposed to 15 in New York? No – unless a bubble-like judgement were made about the long-run superior ability of Japanese manage-ment. True a P/E of 15 in Tokyo might be equivalent to 30 in Western markets when the quirks of Japanese accounting practice and interlocking shareholdings were reckoned with (see Chapter 1, p. 8). But there was still a wide gap to explain. Moreover, a sober analysis of the profits outlook should have contained serious down-side warnings, in that present corporate results were buoyed by a large amount of speculative trading in financial markets. And one note of caution should also be made by the appraiser of Japanese asset prices – has the significant risk of a devastating earthquake in the Tokyo area been at all factored into present valuations?

EVALUATION OF LONG-TERM RISKS

The specific question of how Japanese capital markets should reflect earthquake risk is one example of a general question. How far should present capital market prices discount a substantial risk of a big shock at any point in, say, the next 10–20 years? A related question is the extent to which asset prices should acknowledge a significant risk of a big shock at some point starting from say five years onwards. A specific example of this second type of question is how currency markets should respond to a far-distant risk of war or major political change.

Let us return to the earthquake example. The conventional wisdom amongst seismologists is that a high risk of a major earth-quake in the Tokyo area exists in the decade from the mid-1990s. One factor in that assessment has been the history of around 70-year intervals between the last three great earthquakes. That in itself is not strong evidence – three 'observations' only do not give great insights into the 'true' probability distribution of earthquakes through time. But there is also supporting geological evidence of shifts in the earth's layers affecting Tokyo.

Suppose there were a 5 per cent risk in each of the next ten years (from 1994 onwards) of the earthquake catastrophe (that means the risk of the catastrophe by the end of year 5 is 25 per cent). Estimates of damage to property and loss of life which would be wrought by a Tokyo-area earthquake vary widely and are highly dependent on what time of day it occurs (middle of the night or middle of the day?). But let us take an average estimate of Japan's capital stock (of machinery and buildings) being reduced by an amount equal to 50 per cent of GDP. That estimate is of course far in excess of the damage inflicted by the Kobe earthquake of January 1995 – widely put at 3–5 per cent of GDP (this figure includes not just damage to capital stock but loss of production due

64

to economic dislocation). The recent huge savings surplus would give way to years of savings deficit as a boom in domestic investment (to replace the damage) outstripped current savings. Interest rates and bond yields in Japan would be amongst the highest rather than being the lowest in the G-7 world.

The impact of the earthquake on the yen itself is ambiguous, at least in the short and medium term. In the long-run, years of Japan running a current account deficit (the corollary of savings deficit) rather than huge surpluses (as would have occurred without an earthquake) mean that the yen should come to a lower level than otherwise – corresponding to a depletion rather than a further big build-up of its net foreign investments. But in the short and medium term, the jump in interest rates and bond yields could mean that the yen overshoots (on the upside) the path which would have been followed had an earthquake not struck. Indeed, it is the prospect of the yen eventually falling, as interest rates and bond yields begin to subside from their post-earthquake peaks, which would persuade Japanese investors not to liquidate foreign assets *en masse* despite higher yields now available at home. Increased inflation and political risk in Japan following an earthquake would also deter wholesale repatriation of funds.

The interest rate impact of a Tokyo earthquake would not be confined to Japan. The reconstruction boom there would mean an import boom from the rest of the world. The equilibrium level of interest rates would rise in the main trade partners of Japan as their economies got a lift from Japanese import demand. In the context of a floating yen, the new relationship between Japanese and foreign interest rates and the path followed by the exchange rate would depend crucially on the degree of exchange risk aversion on the part of both Japanese and foreign investors (and borrowers).

If many investors were ready to switch large amounts of capital between the yen and foreign currencies in response to small changes in interest rate spreads (meaning their aversion to exchange risk were low), then the yen might indeed rise initially from pre-earthquake levels. (The interest rate spread moving in favour of the yen would stimulate Japanese investors into considering a big reduction in their holding of foreign assets and foreign investors into looking to increase their holdings of Japanese assets. A jump in the yen, of course, would forestall these shifts, in that a subsequent downward adjustment would be expected.) The stronger yen would dampen inflation pressure and go along with a surge in imports (promoted additionally by their new cheapness relative to scarce domestic production). By the same token, the rise in Japanese interest rates required to prevent the economy overheating would be contained. In sum, low risk aversion means a stronger yen and a smaller spread of Japanese over foreign interest rates than in the case of high risk aversion.

Suppose we could form a guesstimate, based on the above considerations, that an earthquake would bring an immediate 400-basis-point jump in short-term Japanese interest rates (compared to say a 50-basis-point jump in other G-7 economies). Then a 5 per cent chance of earthquake in the next year would be 'worth' 20 basis points on one-year rates. The possibility of earthquake should mean that one-year rates are 20 basis points higher than they otherwise would be. By extension, two-year rates should be 40 basis points higher, three-year rates 60 points. Thereafter the calculation is more complex because if earthquake had struck in year 1, short-term rates might already be subsiding from their peak. Putting the term structure of earthquake premiums together into a yield curve, the illustrative arithmetic might justify as much as 60–70 basis points on ten-year yields compared to where they would be if no earthquake risk existed.

But the range of plausible arithmetic is very wide and we can understand why bond analysts do not make explicit allowance for earthquake risk in their evaluations of the yen markets. Most would agree that earthquake risk justifies some premium on yen rates (compared to where they otherwise would be) and more at the long end of the market than short (in that an earthquake is more likely to have occurred by the end of year 10 than the end of year 2). Whether any such premium exists in reality is hard to determine as we cannot observe what yen yields would be in the absence of earthquake risk. Perhaps the strongest statement we can make is that yields at ten-year maturities in the JGB market of barely 3 per cent (as at end-1993 and again in the second half of 1995) did not provide generous compensation for earthquake risk.

The measurement of how much risk is being priced into the market is sometimes easier in the case of a potential shock which might happen several years from now, but not in the shorter run. As illustration, the possibility of war or revolution is not usually a factor in appraising market values (with the exception of certain hedge assets, including gold). Occasionally, however, war or revolution do enter the screen of possible future scenarios on which the investor or analyst focuses his probabilistic vision. Subsequent events might increase the risk of those particular scenarios becoming reality. We can observe how prices move at these specific periods.

Take the example of the years running up to the outbreak of the Second World War. The possibility of war might have come into focus for a few far-sighted investors as soon as September 1930, when elections to the Reichstag produced a shock result. The Nazis had emerged as the second largest party with around 18 per cent of the vote. But even then the probability of the Nazis coming to power and turning demilitarized Germany into the number one military force on the European continent within six years could not have been rated at even 1 per cent by the most pessimistic of observers. The flows of capital into the US from Europe following the September 1930 elections were not triggered by war risk but by bankruptcy risk. Huge foreign creditors of Germany began to panic that the unstable political situation there, coupled with the ailing condition of German banks (laden with bad debts stemming from bouts of highly speculative lending in the 1920s – first during the hyperinflation and later during the post-stabilization boom of 1925–8) meant they would not be repaid.

The first tentative evidence of capital flight to the USA from Europe on account of war risk came in the years 1934–5 (Hitler became German Chancellor in January 1933). But how much of the flow was capital flight and how much was simply European funds returning to the US now that the Roosevelt Administration had renounced further devaluation of the dollar (against gold) and the US stock market was rising strongly is hard to determine. The first unambiguous evidence of capital flight (other than a brief flurry at the time of German remilitarization of the Rhineland in Spring 1936) came in early 1938 with the *Anschluss* (between Austria and Germany). There followed three great waves of capital flight to the USA as the Second World War approached – autumn 1938 (the Munich crisis), spring 1939 (German invasion of Czechoslovakia), and finally summer 1939 (the growing crisis over Danzig and the announcement of a non-aggression pact between Germany and the Soviet Union). There was a fourth wave in November 1939, two months after the outbreak of war, on fears of an imminent German invasion of France and the Low Countries.

In tracing the impact of growing and approaching war risk on capital flows across the Atlantic in the 1930s it is important to take account of changes in the exchange rate regime. The key exchange rate between the gold bloc currencies (the most important were the French franc, Belga, Dutch florin, and Swiss franc) and the US dollar was virtually fixed from early 1934 to September 1936. Sterling floated. From autumn 1936, 'dirty' floating, broken by intermittent periods of rate pegging, was the rule between the three major currencies (US dollar, sterling, and French franc). During the period of a fixed rate between the gold bloc (led by the French franc) and the dollar (1934–6) a modest increase in the risk of war at least four years away did not justify any substantial rearrangement of portfolios by European investors.

Perhaps in the counterfactual case of a freely floating franc–dollar exchange rate we would have seen some dollar appreciation as early as 1934–5 on the basis of far-off war risk. But any such effect would surely have been small and perhaps totally indistinguishable when set against the larger influence on the dollar of improving economic prospects in the USA. At most, investors might have calculated that if their blackest fears about Germany became reality, the dollar could be 10–20 per cent higher than it otherwise would be, say, two years from now. Actuarially a 10 per cent probability attached to that worst case would justify a 2 per cent premium on the dollar today over its 'peacetime equilibrium' rate. But what speculator would trade in the dollar on the basis of a belief that political events had shifted its 'long-run equilibrium value' by 2 per cent. Our knowledge of equilibrium conditions is so imperfect that no rational investor would act on the basis of a presumed shift in value amounting to so little.

Once war risk loomed large (from spring 1938 onwards), then the (counterfactual) freely floating dollar would have been highly sensitive to changing scenarios of European conflagration. That sensitivity would have been due not just to actuarial calculation by investors but also to the emergence of a hedge premium on the US currency. European investors would have been prepared to pay above the actuarial odds for dollars in order to gain some financial insurance against the eventuality of war. The hedge premium could have been notionally calculated as the amount by which the dollar overshot its actuarial value. The total expected cost of the dollar's insurance service in any period would have been equal to the expected inferiority of its (the dollar's) total return (after adjustment for exchange rate change during the period) below that, say, on the French franc if indeed war did not erupt and war risks did not increase with respect to future periods. (The calculation assumes that it was indeed French francs that were displaced in the portfolio to make room for additional dollar holdings as war insurance.)

In the five decades since 1945 conflagration risk has been a minor sporadic factor in the dollar's international valuation, particularly at various crisis points of the Cold War. More important as a phenomenon in currency markets has been the role of far-off domestic political risks in influencing exchange rate behaviour. For example, in the 1970s and early 1980s the political scene in both France and Britain was marked by a close contest between a large centre-right formation (the Conservative Party in Britain, The RPR and UDF parties in France) and a Socialist Party (Labour in Britain, the Socialists in France) still committed to highly redistributive taxation and stiff controls on domestic residents investing abroad. In the run-up to elections, the national currency became highly sensitive to the fluctuating probability of the Socialist Party emerging as the next government. For example, in spring 1978, huge capital flight depressed the French franc ahead of parliamentary elections at which the polls were predicting a Socialist victory (in the event, the incumbent centre-right government emerged as victor, defying the polls' predictions).

Well ahead of scheduled election dates (say two to three years), political risk should not have been ignored in any fundamental appraisal of the currency (British pound or French franc). For example, in 1976, French parliamentary elections were still two years away, and the next presidential elections five years ahead. But given the economic crisis of the mid-1970s (the first oil shock of 1973–4 had been followed by severe recession), a rational investor should have put some significant probability, say 20 per cent, on the Socialists being in power within two years. Suppose a Socialist victory would bring a 10 per cent devaluation of the French franc (and indeed this occurred soon after the election of the Socialist candidate, François Mitterand, as President in May 1981). Then actuarial calculation would have justified the franc falling by 2 per cent below its otherwise equilibrium value. As we saw in the pre-Second World War example (the franc–dollar rate in the period 1934–5), such small adjustments in calculation of the fundamental equilibrium exchange rate are neither clearly discernible in practice nor likely to be a trigger to long-term speculative action in the marketplace.

A much bigger chance (than the 20 per cent above) of a major political change some two years or more ahead *could* have a discernible influence on currency value. Take the example of the

UK in 1977, when already the weight of opinion poll evidence and by-election results suggested that the Labour government had little prospect of climbing over the mountain of unpopularity which had built up in consequence of runaway inflation, recession, and sterling depreciation. The final straw had been the ignominy of calling on the International Monetary Fund (IMF) to oversee a programme of budget and monetary austerity. The perceived probability of the Conservative Party under its new charismatic leader, Margaret Thatcher, winning the next general election (due by spring 1979 at the latest) was perhaps as great as 80 per cent. That possibility would have justified actuarially a, say, supplement of 8 per cent on sterling's price (in the currency markets). Indeed, from mid-1977, the pound was in growingly strong international demand. (Note, however, that another medium-term factor which was simultaneously positive for sterling was the prospect of sharply rising oil production from the North Sea.)

Even in the case of Sterling in the late 1970s, it was not until close to the eventual election data (spring 1979) that fluctuations in the probability of political change became a subject of short-term speculation in the marketplace. The same observation could be made with respect to the pre-election period in France (1976–8). Medium-term political scenarios do not in general change by enough over several weeks to become the only major influence on exchange rate determination during that period. Opinion poll ratings might fluctuate by a significant amount from month to month. But it is not until the elections appear on the short-term horizon that short-term changes in opinion-poll readings are treated as implying an important shift in probability with respect to the final outcome.

During the election campaign itself (and sometimes during the pre-campaign weeks) politics can become the dominant influence on currency behaviour if the race is seen as close. A wide-open race three months before election day may have turned into an 80 per cent probability of a Socialist victory with only two weeks to go. Still assuming as a rule of thumb that the currency (franc or pound) would be 10 per cent lower in the event of a Socialist than a Conservative victory, the changed odds would justify on a simple actuarial basis a 3 per cent fall over the two and a half months to date. Thus short-term traders and investors could not ignore the political risk. Indeed, politics might become the dominant influence on exchange rate determination during the final run-up to the elections. Then foreign currency might be sought as a hedge asset by domestic investors. They would calculate that in the event of a Socialist victory profits from their holdings of foreign currency would be an offset to losses on other assets and to increased potential taxes. Foreign currency, as a 'bad news good' could be bid up to a significant premium above its actuarial value.

SHOCK – FOCUS ON LONG-RUN

Domestic political change, earthquake, war – these are all examples of 'shocks' which should be within the span of investors' probabilistic vision well before they occur. Occasionally, however, a shock occurs which could not have been included for long within the range of possible scenarios focused on even by those investors and commentators with the keenest probabilistic vision. In the aftermath of the shock, a completely new consensus long-term view has to form in the marketplace as a basis for revised valuations of the different asset classes. Whilst the consensus view is in the melting-pot, and some considerable divergence exists between commentators on how the present and future possible realities have changed, even short-term investors have to concern themselves with long-run analysis. Which of the competing hypotheses about the implications of the shock event is going to win through to become the new conventional wisdom? Market economists find their work on possible long-run scenarios in unusually strong demand!

Perhaps the best examples of such shocks are the quadrupling of the price of oil in the winter of 1973/4 and the announcement of German monetary union in February 1990. Neither event came totally out of the blue. For example, already in December 1970 the OPEC cartel had displayed some new strength, calling for a 'joint production programme' and a general increase in posted prices. In February 1971 the oil companies, under the threat of production cutbacks, had agreed to an immediate 35 per cent rise in the price of a barrel to $1.30. And in the German case, ever since the trainloads of East Germans had started coming to the West via Hungary in summer 1989, the early demise of the GDR (Democratic Republic of Germany) had been a real possibility. Even so, both shock events were well out of focus on the film of future possible scenarios which investors and commentators were playing to themselves just weeks before their occurrence.

The instant macro-economic analysis written in the immediate aftermath of the oil shock took as a premise the sustainability of the price increase – albeit that some lone voices warned that the cartel would eventually fall apart. Much was written about the absorptive power of the oil-exporting countries being limited at first (their spending would rise only with a considerable lag behind their revenues). Hence the shock would be deflationary on the world economy (unless offset by monetary stimulus). After an uncertain period, however, the oil-exporting countries would be spending their revenues – and maybe overspending them (borrowing against oil in the ground). Then the equilibrium level of interest rates in the world economy would rise. Some historical parallels were drawn between the oil-importing nations paying oil tax to OPEC, and Germany paying reparations to the Allies half a century earlier.

Whilst most economists could agree on the method for analysing the implications of the oil shock (including its influence on interest rates), all were 'in the dark' as to the range within which key parameters would lie. How quickly would the oil-exporting nations build up their spending? How far would households in the oil-importing nations cut back their spending? Even though the rise in oil prices was a real phenomenon (having its origin in the action of a cartel) could it be a catalyst to monetary inflation? Central bank officials, concerned at the evidence of a looming recession wrought by the energy crisis, might not seek to reverse the impact effect of higher oil prices on the overall price level (by allowing monetary conditions to tighten enough to deflate non-oil prices). In turn, inflation expectations, taking account of the likelihood of monetary accommodation, would rise. A vicious circle of inflation, starting with an increase in the price level, on to monetary accommodation (actual or supposed), and on to claims for higher pay in the labour market, could develop.

Given the wholly rational lack of conviction of any market-participant (including the commentators themselves) in the central case forecasts which were quickly distilled in the aftermath of the shock, it is easy to explain the extreme volatility of all market prices at that time. New pieces of data, changes of nuance in policy-makers' statements, could and did have major consequences for market movements.

A similar volatility marks the period following the announcement of German monetary union. Bonn's offer of currency union (6 February 1990) to East Germany (GDR) just three months after the opening of the Berlin Wall brought an immediate 100-basis-point rise in ten-year German government bond yields amidst frenzied trading in the London futures market which Bundesbank spokesmen described as 'destabilizing'. But how could the market conditions become anything other than unstable?

The initial reaction of analysts to the shock of imminent German monetary union (GMU) was to look at the recent experience of Reaganomics (in the mid-1980s), where an explosion of the budget deficit and buoyant investment spending had galvanized the dollar and US bond yields. Now a big expansion of state borrowing in the German capital market and very strong private spending (both consumer and investment) following monetary union would surely send German interest rates and bond yields, together with the Deutschmark, higher. Only wild estimates could be made of the burden which economic and monetary union would place on the Federal Republic's budget. How skilful, and how free of political constraint, could the Bundesbank be in the task of containing any inflationary pressure which might build up following the distribution of Deutschmarks to East German citizens?

In principle, the Bundesbank could 'squeeze' the growth of money circulating in West Germany to 'make way' for the oversupply of Deutschmarks in the East. Any estimate, however, of excess money creation in East Germany, was hazardous. Who knew what the East German demand for money would be (equivalently, how much of the Deutschmark manna from heaven would they spend and how much would they save?) or how large would be East Germany's productive potential? The chances of a major mistake in monetary policy being made in an inflationary direction, even given the best of intentions, were considerable. Even those analysts attracted to the 'Reaganomics' model as a precedent for contemporary events in Germany could not argue that the Deutschmark was a sure one-way bet upwards. Perhaps a big inflation mistake was already in the making and would tarnish the Deutschmark's reputation as a hard currency for a long time to come.

Another large element of uncertainty in assessing Deutschmark markets in the aftermath of monetary union between East and West Germany was the nature of economic interdependence between the German and other West European economies. How far would the boom in demand for goods and services emanating from unification extend to neighbouring economies? In technical jargon, how close would be the substitutability of French or Italian consumer and capital goods for German? And how great a barrier would exchange risk be to capital inflow from other EC countries into Germany? At one extreme, all West European capital markets could perform virtually as one integrated whole. At the other extreme, wide yield spreads and interest rate spreads could open up. The answer to these last questions would turn in part on the credibility of continuing fixed exchange rates at an unaltered parity within the European Monetary System.

Did the economist have anything useful to say to investors in the wake of German monetary union? Or were the uncertainties, the 'ifs' and 'buts', so great in any comprehensive analysis of the possible outcomes that the 'practical man' could have saved himself the trouble of reading through the pages of analysis? The same type of question could of course have been asked about the value of economic analysis in the wake of the first oil shock.

In both cases, the answer depended on the attitude of investors. They had the best chance of extracting benefit from reading the analyses if they acknowledged that economics could not open up before their eyes one scenario of such high probability that it should be followed through 'thick and thin' over an extended period of time. Good economists offered opinions which were formed one step back from the excitement of the marketplace. The economists' carefully considered alternative scenarios with probabilities of occurrence attached should have helped their clients appreciate the risk parameters within which their portfolios were being managed. Investors could have looked to economists to press the alert button when market prices were putting a greatly exaggerated weight on one scenario as against several other possible future realities. Then the investors should have been ready to spring into action, hoping to take their profits when the price shifted towards a more appropriate weighting of future possibilities.

When Deutschmark bond yields shot up immediately following the announcement of German monetary union, the market-participant aware of the range of possible scenarios could question whether large enough probability weights were being given to large-scale financing of the German budget deficit through foreign capital inflows or to the Bundesbank being able eventually to correct any inflation error arising from excess creation of Deutschmarks in the East. In this questioning mood, the investor could have taken advantage of the panic in the futures pits. Success would be far from guaranteed – the Bundesbank might indeed make severe errors, and Deutschmark yields might have to rise to show a large risk premium over other European yields before Germany would attract large-scale capital inflows from abroad.

4

PROPHETS OF THE
BUSINESS CYCLE

The rigour of academic discipline has not been proof against the best of economists having their judgement swayed by the course of the business cycle. Thus Nobel prize winner Paul Samuelson, just before the peak (December 1969) of the long economic upswing in the USA which started in 1961, was so moved by the experience of continuous prosperity to remark that the National Bureau of Economic Research (long established as the primary 'measurer and referee' of the US business cycle) 'had worked itself out of its first job'. In the same year (1969) a conference volume appeared under the title *Is the Business Cycle Obsolete?* This was the heyday of fine-tuning, when most economists and market-participants really did believe that governments could prevent the economy from slipping into recession or overheating by timely changes in monetary and fiscal policies.

Now, after a quarter century of considerable fluctuations in economic activity, including five recessions in the USA, denying the existence of the business cycle looks an absurd proposition – and most of all before an audience of economists active as commentators, practitioners, or advisers in financial markets. The language of the marketplace is largely that of business-cycle economics. Troughs, peaks, growth-recessions, growth pauses, contractions, leading and lagging indicators – these are part of the everyday jargon. Many asset prices, including exchange rates, have become hypersensitive to changes in the perception of where the respective economies are situated in the cycle.

The business cycle is not just a question of belief for market economists. They are likely to find that a large amount of their work is concerned with monitoring the economic fluctuations out of which the cycle is formed stage by stage. Market-participants look to economists for a view on where the given economy (or economies) is situated presently in the business cycle, on how far off is the next phase, and on how large the fluctuations 'around trend' are likely to be. The economist who is skilled at in-depth reading of the cycle should also be in a good position to distinguish economic changes which are long term in nature (transcending the current business cycle) from short-term fluctuations. In turn, market-practitioners might look to the economist for guidance as to which hypotheses about the long-run currently popular in the marketplace are in fact only a passing reflection of the present stage in the business cycle.

CHANGING PERSPECTIVES ON THE CYCLE

Skill in reading the business cycle (including the assessment of current conditions and what phase lies ahead) involves much more than understanding how cycles are identified. None the less a familiarity with the process of identification is an essential first step. As an introduction to defining the concept of business cycle we could start with the authoritative description of A.F. Burns and W.C. Mitchell (*Measuring Business Cycles*, Vol. 3, New York: National Bureau of Economic Research, 1946):

> Business cycles are a type of fluctuation found in the aggregate activity of nations that organize their work mainly in business enterprises: a cycle consists of expansions occurring at about the same time in many economic activities, followed by similarly general recessions, contractions, and revivals which merge into the expansion phase of the next cycle; this sequence of changes is recurrent but not periodic; in duration, business cycles vary from more than one year to ten or twelve years; they are not divisible into shorter cycles of similar character.

This description makes clear that the business cycle is not a regular fluctuation (of economic activity). The length of the total cycle and of its various phases is distinct on each occasion. The totality of economic activity through time can be broken up into a series of business cycles. These cycles are more than an *ex post* classification of economic data into sub-periods whose markers are set by various random interruptions. The same observations hold with respect to the concept of the growth cycle, encountered widely in market analysis. The growth cycle relates to trend-adjusted economic data. A strong phase of the growth cycle is marked by the economy expanding at a faster than trend pace, and a weak phase by slower-than-trend expansion. Sometimes two or more growth cycles overlap one business cycle. The turning points of the growth cycle are generally not synchronous with those of the business cycle, though quite often the troughs coincide (as happens when the upturn from recession is sudden and strong). The peak of a growth cycle is when the economy is farthest above its long-run trend path. The trough is when the economy is furthest below.

For example, in the almost nine years from the business cycle trough of February 1961 to the peak of December 1969, the US economy experienced several growth cycles (first peak May 1962, trough October 1964; next peak June 1966, trough October 1967; next peak March 1969, trough November 1970). The trough of the growth cycle ending in November 1970 was simultaneous with the business-cycle trough. The next long business-cycle upswing, from the trough of autumn 1982 to the peak of summer 1990 overlapped two growth cycles (first peak June 1984, trough January 1987; next peak March 1989).

The fact that growth cycles are of shorter average life than business cycles and that they often involve milder fluctuations in economic activity means that positive identification of a new phase (for example, strong expansion giving way to a 'growth-recession') can often not be made until well after the next turning point. Contemporary observers may suspect that the economy has turned a corner in the growth cycle. But by the time that statisticians can be reasonably confident of their measurements with respect to this particular growth cycle it may well have long since passed from actuality into history.

For example, in spring 1995 the great weight of current data and anecdotal evidence suggested that the US economy was now expanding at a slower pace than during 1993-4. But it was far from clear whether the slowdown was to a below-trend pace and whether that slackness would be sustained for two quarters or more (the definition of a 'growth recession'). By end-1995, the 'mainstream' view of commentators was that the US economy had passed through an exceptionally mild growth recession starting in late 1994 (November or December) and ending in mid-1995. But there were also strong minority counterviews – first, there had been no growth recession at all (the Mexico 'shock' and an inventory correction in the automobile sector had brought growth below trend for one quarter only in the spring); and second, the growth recession was continuing and might even deepen into a full-fledged recession. By spring 1996 most commentators agreed the mild growth recession was over, but disagreed whether the present growth cycle upturn had started already in summer 1995 or was a much more recent phenomenon.

The growth cycle, like the business cycle, is a living entity. There are forces, whose source lies at the heart of the capitalist process, which drive the economy from one phase of the cycle on to the next. In addition to these forces from within, a variety of outside forces (so-called 'shocks') influence the extent of fluctuation. In the language of business-cycle economics, the cycle is driven by a combination of impulses and propagation mechanisms (these terms were coined by Ragnar Frisch and Eugene Slutsky in the late 1920s). In the history of economic thought there has been a large swing in emphasis between the two motors driving the cycle.

The 'classical economists' were concerned primarily with the propagation mechanism and focused on the internal dynamics of the economic system. Examples include the various 'underconsumption theories' (excess profit accumulation meaning excess savings and a rate of consumption which becomes inadequate to absorb what is supplied). Neo-classical economists similarly focused on the endogenous processes (internal dynamics) behind the business cycle. In some accounts the most important process was monetary – for example, inevitable deviations which open up, then close, and then go into reverse, between the 'market rate of interest' and the natural rate of interest (Wicksell). Other accounts put emphasis on real factors – a growing imbalance between production of long-lived and short-lived capital goods (the Austrian theory), or changes in unit labour costs relative to output prices (Mitchell).

Keynesian economists, in the first years of excitement in pioneering with mathematical accounts of the business cycle, excluded outside shocks from their analysis. They struggled to build models of a self-generating no-shock business cycle which could correspond with observed reality yet incorporate the key Keynesian concepts of income 'multipliers' and 'accelerators' (investment spending expressed as a function of change in overall output level). The struggle did not meet with success.

The 'monetarist' economists starting in the early 1960s shifted the emphasis in cyclical analysis to 'impulses' – albeit that the impulse on which they focused was largely restricted to monetary shock (meaning big changes in monetary policy, intentional or otherwise). A large variety of reduced-form, single-equation models appeared that linked fluctuations in economic activity directly to prior fluctuations in the growth of money supply. Then the 'oil shocks' of 1973–4 and 1979–80, and a decade later the 'German unification shock', reinforced economists' interest in external impulses as an important source of business-cycle fluctuation. Attention shifted away from just the budget or the central bank as the motor.

In the 1970s and 1980s a group of macro-economists (Lucas and his disciples) sought to build a model of the business cycle – including possible shocks ('impulses') and 'propagation mechanisms' – which was consistent with rational expectations of individual agents in the economy and also continuous market clearing, but which allowed for a time-lag between the shock occurring and agents obtaining full information about its aggregate impact. Thus 'information barriers' were the sole source of business-cycle fluctuation in the Lucas model.

A CURRENT SYNTHESIS

The Lucas approach has failed to generate much enthusiasm amongst commentators and analysts near to the marketplace. They have been unconvinced that an information barrier of a month or two could generate the swings in output observed. Moreover, the hypothesis that most unemployment in recessions is 'voluntary' runs counter to 'common-sense' observation, even if we allow for a significant section of the labour force which 'accepts' that periods of unemployment in business downturns are a normal experience (for example, those who chose to become construction workers realized that during recessions they will be at high risk of unemployment; when, in fact, they become unemployed they might well 'bide their time' until the upturn, rather than intensely searching for any full-time probably low-paid job).

In practice, economists near to financial markets form eclectic views of the business-cycle process, drawing together various themes from alternative models into a new whole which is their own. A starting point is the defining of various phases of the cycle. Most contemporary economists would go along with a more elaborate list of phases than that in the Burns and Mitchell description already cited. The 'rudimentary' phases include first, the peak, then the downturn, then the trough, then the recovery back to the previous peak level of output, then expansion. Otto Eckstein and Allen Sinai suggested a breakdown into phases as follows – (1) recovery and expansion; (2) boom; (3) pre-crunch period/credit crunch; (4) recession/decline; and (5) reliquefication. An occasional cycle may omit one or another of the stages, and there could be some overlap in their timing. But the typical cycle seems to run through all five stages.

The Eckstein and Sinai elaboration draws together financial and real concepts – and most economists whether of monetarist, Keynesian, or 'agnostic' leaning, would go along with the advantages of this hybrid approach. Indeed, Milton Friedman's popularizing of the quote from J.S. Mill that 'money is the monkey wrench in the machine' would command broad agreement from analysts of the business cycle. Mistakes (even if 'unavoidable') of monetary policy-makers have been a pervasive phenomenon of business-cycle history under fiat money regimes (where money is not convertible into gold at a fixed price). Under the gold standard regime, lack of synchrony between money-market rates determined by the relative abundance or shortage of metal and the (non-revealed) natural rate of interest (the rate consistent in the long-run with price stability and unemployment at its natural level) was a pervasive story behind economic fluctuations.

Monetary mistakes – with a considerable bias in the inflationary direction – are virtually inevitable given the way in which central banks (or their masters at the Finance Ministries) conduct policy. Essentially the monetary authorities peg short-term money-market rates – adjusting the peg upwards or downwards at irregular and usually infrequent intervals in line with changing 'economic fundamentals'. The authorities operate as any bureaucratic organization – slowly and generally too late. And whatever their constitution (independent, autonomous, or agent of the Finance Ministry), they are subject to political pressure, albeit to varying degrees.

During the expansion phase of the business cycle, the central bank is likely to hold the interest rate pegged at a level below the new natural rate. The members of the policy-making council cannot reach a consensus on sizeable upward adjustments of the peg until there can be no reasonable doubt that expansion is indeed well established. But allowing for the lag between what is happening 'on the ground' and its confirmation in indisputable statistical evidence, the central bank may be at least one year late in beginning to adjust the peg up. So-called cautiousness might mean that a further six to twelve months elapse before rates rise to the neutral (or 'natural') level.

It is difficult for the central bank to effect a big rise in rates without the alibi of rising inflation, at least at the level of producer prices (consumer price inflation lags producer price inflation). But inflation usually takes off with a long lag after the seeds were sown by over-easy monetary policy. By the time the central bank begins to correct its earlier error an inflationary boom might well be already in the making, and a sustained period during which short-term rates are above the natural rate could be necessary to 'cool the economy down'. Hence follows the pre-crunch/credit-crunch phase of the business cycle, during which the central bank at last acts forcefully to break the vicious circle of inflation and inflation expectations feeding off each other. Such action typically falls far short of the aim which some 'orthodox' central bankers might see as desirable – bringing the general price level back down to its pre-boom level and so achieving zero inflation over the cycle as a whole.

Already when inflation has fallen back to below 3 per cent, say, the monetary authority comes under usually irresistible political pressure to shift policy towards stimulus, bringing the economic downturn to an early end. Even so the lags in the system are such that central bankers get nearer to their desired aim (albeit still not very close) than if a much fuller accountability were possible. The earlier sharp monetary tightening might not bring clear evidence in data form of a cooling in economic activity until eighteen months have elapsed, and the big fall in inflation could be a further year beyond then. Hence there is a risk of 'overkill' (measured relative to the objective of breaking the vicious circle of inflation rather than of achieving price stability over the cycle).

The contribution of interest rate pegging to fluctuations in the economy has been a principal argument of those economists calling for central banks to abandon discretionary policy-making in favour of operating according to an automatic rule. Indeed the 'adjustable interest rate peg' method of monetary control is far from being the historical norm. Under the international gold standard as it operated in the forty years up to the outbreak of the First World War, central banks were largely passive in their money markets – draining liquidity when gold reserves were falling and adding

81

liquidity when they were plentiful. Historical evidence allows us to reject the hypothesis that money rates determined under the gold standard or longer-term interest rates (which were influenced by the path of money rates) glided along in perfect harmony with the changing natural interest rate, so suppressing economic fluctuations. In the interwar period, the Federal Reserve became the leading 'fixer', pegging rates at what seemed to be an appropriate level given business conditions. Milton Friedman and Anna Schwartz have documented the policy errors of the newly powerful Federal Reserve – the biggest of all being from 1929 to 1932.

Under the Bretton Woods international monetary system, the Federal Reserve continued to be largely free of external constraints in the pegging of interest rates. The demise of the system, and the floating of the dollar–mark and dollar–yen rates, gave new power to the Bundesbank, some other European central banks, and the Bank of Japan to peg short-term interest rates in their domestic markets. In practice, however, in the first decade of floating, both the Bundesbank and Federal Reserve experimented for lengthy periods with unpegging rates and allowing them to find their own level. They were drawn into experimenting by the surge of inflation to double-digit levels. Rate-pegging was abandoned in favour of setting short-term target growth paths for non-borrowed reserves (US) or for central bank money stock.

Once the inflation storms were over, both the Federal Reserve and Bundesbank reverted to forms of rate-pegging, even if growth in monetary aggregates was sometimes a key determining factor in whether to change the level of the peg. Neither institution could resolutely resist all the normal pressures of an open society to suppress counter-intuitive rate fluctuations which would follow from blind adherence to a monetary rule, especially when senior officials themselves admitted there could be substantial instability in the demand for money when considered over short periods of time. Rapid growth in the monetary aggregates during a downturn would bring a rise in rates (as much as during an upturn) under an automatic rule. Yet in a low-inflation environment, a rise would be politically unacceptable. It was different under the gold standard, where convertibility of the national money into gold was an axiom of policy with broad popular acceptance which transcended any particular phase of the business cycle.

NON-MONETARY SOURCES OF FLUCTUATION

In an eclectic account of the business cycle, real factors must range alongside the powerful monetary disturbances described above. Some of the real factors are in the nature of impulses. The 'oil shock' and 'German unification shock' have already been mentioned as real disturbances, albeit that both involved strong monetary elements; the 'compasses' which usually guide monetary policy-makers were sent haywire by both shocks. In the aftermath of the oil shock, many of the major central banks eased policy at first, believing first-round effects would be deflationary. They underestimated the excess of monetary growth still hanging over from the past two to three years and also the direct effect of oil prices on inflation expectations.

In the run-up to monetary union between East and West Germany there was much discussion about what proportion of the new DMs created (via conversion of GDR-marks) would be saved rather than spent. The failure of the Bundesbank to raise rates for eight months following union suggests considerable sympathy amongst members of its policy-making council for the view that the explosion of money supply had a counterpart in increased demand for real money balances (from East Germany). In reality the inflationary boom in the West German economy fuelled by East German spending suggests that the monetary overhang was greatly underestimated.

The monetary sector of an economy can itself be a non-monetary source of impulse to the business cycle. Examples here include a burst of financial innovation, perhaps triggered by deregulation. Increased access of both consumers and corporations to debt finance might bring a bulge in demand for consumer and producer durables. Yet there may be no corresponding surge in monetary growth if deregulation is simultaneously allowing non-bank intermediaries to gain a much larger share of credit markets. Alternatively, policy-makers might confront a situation where deregulation is increasing the demand for real money balances, as the narrowed spread between borrowing and lending rates encourages households to hold larger liquid reserves. The monetary authorities might overestimate the influence of spread narrowing on the demand for real money balances, and so tolerate too rapid a rate of monetary growth for price stability.

There are many other types of real shock which have been

impulses for economic fluctuations and which should be included in any eclectic account of the business cycle. These include natural disasters (hurricane or earthquake, for example) and product innovations. Colour TVs, videos, micro-computers – these are all examples of new products which stimulated business or consumer demand as households and corporations introduced them for the first time into their portfolio of assets.

More generally, consumer and producer durables play a crucial role in the generation of the business cycle. A look at the particular nature of the supply and demand of durables can illustrate why activity in the industries making these is uneven and so is an important propagation mechanism in the business cycle. An increase in demand, for example, for housing, or private transport, is usually reflected both in spot and forward markets simultaneously (these exist only as theoretical constructs). New production of housing or private transport services in the present period cannot be technically separated from production for future periods.

A more optimistic view of the economic future and an improved balance sheet (the consequence of some retrenchment during the early stage of recovery from the trough) might cause many families to revise-up their demand for residential accommodation (in terms of space and/or quality). Rents move higher. Future rents, quoted in multi-year lease contracts, also rise – after all, increased demand for space is most probably more than a one-year affair. In turn capital values of residential real estate rise, making it again profitable eventually (after the excess inventory of unsold homes has been in part cleared) to build new houses and apartment blocks.

Producing the new residential accommodation occurs over a concentrated period of time, even though the accommodation is consumed over a half century or more. The telescoping of production of multi-decade services into one or two years, when taken together with considerable volatility in demand (for these services), is a source of fluctuation in economic output. Volatility derives from the considerable scope which households have to vary their consumption levels even in the short run (despite the fact that there are many practical obstacles in the way of instantaneous adjustment).

When times are bad, households can 'make do' with somewhat small and shabby accommodation. As optimism returns, they decide to upgrade their conditions, but transaction cost considerations force them to make a multi-period commitment. Hence adjustments in demand are non-continuous through time. The fluctuations in demand, and the discontinuous way in which these occur together with the telescoped production process, lie behind the endemic cyclicality of construction activity; the swings in inventories of unsold homes form a further factor.

The business cycle analyst in focusing on demand for durables goods – whether housing or much smaller items (including household appliances) – as a source of business fluctuation realizes that swings in consumer confidence (between optimism and pessimism) are themselves often induced by parallel developments in the economy. Often the state of consumer confidence might not be an 'original source' of cyclical motion, but one of several interrelated propagation mechanisms. Sometimes, however, 'consumer sentiment' can be more like an impulse from without.

Harvard professor, Benjamin Friedman, has commented that one of the things economists most dislike talking about is people's attitudes. But that does not make these any less important in accounting for the behaviour economists seek to understand. Friedman was referring specifically to the readiness of individuals and businesses to take on debt and why this has been so variable through time. The same observation applies to consumer confidence and the readiness of households to enter into new commitments with respect to housing and private transportation (car purchase).

Indeed the same story can be told about cyclicality of demand for cars as for housing, despite the markedly different economic lifetimes for these two types of consumer durable. When the economic mood is sombre, households can postpone replacing their four-year-old car with a new one and thereby delay enjoyment of the latest advances to speed control, comfort, and safety. As optimism about the economic outlook returns, and households become more ready to enter into a multi-period commitment (either via outright cash purchase or entering into lease contracts) car production bounces.

The increase in production is not just to meet final consumer demand. Stronger consumption (and thereby retail turnover) means that distributors and manufacturers adjust upwards their desired level of inventories. Demand from inventory builders (who are bringing their inventories into line with revised target levels) is typically volatile (sometimes negative, sometimes hugely positive, on a quarter-by-quarter basis) and can be a powerful influence on the overall economy. Indeed, in some accounts of the business cycle, inventories have prime place. Retail and manufacturer inventories are more important as a source of fluctuating demand (for current production) in the case of, say, cars than buildings. Retail distribution out of inventory is not the general rule for houses, apartments, offices, or warehouses. Swings in the volume of unsold space (second-hand and new), however, are an important specific source of fluctuations in output, sometimes violent, in the construction sector.

The role of asset prices as a source of fluctuating demand is at its most dramatic in the case of construction. Real estate booms and busts are part of the folklore of business cycles as are the remarkable changes in attitude of the lenders involved. By contrast, there is no phenomenon in the car sector of speculative expectations with respect to prices driving production. The time taken to manufacture cars is too slight and the flexibility of production too great for an asset price bubble (in this example, car prices) to take off. Demand for cars, however, can be sensitive to the behaviour of asset prices generally in the economy. A real estate and equity boom might fuel demand via the so-called wealth effect (consumers feeling better off).

Equity and bond market fluctuations can also have a direct and important bearing on business investment spending. A lower cost of capital means a wider range of potential investment projects satisfying the criterion of having a positive net present value. Lower interest rates mean generally a higher optimum ratio of inventories to sales. In sum, a two-way chain of causality exists between asset prices and the business or growth cycle.

FROM CYCLES BACK TO MARKETS

Analysts of market prices are most concerned with the direction of causality running from the business cycle back to asset prices. They seek to identify any general rules for how various asset classes – equities, real estate, bond yields, and currencies – move in price through the cycle. If they have above-average insight into where the economy is now positioned in the cycle and where it is going next, they should be at some advantage in projecting investment returns. Sensitivity to the progression of the often smaller 'growth cycles' which overlap the business cycle, together with an ability to distinguish the two, are added bonuses.

Knowledge of general rules relating asset prices to the business cycle is far from a sufficient condition for investment success.

86

A good appraisal of where in the cycle the economy is now situated, what stage is likely to come next, and how much of this 'central case' is already discounted in market prices, are additional requirements. The analyst must also reckon with the full range of non-cyclical forces operating on markets.

An example of the difficulties in reading the business cycle can be illustrated by the experience of the US economy in the four years from the peak of the 1982–90 cycle (in summer 1990). Through late 1990 and early 1991 the contemporary 'consensus' perception was that the US economy was in severe recession. A brief period of optimism in the aftermath of the Gulf War (spring 1991) was followed by eighteen months (to winter 1992/3) of commentaries to the effect that the US economy was in a quarter- to half-speed recovery following one of the severest recessions since the war. Only in winter 1993/4 did the view shift to seeing the US economy in a classic expansion.

The erroneous view in the marketplace can be attributed in some parts to the normal delays between changes in economic reality and when these show up in the data. The acceleration in the pace of US recovery during the second half of 1992, for example, was not reflected definitively in the data until early 1993 (unfortunately for the incumbent US president, George Bush, who was defeated at the elections of November 1992 by Bill Clinton). There was an additional problem of faulty data. Already by spring 1993 big backward revisions had turned the 1990-1 recession into one of the mildest post-war downturns.

The investor who had correctly suspected that contemporary data in 1991 overstated the depth of the recession would have only got faint cheer (and little, if any, market recompense) from being proved correct two years later. More important was to recognize turning points for the economy as it passed from one phase of the cycle to the next (whether recession to recovery, or recovery to expansion), ahead of the market consensus. A knowledge of history and theory could provide help in the essential next step of going from the appraisal of the economy's present situation in the business cycle to a prediction of asset prices.

Money-market rates and bond yields are themselves often described as following a cycle which is closely aligned to the business cycle. When more than one growth cycle overlaps the business cycle, interest rates also tend to follow sub-cycles. Typically rates peak at a point close in time to the cyclical peak, whilst they reach a trough in the early recovery phase. Where the growth cycle trough comes long after the business cycle trough (as happens in the case of a weak recovery), then the interest rate trough is usually similarly delayed.

In principle, and sometimes in practice, bond yields can lead the business cycle, starting to fall ahead of the peak and rising very early in the recovery phase or even just ahead of the trough, in anticipation of later similar moves in money-market rates. It is rare, but not unknown, for bond yields and money rates to move in contrary directions. After all, bond yields are an average of spot and forward short-term interest rates. The latter are pegged, as we have seen, for long periods of time by central banks who habitually are slow in their reactions.

The theoretical basis for a link between the interest rate cycle and the business (or growth) cycle turns partly on the evolving balance between savings and investment and partly on inflation expectations. During a recession, business investment falls whilst households raise their savings ratio in response to raised fears of unemployment. The tendency towards a glut of savings (even despite increased 'dissaving' by the government in the form of a widened budget gap) is reflected in the equilibrium real rate of interest (the so-called 'natural' rate) falling to a low level.

During the expansionary phase of the cycle, investment spending tends to run ahead of the supply of savings as households become more confident about the economic future and become readier purchasers of consumer durables and businesses see greater opportunities for profitable investment (therefore increasing their expenditure on plant, machinery, and equipment). The natural rate of interest rises. Some increase in inflation expectations, typical of the late stage of a business cycle expansion, means that nominal interest rates rise relative to real rates.

Actual interest rates do not follow natural (equilibrium) rates continuously throughout the cycle. Indeed, if perfect synchrony did occur, cycles would be of considerably smaller amplitude than what has been observed historically. In practice, interest rates set in the money market and longer-term rates (which are influenced by expectations of money rates in the future) can be out of line with natural rates for considerable periods of time.

Money rates come under upward pressure when the supply of reserves (in the form of deposits at the central bank or of banknotes) runs behind demand or equivalently when banks are expanding their loan and deposit base at a faster pace than is consistent with the monetary growth path set by the authorities. There is a clear tendency for cyclical forces to create a new momentum behind monetary growth during the expansion phase – typically stemming from the side of credit demand, and so money-market rates ultimately come under upward pressure. But there is no one-to-one relationship between a shift in equilibrium rates in the money market and the natural rate. Over long periods of time the two tend to average the same (when adjustment is made for inflation expectations). Periods when money rates are below natural rates (meaning that inflationary pressures are bound to build up) are followed by periods when the reverse holds.

The analyst who is forming a view on the outlook for interest rates has to make at least a two-stage judgement with respect to the influence of the business cycle. First, how is the natural rate likely to be influenced by the cycle over the period in question? Second, how far, if at all, will money rates diverge from the natural rate? The fact that he/she and fellow-analysts foresee long stretches of time during which interest rates are following a trend should not jolt even the firmest believer in efficient markets. The recognition of an interest rate trend is not a sure step to trading profit.

Most likely the trend is already discounted in the term structure of spot and forward interest rates which are built into the yield curve. No simple rule can be devised in the form of buying bonds at a point in time x months after the rate trough and selling them y months after the rate peak. Indeed, successful investment may well involve buying bonds when the trend of rates is up and selling bonds when the trend is down. For example, at end-May 1994, the dominant view in the marketplace was that the interest rate peak (both for short and long maturities) in the USA lay some distance ahead. But an investor could none the less justify buying, say, ten-year T-bonds then (at 7.25 per cent annual yield) so long as yields had not risen above 7.65 per cent a year from then or 7.85 per cent two years hence.

The basis of calculation of these so-called notional break-even rates is trading of income gain (from the extra yield on bonds compared to, say, one-year bills against capital loss (the fall in the price of the bond as yields rise, taking account of the steadily decreasing life of the bond, meaning that the relevant yield for calculation comes lower down the yield curve – on the assumption that this is positive sloping).

The efficient marketeer, though accepting the notion of an interest rate cycle, would be at the forefront of sceptics about any analyst's ability to produce systematically better forecasts than 'the market'. First, he/she might question whether the analyst could consistently come to a better appraisal of the economy's cyclical situation than the consensus view discounted in market prices. Second, he/she can point out that the relationship between money-market rates or bond yields and the business cycle is too imprecise for either to have qualified for inclusion in, say, the US index of leading, coincident, or lagging cyclical indicators. An administered rate – the prime rate set by banks as a benchmark for fixing the cost of borrowing by commercial customers – is one component of the index of lagging indicators. The key overnight rate, the Federal funds rate, has been found to have some reliability as a lead indicator towards the peak of a cycle (or growth cycle) but not more generally.

In some countries, the shape of the yield curve, say the ten-year minus the two-year yield, is one component of the index of leading indicators. In principle, the yield curve reaches its peak steepness during the recovery phase of the business cycle. Long yields rise as the economic pessimism which built up during the recession fades, and investors anticipate much stronger demand for capital. Short rates, by contrast, continue to reflect monetary ease.

At some stage during the blossoming of economic recovery into a full-scale expansion, markets begin to discount a near-term tightening of monetary conditions and the yield curve begins to flatten (as measured by the spread between two and ten-year yields). During the late part of the expansion as the business cycle peak approaches the yield curve turns negative sloping (say two-year yields above ten-year). The rise in short-term rates necessary towards cooling the economy down is not seen as sustainable over the long-run.

The relationship between the yield curve and the business cycle is none the less quite loose. Some analysts claim a better fit can be found between the growth cycle and the yield curve. Indeed, in the US business upturn from early 1991 it seemed that way. The National Bureau (NBER) dates the recovery as starting in spring 1991. It was not, however, until summer 1992 that growth was at a sufficient pace to begin narrowing the so-called output gap (the amount by which actual GDP is below trend GDP). Already in autumn 1992, just a few months after the trough of the growth cycle, the ten-year vs two-year yield spread started to narrow from its peak of around 285 basis points.

That early tendency, however, towards yield curve flattening, was not clearly attributable to cyclical developments. The first year of flattening (to summer 1993) was powered initially by a decline in inflation expectations and by a big announced tightening of fiscal policy (in the Clinton Administration's first budget). Then came the great speculative run-up of bond prices which brought ten-year US T-bond yields down to almost 5.25 per cent in summer 1993 (compared to 7.5 per cent just nine months later). Only from autumn 1993 onwards did the prospect of a normal mid-cycle monetary tightening take over as the principal force behind yield curve flattening. The collapse of the two- to ten-year yield spread to barely 10 basis points in December 1994 was seen by some analysts as a powerful predictor of a growth-recession ahead (and, indeed, economic data showed subsequently that late autumn 1994 was the peak of the growth cycle upturn starting in summer 1992).

Much more reliable historically than the relationship between either the yield curve or the absolute level of yields on the one hand and the business cycle or the growth cycle on the other is the relationship between the business cycle and the equity market. Generally equity prices are a leading indicator with respect to the business cycle. They tend to start weakening ahead of the business cycle peak and turn upwards ahead of the business cycle trough. The indicator property of equity prices stems in considerable part from the pro-cyclical behaviour of corporate earnings (rising at a typically strong pace in the recovery phase, growing more slowly from the mid-expansion phase, and falling during the recession) and the tendency of market valuations to be highly sensitive to projected earnings over the next two years or so.

The biggest change in expectations of corporate earnings occurs around turning points in the business cycle. The realization that the economy is about to come 'out of the tunnel' usually dawns in a sudden fashion. (In theory, dawn could occur as a gradual rise in the probability of economic recovery by, say, spring 1996, from 0 in summer 1995, to 25 per cent in autumn 1995, to 50 per cent in winter 1995/6, to 75 per cent in early spring 1996 – but this is rarely what happens.) Just a month or two before the realization, market-participants may well have been discounting a further year of recession with a continuing decline of corporate earnings.

There are several factors behind the pro-cyclical pattern of corporate earnings. One is their 'residual nature'. There are many semi-fixed charges on value-added in the corporate sector – in particular, the wage bill (not very flexible in the short run), rent, and depreciation. Hence an upturn in demand in the given economy (or economies) is reflected in a profits jump, whilst a decline in demand brings a big fall in profits. An unanticipated shrinking of the economy means that recent investment decisions of the corporation turn out to be costly – equipment lies idle. Returns to the newly deployed capital fail to materialize. If the capital came wholly from equity sources, overall earnings might remain unchanged but earnings per share would fall even if overall earnings remained unchanged. In fact, the unused equipment might well require considerable maintenance. At best, the unused equipment produces no income. At worst it is the source of large negative income.

During the recession the corporate sector is likely to be using its labour force less efficiently than during economic expansions. Ruthless hiring and firing policies, together with linking pay to profits and hours worked, can considerably reduce the extent to which labour costs are a fixed charge on value-added within the corporate sector. But there are both legal and micro-economic considerations which limit such flexibility in labour payments. Transaction costs (including search costs for specific skills) in the labour market are high. It may well be cheaper in the long-run to accept some element of underutilization of labour during periods of slack economic activity than radically pruning all inputs. Anyhow, many wage contracts are for an extended period of time.

Two further fixed charges on value-added within the corporate sector are usually mentioned as important contributors to the cyclicality of net corporate earnings. First, there are net interest payments. The extent to which these accentuate pro-cyclical behaviour (or reported earnings) depends on the ratio of fixed rate to floating rate debt. In principle, floating rate payments would tend to fluctuate with the cycle (low during recession and high during boom) and so may well not be a systematic source of cyclicality in earnings.

Even so, changes in the level of interest rates, either short or long (fixed rate), can be relevant to equity market prices. For example, a cut in money-market rates, if not wholly discounted already, can bolster earnings expected over the next year from corporations with a large amount of floating rate debt outstanding. A fall in bond yields, taking place against the background of unchanged expectations of earnings (both yields and earnings measured in real terms), is a fillip to equity values in that bonds are a competitor of equities in investment portfolios. Equity values of corporations with large amounts of fixed rate debt outstanding would gain less from the fall in bond yields.

The importance of how bond yields and money-market rates move in different phases of the business cycle to determining the overall cyclical sensitivity of equity prices is instructive for real estate market analysts. Adverse cyclical variation in rental income prospects may sometimes by substantially mollified by bond yield and interest rate developments. In particular, when rents are still falling in the early stages of a business cycle upturn, real estate values might none the less climb considerably, influenced not just by better prospects for rental income, say two years from now, but also by lower interest rates (and bond yields), and easy money.

Rents are indeed the second further fixed charge on corporate income. Newly negotiated rent levels, like interest rates and corporate earnings, are subject to the influence of the business cycle. But total rental costs of business (including some rents established during the last boom) are fixed to a considerable extent over the short and medium term. Commercial rents tend to lag rather than lead the business cycle. Commercial real estate values, by contrast, might well not lag, as investors discount rental growth starting from, say, the mid-expansion phase on, and the discount factor (used for capitalizing rents) falls.

It is not until expansion becomes well established that corporations increase their space requirement. In the case of offices or warehouses, they must feel confident enough to expand their input of labour and machinery. At first it is a question of simply putting idle machinery to work. Then there is probably some margin of spare space where they can put their extra resources. In the case of retail space, a threshold of business confidence must be passed before serious demand from potential entrants appears. Residential rents, by contrast, tend to harden quite early in a business recovery. Individuals, more optimistic now about the economic future, are ready to enter into medium- or long-term commitments to increase the quality and quantity of their residential accommodation.

CURRENCIES AND THE BUSINESS CYCLE

Much more speculative than the relationship between the business cycle and various asset markets (especially bonds, equities, and real estate) is that between the business cycle and the currency markets. A hypothesis which came into considerable 'vogue' in the mid-1980s and which has remained popular since is that the US dollar behaves pro-cyclically – strengthening when the US economy pulls out of recession well ahead of other major economies (Europe and Japan) and again during the late expansion stage when US monetary conditions are very tight compared to those abroad. By the same token the dollar weakens when the US economy slips into recession well ahead of other big economies.

The cyclical hypothesis appeared to fit the facts admirably during the dollar's spectacular rise and fall from 1982 to 1987, and in the subsequent five-year period. From DM/$2.35 in late 1982 (at the trough of both the US business and growth cycle) the dollar rose to a peak of DM/$3.45 in February 1985, just two quarters past the peak of the US growth cycle. The dollar fell back to DM/$1.78 by spring 1987, just past the growth cycle's trough (January 1987). In spring 1989, the peak of the next US growth cycle, the dollar was back to almost DM/$2.05, from where it fell to DM/$1.40 by autumn 1992, just past the trough of the next US growth cycle.

The German growth cycle followed a significantly different path from the US during these years. The German economy emerged less strongly than the US from the recession of the early 1980s (1980–2) and the peak of the first growth cycle was not reached until mid-1986. The trough followed in mid-1988. The next peak was in spring 1991 (two years after the US), followed by a growth cycle trough in winter 1993/4 (more than eighteen months behind the US).

The pro-cyclical behaviour of the dollar against the mark during the 1980s encouraged economists to look back at earlier periods this century for evidence of the same phenomenon. Some support could be found in the first year of US recovery from the sharp recession of 1974–5. Before that, evidence relates to periods when the exchange rate between the dollar and mark was not freely floating, and the analyst must look at movement of foreign exchange reserves as a surrogate for currency strength or weakness.

For example, a considerable lack of synchrony between the US and German business cycles was a key feature in the huge flows of 'hot money' which culminated in the floating of the mark (against the dollar and most other currencies) in May 1971 – the forerunner to the complete breakdown of the Bretton Woods System in August of that same year. During 1970 the US economy was in recession, whilst the German economy was overheating (following excessive monetary ease there during the European currency crises of 1967–9). The trough of the US business cycle (and growth cycle) as reached at end-1970, but the Federal Reserve continued with an aggressively easy monetary policy through the early stages of recovery.

The brief period of 'normality' in the interwar years, between 1924 and 1930, also provides supporting evidence for the strong influence of mismatch between the US and German business cycles on capital flows between the two countries. The peak inflow of funds into Germany from the US was in the period 1926-8. German recovery was in full swing whilst the US economy was in mild recession from October 1926 to November 1927. The peak of the German business cycle came already in early 1929, some two quarters ahead of the US. As the Federal Reserve continued to tighten monetary conditions through spring and summer of that year, Germany suffered a large drain of gold reserves. The Wall Street Crash (October) and subsequent cut in US interest rates brought relief, albeit short-lived.

Indeed, the influence of business cycle mismatch on international capital flow should be at its strongest in the context of a fixed exchange rate system where currencies can float only within narrow margins around an official parity and where there is virtually complete confidence in that parity being maintained. Such was the situation under the pre-1914 gold standard – where the limits to fluctuation were set by the costs of transporting gold and the parities set by comparison of gold content of the respective national coinages.

If (under the gold standard) the US economy were well into the expansion phase of its business cycle whilst Europe had not yet started to recover, the dollar would be near or at its ceiling against the European currencies, and the latter would be at their floor (gold export point) against the dollar. Money rates in the US would be above those in Europe, but the spread between the two could be no greater than the expected recovery of European currencies over the relevant time interval.

Hence if the cyclical mismatch were seen as narrowing sharply within two years and the exchange rate between the dollar and

European currencies returning to parity within say the same period (implying an illustrative cumulative climb of European currencies by 2.5 per cent), then money rates in Europe could be 100 basis points below those in the US without any gold flows being triggered. European central banks could stretch the limits of the possible, lowering their rates slightly more, if they were ready to accept big transitory losses in their gold reserves (whilst not allowing the losses to impact on the monetary base). But if capital outflows were highly elastic with respect to small interest rate changes (the norm under a fixed exchange rate system – based on gold or another anchor – where there is total confidence in the system being maintained) the scope for European central banks to ease rates by any more than the differential representing recovery prospects (for their currencies) would be very slight.

Note that in the discussion about the influence of business-cycle mismatch on interest rate spreads and exchange rates under the gold standard (or any other fixed exchange rate system in which the parities enjoy the full confidence of market-participants) no mention has been made of trade flows. Under fixed-rate systems capital flows generated by small changes in interest rates dwarf net trade flows. Thus, in the above example, Europe might well be running a trade surplus and the US a trade deficit, each say of around 1 per cent of GDP, as a consequence of cyclical mismatch. But an interest rate spread in favour of the US should generate capital flows into the dollar and out of Europe that would potentially dominate the net trade flows.

Under a freely floating exchange rate system, capital flows are typically less elastic with respect to changes in interest rate spreads. Exchange risk is a powerful break on capital flow. A 1 per cent spread in favour of, say, US money rates might not generate substantial inflows against the background of an exchange rate between the Deutschmark and the dollar which swings by, say, an average 3 per cent per month. Could the strength of European trade balances and the large deficit which emerges in US trade at a time when the US economy is well into a business expansion whilst Europe is far behind not mean that the dollar could be weak then – in contradiction to the cyclical hypothesis?

The history of the Deutschmark–dollar exchange rate in the 'floating' era does not reveal a period when trade flows were the dominant influence. Whilst exchange risk is an obstacle in the way of capital flow, we must remember that the scope for interest rate spreads to open up under a floating exchange rate system is much greater than under fixed. Moreover, large bond yield spreads can develop in favour of the currency backed by a cyclically strong economy.

Bond yield spreads are more important than short-term interest rate spreads as a motor driving international capital flow under a floating exchange rate system. The Bundesbank, for example, has published research suggesting that during the twenty years from 1974 to 1994 the real yield spread between long maturity US and German government bonds was the most important variable explaining quarterly changes in the real exchange rate between the dollar and the Deutschmark. If investors are going to transfer funds across a currency frontier and assume thereby the hazard of large exchange loss in order to obtain interest income advantage, they must presumably be quite confident that the advantage will persist for some considerable time. A key measure of consensus expectations regarding the future path of interest rates is the term structure implicit in the bond market yield curve.

Bond yields are sensitive to the business cycle in two main ways. First, as we have seen, interest rates follow a cycle which has links to the business cycle. Second, views about the secular development of the economy and so of the average natural rate of interest over the long run (likely to span several business cycles) can be influenced by the present situation in the business cycle. When the economy is languishing in recession, long-run hypotheses about vanishing of investment opportunities, Kondratieff downturns and the like, make their appearance, and provide at least some rationalization for a fall in bond yields below what would be justified by a cyclical dip below an unchanged long-run trend line. Conversely, when the economy is in a strong expansion phase of the business cycle, hypotheses appear about the dawn of an era of dynamic growth, in which capital will be in persistent short supply, and so the average natural rate of interest over the long run would be much higher than in the past.

Under a fixed exchange rate system, bond yield spreads between currencies cannot move freely to express changes in perception about the long-run dynamism of one economy relative to another. Market-participants realize that uncovered interest arbitrage should keep the spread within fairly narrow bands. As illustration, if a business-cycle recovery led to the view becoming popular that the

US economy was now the dynamic growth centre whilst Europe was the 'sick man', US yields could not rise far above European.

Any widening of the spread would trigger arbitrage in a variety of forms, all of which equate to some combination of a long position in European interest rate futures and a short position in US interest rate futures. A substantial bond yield spread, after all, means that short-term interest rates discounted in the medium and long term are quite different on both sides of the Atlantic. The arbitrager takes his position in the conviction that international capital flow would prevent such short-term rate spreads ever becoming effective in the spot money markets.

By contrast, under a floating exchange rate regime, where currency risk looms large, bond yield spreads between countries opened up by cyclical divergence as catalyst, but magnified by extrapolative expectations about the long-run economic future, can be substantial in size (before even considering any difference in inflation performance). But before the economist boldly trumpets the cyclical hypothesis of exchange rate motion in his/her daily, weekly, or monthly market analysis, he/she should draw up a list of several qualifications.

A case-study from the currency market in early 1995 points the way to drawing up the list. The US dollar, having risen to almost 1.60 against the Deutschmark in November 1994 (from DM/$1.50 in early autumn 1994), fell sharply to almost 1.35 in spring 1995. Almost simultaneously the perception in the marketplace of where the US economy was positioned in the growth cycle changed radically. In late 1994 the consensus view was that the US economy would probably remain in a strong upward phase of the growth cycle through the first half of 1995 and that further tightening of Federal Reserve policy would be essential to avoiding a serious upturn of inflation. Already by February 1995, the consensus view – partly under the influence of the 'Mexico shock' (in the wake of which exports from the US to Mexico would plummet) – had changed to the US economy being in a growth recession which might already have started the previous November. Correspondingly ten-year US Treasury bond yields which had been as much 75 basis points above Bund yields the previous autumn fell to 50 basis points below by spring 1995.

Surely this was a perfect illustration of cyclical forces determining the mark/dollar exchange rate. Perhaps. But there were competing hypotheses to explain the same piece of currency market action and these were put forward by serious analysts at the time. Was the sudden weakness of the dollar symptomatic of US monetary policy being too easy? Double-digit US credit growth and rising wholesale price inflation was consistent with that explanation. Some analysts voiced the suspicion that the Federal Reserve was deliberately pursuing a soft money policy so as to depreciate the dollar and join with the Administration in putting maximum pressure on Tokyo to make concessions in the increasingly bitter conflict between the two countries concerning allegedly unfair barriers to imports into Japan. A flight of capital out of the dollar led by Japanese investors fitted the fact of the yen being much stronger than the Deutschmark.

Finally, a small minority of contemporary analysts suggested that the key fault triggering the sharp decline of the dollar in early 1995 was excessively tight monetary policy in Japan and Germany. What sense did it make that Japanese money rates were at 2–3 per cent p.a. when the economy was in deep deflation (the price level falling by 2 per cent or more when measured correctly to take account of the shift in private consumption towards discount outlets)? The German economy, though recovering, had not yet created any new jobs since the recession of 1992/3, and had barely achieved trend growth.

With the benefit of hindsight, the hypotheses which stand up best in explaining the dollar 'crisis' (of early 1995) are first, the cyclical (unexpected slowdown of the US economy) and second, overtight monetary policy in Japan and Germany. Over-easy US monetary policy cannot be sustained as an explanation rooted in reality, given the substantial easing of inflation pressure in the US economy through the remainder of 1995. Even so, factually wrong perceptions (which are none the less reasonable hypotheses at the time) in the minds of market-participants can hold sway over short periods, and that may have been the case with respect to Japanese fears of the Federal Reserve being a monetary accomplice of the Clinton Administration's trade policy.

The strongest lesson in hindsight from the illustration of the dollar crisis in spring 1995 is the sceptical response which any monocausal explanation of currency market behaviour deserves. Most probably the US growth cycle had a lot to do with the dollar's sharp decline. But the cyclical story could not stand on its own. More generally, the analyst when advancing a cyclical hypothesis as a main basis for his/her particular currency view, should check through the following points.

First, are there monetary influences of such strength as to outweigh the cyclical influence on the exchange rate under consideration? Second, although the focus of the cyclical hypothesis is often on the degree of mismatch between the US and German economies and the implications of this for the mark–dollar exchange rate, the situation of the Japanese economy must not be overlooked. The exchange rates between the leading three currencies in the world (dollar, mark, and yen) are determined multilaterally not bilaterally. Third, the power of cyclical divergence to affect exchange rate movement is not even, but is greatest at turning points (in either the business cycle or growth cycle). Let us look at each of these three issues in greater detail.

Certainly monetary policy can play a key role in jump-starting an economy out of recession. But sometimes the monetary authorities continue with an aggressively easy policy well into the recovery phase. Then money-market rates might not rise either in absolute terms or relative to those abroad. And though bond yields may well rise, their total climb might be no more than the rise in long-run inflation expectations. Concern about the implications of monetary aggression for the long-run stability of the currency might cause it to lose some stature amongst international investors as a safe store of value, causing its exchange rate against other currencies to weaken.

Perhaps the best example of inflationary monetary policy more than offsetting the influence of a strong business recovery on a currency was the behaviour of the dollar through 1977 and early 1978. The US growth cycle had troughed back in spring 1975 some six months ahead of the European, and the dollar had gained correspondingly. Then in late 1976 and 1977, the European recovery slowed sharply, whilst the US expansion went full-steam ahead. The failure of the dollar to gain from this cyclical mismatch was an early indicator of the emerging huge error in US monetary policy which culminated in a brief episode of double-digit inflation at the end of the decade and the severe shock therapy of Paul Volcker (who as Federal Chairman presided over a period when short-term US interest rates exceeded 20 per cent p.a.).

The rapid expansion of the US economy from the growth cycle trough of spring 1975 to its peak at the end of 1978 completed the last cycle during which Japanese capital flows were still heavily restricted. By the end of 1980 controls on exporting capital from Japan had been almost fully lifted. The 1980s saw the emergence of Japan as the number one international creditor as a huge structural savings surplus became characteristic of its economy (reflecting a big dip in the ratio of investment spending to total output) with the counterpart of a massive current account surplus.

The unleashing of capital outflow could have disturbed the Japanese yen's prior pattern of sensitivity to the business cycle. In practice, the same relationship between the yen and the cycle has persisted. The Japanese yen tends to rise against all currencies during the early recovery phase of the US growth cycle and weaken as the Japanese growth cycle reaches its peak. This pattern reveals the dominance of net trade and equity flows generated by the business cycle in the case of the yen.

US recovery brings a surge in Japanese exports not just to the US itself but also to other East Asian economies which themselves are highly geared to the US. Commodity prices are still depressed at this stage of the cycle, meaning that the terms of trade are favourable to Japan. The prospect of strongly rising profits in the export sector pulls in foreign capital to the Tokyo equity market. By contrast, direct investment outflow from Japan remains at a low ebb reflecting depressed actual profits and excess capacity at home.

Just as the Japanese trade balance is more sensitive than the European (relative to economic size) when the US economy is leading the world out of a period of weak activity, so it is when expansion spreads throughout the OECD area, including the Japanese economy. At that stage the Japanese trade surplus moves on to a falling trend, as imports into Japan rise and the terms of trade begin to move adversely (as commodity prices rise).

The missing part of the yen story told so far is capital flow driven by interest rate spreads. As rate spreads widen in favour of the US during the early recovery phase of the US economy, could huge capital outflows from Japan (into dollar money markets and bonds) not outweigh the trade and equity flows in favour of the yen and mean that the yen–dollar would move in similar fashion to the mark–dollar rate with respect to the business cycle? Experience so far (until the mid-1990s), however, suggests that the flow of capital between yen and dollars does not respond as smoothly or with the same elasticity to changes in interest rate and bond yield spreads as those between European currencies and the dollar.

One explanation could be the fairly minor role still played by the yen in the mass of international money and bond portfolios managed in Europe. The dollar, but not the yen, are core components of those portfolios. Japanese investors themselves reveal a high degree of risk aversion with respect to currency exposure. Outflows of capital into foreign money and bond markets from Japan has occurred typically in bursts followed by periods of inaction, rather than smoothly. If one of these inactive periods coincides with the US economy passing through its trough, then the dollar would come under upward pressure on account of interest-rate-driven capital flows.

Even in the case of the mark–dollar exchange rate, the influence of the business cycle factor on capital flows does not wax and wane in continuous fashion. Rather, the cyclical influence is greatest at turning points in the business or growth cycle. When the US economy passes through the trough of the growth cycle (usually very near the trough of the business cycle), a discontinuous change in expectations occurs about future economic prospects. The passing of the US economy through the trough of its growth cycle in the third quarter 1992 was followed by a near 20 per cent jump of the dollar against the Deutschmark over just a three-month period. The earlier and faster than expected recovery of the German economy in early 1994 brought a 10 per cent rise of the DM against the dollar in less than three months. The economist who can recognize the passing of a cyclical turning point ahead of the consensus in the marketplace and who is also aware of the significant links between the cycle and the currency markets should be able to make a valuable input into international investment strategy.

5

VIEW FROM THE BRIDGE

Down in the marketplace it is often quite difficult to see from where demand and supply is coming. One function of market economists is to periodically step up on to the bridge and take a wider look. The information they return with can be crucial to market-participants' appraisal of current prices. Other times, the information can be superfluous. Skilled economists, in contrast to the statisticians collecting the raw data, should have an insight into the market significance of what they are bringing back.

Economists take their broadest view of supply and demand in financial markets when setting their sights on the global flow of funds. The data readings which come to them include national balance of payments (broken down into current and capital accounts). Much of the information in international payments data is fairly 'sketchy' especially as regards capital flight or so-called hot money flows. Moreover, even the most recently published capital flow data is usually several months out of date and the economist must be used to putting together a combination of fragmentary and hearsay evidence.

Economists, in forming their view from the bridge, should also know currency geography well. Which of the three big monies (US dollar, Deutschmark, and Japanese yen) are presently at the poles of the dominant axis around which exchange rates are turning? What polar power is being exercised on other currencies? Where on the map are the main currency zones? Which are the currency islands? Have any hedge currencies erupted? Are there any cross-winds in the form of capital flight or hot money flows?

CURRENT ACCOUNT SIGNPOSTS

Let us return to the first conventional 'reading' on the international flow of funds – the current account of the balance of payments.

A current account surplus for a given country means that its exports of goods and services together with income received from abroad (on the part of both labour and capital) exceed imports of these same items. A significant surplus on current account means that the transactions listed give rise, in total, to a net flow of payments towards the given country from abroad.

The current account is typically divided into several sub-accounts. These include the merchandise trade account (goods), services (for example, insurance, banking, travel, transport, technology transfers), income (investment income from abroad, payments of interest and dividends to abroad, income received by residents from foreign buyers of their labour, payments of wages and other income to foreign labour), and transfers (government grants – for example, aid – to foreign governments, immigrant remittances, restitution payments, pensions to and from abroad). It is hardly surprising given the impressive catalogue of what should be included in the current account of the balance of payments that huge errors in recording occur. The errors, however, tend to be systematic. In particular, investment income from abroad is seriously under-recorded by the statisticians. They cannot capture in their data the large flow of income that goes into offshore centres and tax havens, and is not visibly received by investors in any particular tax jurisdiction. This 'black hole' is the source of most of the $100 bn plus error in the total of current account recording (if the current balances of all nations are added up they come to a negative amount of over $100 bn, rather than summing up to zero).

The aggregate error in current account recording, because it is non-random and largely explicable, is not grounds for ignoring the data. But what do economists aim to distil from their study of current accounts (including the 'black hole' in world payments data) towards putting together an interesting story for market-participants? One of the simplest stories that economists have sometimes told is that a large current account deficit means down-ward pressure on the national currency because the demand for foreign exchange to make payments for foreign goods and services (including income payments) far exceeds the supply (from the sale of exports of income receipts).

The 'simple story', however, is far from simple. The value of a currency, as any other asset, is determined in 'stock equilibrium'. At the given exchange rate and international yield spreads, investors must be 'comfortable' with respect to the distribution of their portfolios between the different currencies. The stock of assets in any particular currency dwarfs net flows through the current account.

Of course most investors do not operate a precise sliding scale recalculated continuously to tell them what proportion of their portfolio to hold in each currency according to how exchange rates and interest rates move. Nor do they continuously adapt portfolio proportions to optimum levels. Thus considerations of 'stock equilibrium' set a range rather than a precise point for exchange rates. Within that range, big changes in net flows via the current account can influence the path of the exchange rate. But that influence cannot be sustained unless the current account data holds a deeper message relevant to appraising the investment merits of one currency against another.

One deeper message could concern the possibility of 'overheating'. The sudden appearance of a huge deficit on current account could be symptomatic of capacity constraints having been reached in the domestic economy as aggregate demand outruns supply. Before excess demand becomes evident in an acceleration of inflation, imports could surge. Holders of the currency might be concerned in the light of the current account data that inflation risks are increasing and its exchange rate would fall correspondingly.

Not every sudden widening of the current account deficit portends increased inflation risk. 'Normal' cyclical forces may be at work. For example, the US economy has often 'led' recovery elsewhere, and so two years past its cyclical trough its current account balance might be in huge deficit. The red ink would reflect the fact that US monetary policy was eased ahead of policy in Europe and Japan and perhaps with more aggression. The earlier recovery does not mean that an inflation time-bomb is ticking. Market-participants should reject panic prognoses that the red ink will fuel a big increase in the supply of dollar assets relative to those in other currencies which have to be absorbed in portfolios of international investors. Long before the net flows were capable of significantly changing the distribution of outstanding stocks, the cyclical position should have swung round. In the late expansion phase of the US business cycle, exports have often taken off, as the growth of domestic demand in the rest of the OECD world overtakes that in the US.

A current account deficit which is seen as a secular rather than a cyclical phenomenon could have a big influence on the exchange rate – not via the 'mechanical' effect of flows of the given currency coming onto the market in any period (which would be small relative to outstanding stocks) but via expectations of an important long-run cumulative change in the outstanding external liabilities (over, say, a ten-year period) of the economy in question. In turn, investors could become concerned at the burden placed on the economy in servicing its increased international indebtedness. As illustration, take a country which has a large national savings deficit (private sector savings – both by households and corporations, the latter in the form of non-distributed profits – amount to considerably less than private investment spending plus the budget deficit). The current account in the balance of payments is correspondingly also in large deficit. (It is an identity of national income accounting that the current account deficit equals the national savings deficit.)

The path of future deficits might appear unsustainable at current exchange and interest rates. For example, the stock of net external liabilities of the given country could be set to expand at a much faster rate than its economic size or international investor wealth. A long-run decline in the exchange rate together with some rise in interest rates might be seen as essential to maintaining the growth of its net external liabilities, denominated in domestic and foreign currency, in line with investor demand. The lower exchange rate would promote the production of tradable goods and encourage a switch in domestic consumption towards non-tradables – essential components of a long-run narrowing of the current account deficit. The rise in interest rates would encourage higher savings and be consistent with no inflation accompanying the shifts in consumption and production.

If, however, the secular savings and current account deficit has its source in dynamic investment spending relative to a normal domestic savings rate (relative to other economies at a similar stage of development) rather than low savings and budget deficits, then there may be no implication for the long-run path of the exchange rate or interest rate. Extra economic growth resulting from the high level of investment might mean that the stock of net external liabilities of the given economy (both in domestic and foreign currency) is set to grow unsustainably were the exchange rate and interest rate to stay on a flat trend. Thus in assessing the market significance of a secular deficit prospect the economist must seek to discriminate whether or not its source is productive.

106

Shifting sights back from the secular to the shorter term, the emergence of a large current account deficit could sometimes be symptomatic of a loss of competitiveness by the given economy, which might mean the currency would be devalued eventually. Expectations amongst investors of that end-of-the-road devaluation could bring immediate downward pressure on the currency in the spot market. There is no inevitable link, however, between loss of competitiveness and devaluation. The link depends on a particular policy being followed by the monetary authorities.

For example, take the British economy, which has been frequently diagnosed as having an ailing manufacturing sector whose survival depends on a continuous cheapening of domestic labour costs relative to those in most other West European countries. Were the authorities to pursue a hard exchange rate policy (maintaining a fixed link to the Deutschmark, come what may), then the British economy could yet achieve internal and external equilibrium via the domestic price level falling, or at least rising more slowly than in other major economies (and there could be some fillip to the overall current account from a growing comparative advantage of the British economy in services trade). The tendency of the current account to move into large deficit would be contained by the Central Bank exerting continuous deflationary pressure on domestic prices and costs. In practice, exchange market-participants would be sceptical about such a policy course being adhered to over the long haul, and they would speculate on some monetary accommodation with its corollary of currency depreciation.

The opposite case to a country running into current account deficit as its competitiveness declines is the emergence of surpluses as export demand runs high. The German economy in the late 1950s and 1960s provides a case-study for analysis. These were the years of the German post-war economic miracle. The rapid productivity growth in German industry and its skill at product design were winning many admirers. In principle external and internal equilibrium (meaning no strains in the balance of payments, full employment and low inflation) could have been maintained by the Bundesbank accepting a steady-state rate of inflation modestly above the very low rate in Germany's major trading partners, so that at an unchanged nominal exchange rate the real exchange rate of the Deutschmark would have been rising. In practice, the Bundesbank was not willing to follow an accommodative monetary policy and thereby 'condemn' the German economy to a worse-than-average inflation performance. Realization in the marketplace that the authorities were 'unhappy' about the dangers posed by the huge external surplus for inflation fed recurrent speculation on an imminent revaluation of the Deutschmark. This indeed occurred in 1961 and again in 1969.

The huge Japanese current account surpluses of the past quarter century (1970–95) can be explained in certain periods by gains in product competitiveness (a leading position in many high technology goods). But the permanence of the huge surpluses (with only transitory interruption, as during the oil shocks or at the peak of the bubble economy) reveals other factors than competitiveness at work. 'Permanent' surpluses must reflect a secular excess of domestic savings over investment opportunity. A surplus which emerges due to a bounce in competitiveness (including good product design) but which is not underpinned by savings–investment imbalance would wane (as real exchange rate appreciation changed the composition of domestic consumption towards imports and reduced the profitability of export production).

The factors behind the long-run giant savings surplus of Japan are well known – the fast-ageing population (meaning a build-up of pre-retirement savings), restricted supply of residential land (high prices of homes means that 'salarymen' must save at a high rate to provide themselves and their families with living accommodation), long working hours (meaning little time to spend on leisure), and a highly inefficient retail distribution system.

A huge current account surplus with its source in a secular savings–investment imbalance (savings, net of any budget deficit, well in excess of investment spending) has a much lower order of implication for the path of the real (and probably nominal) exchange rate over the short or medium run than does a similar size surplus which reflects a sudden blossoming of competitiveness (with no accompanying change in the long-run imbalance between savings and investment). The first type of surplus, cumulated over many years, could mean that investment income from abroad would rise substantially (in line with the stock of foreign assets), and become a significant proportion both of total export receipts and of national income at some point far into the future. An appreciation of the real exchange rate could be essential over the long-run to external and internal equilibrium (squeezing out marginal exports to make way for rising investment income), and if this is to be achieved without a rise in the domestic price level then a nominal appreciation must also occur. But the trend rate of appreciation per annum would be slow.

The identification of a huge current account surplus as secular (having its origin in an equally large 'structural' savings surplus) should go along with a presumption that interest rates will be low (on the given national money) by international comparison. Huge capital exports are the counterpart to the surplus. Some market-participants would be interested in the economist's analysis of what form these capital exports are likely to take (in particular, are there any markets which should gain from investment inflows out of the surplus country). Capital export analysis would be of interest for similar reasons in the case of huge transitory current account surpluses (for example the OPEC surpluses following the oil shocks, or Italy's mega-surplus following the 30 per cent fall of the lira from 1992 to 1993) – even though the interest would be qualified by the short expected life of the phenomenon.

CAPITAL: THE TAIL WHICH WAGS THE DOG?

Looking to current account data for an explanation of observed capital flows runs counter to so-called 'common sense' of both market-participants and commentators. We all know that in today's currency markets, trade-related transactions are only a small proportion of total turnover. It is important, however, to distinguish net from gross capital flows. Much of the activity in currency markets is zero-sum – banks trading with each other and standing to make offsetting profits and losses from any given exchange rate movement. The net flows of capital under the broad headings which feature in balance of payments analysis (for example, direct investment, portfolio, loans) make up only a small share of gross foreign exchange transactions.

Even so, the instances where a big change in the current account position is the autonomous event explaining a new observed pattern of capital flow are quite rare. The example of a temporary bulge in the current account surplus or deficit bringing a sharp change in capital flows is most usually associated with commodity price fluctuation, or a 'natural disaster'. As illustration, a big decline in commodity prices might push Canada into huge current account deficit. Depression in the primary commodity sector of the economy would not go along normally with higher interest rates.

The analyst of the Canadian dollar would ask in such circumstances how far its exchange rate (against the US dollar) must fall to induce sufficient capital inflow to bridge the widened current account gap. The incentive to the inflow would be the expectation of an eventual bounce-back of the Canadian unit once commodity prices returned to a 'normal' level.

The hypothetical illustration of Canadian payments adjustment does not provide an exception to the rule of simultaneous determination of the current and capital accounts. Indeed simultaneity is a tautology – all economic variables are determined in a general equilibrium set of equations embracing all markets in the economy. But in some situations, one part of the simultaneous process is so dominant that the economist can usefully focus his attention there, drawing out a so-called partial equilibrium analysis. Consistent with that approach, he can occasionally draw a chain of causality from the current account to the capital account, and sometimes from the capital to the current account.

More usually the current and capital accounts can be viewed as determined by differing national propensities to save and investment opportunity. When different nations, however, produce goods and services which are imperfect substitutes for one another, and some goods (and services) which are not traded internationally (the so-called non-tradeables), and where exchange risks (and political risks) are significant, the concentration on the savings–investment balance should be viewed as a simplification, with more or less validity according to circumstance.

Let us start with the simplified description of joint determination of the current and capital accounts in the balance of payments. A country where savings tend to run ahead of domestic investment opportunity should run up current account surpluses and capital account deficits. The low interest rates brought about by the downward pressure of a savings glut are the motor behind capital exports. If a 'savings excess' is indeed the common cause of an observed combination of current account surplus, capital account deficit, and low interest rates, then we may also observe a relatively high ratio of traded to non-traded goods prices in the given nation (non-traded goods seeming cheap by international comparison). The high ratio would induce domestic enterprises to switch production away from the low-consumption domestic market.

In practice, two prominent examples of countries with huge savings and current account surpluses (relative to economic size) –

Switzerland and Japan – do not demonstrate a relatively high ratio of traded to non-traded goods prices. This is because both countries have ostensibly low productivity in their non-traded goods sectors (marked by widespread restrictive practices and associated high margins in retail distribution), and international trade tends to equalize prices across frontiers in the high productivity traded goods sector.

Moreover, Switzerland has been a surplus nation for so long that it has progressed to the mature stage where investment income from abroad is such a high proportion of GDP that the trade balance has been forced into deficit (when considered over the business cycle as a whole). A steady deterioration in the trade balance to make way for growing investment income (and so hold the current surplus ratio steady) normally means a rising ratio of non-traded to traded goods prices.

Both Japan and Switzerland have not had persistently weak capital accounts as the simple account of simultaneous determination of current and capital balances for a high savings surplus nation would have it. Some of the deviations from the simple case can be explained episodically – refuge demand for the Swiss franc, varying risk aversion of Japanese investors with respect to foreign assets, foreign 'volatility' in purchases of Tokyo equities. These episodic explanations all involve factors which are ruled out by the initial assumptions of the simple model describing how current and capital accounts are determined jointly by savings and investment behaviour.

A big shortfall of the simple model is its exclusion of monetary influences. As we have already seen, money rates of interest and the so-called natural rate of interest tend to equal each other when calculated as averages over many years. But over shorter periods, large deviations occur. Hence, though the natural rate of interest in the savings surplus country should be low by international comparison (especially relative to the natural rate in the savings deficit countries), sometimes money rates will be in reverse relationship.

As an example, during most of 1993 and early 1994 real money and bond yields in Japan were far higher than in the US (when consumer price data in Japan were corrected for the shift towards discount outlets), despite Japan being in huge savings and current account surplus whilst the US was in the opposite situation. The Bank of Japan under Governor Mieno was following a very cautious policy, holding money-market rates even in the first half of 1993 at above 3 per cent – similar to the level of rates in the US, where a good recovery was underway and the rate of inflation still significant, albeit low. Moreover US investors were intermittently huge buyers of Tokyo equities. Thus Japan's capital account was strong at the same time as its own current account was in large surplus – illustrating an exception to the simple hypothesis of savings imbalance being reflected in simultaneous divergent tendencies in the current and capital account balances. Excessively tight Japanese monetary policy and distrust of Federal Reserve policy (in view of the running trade conflict between the US and Japan many investors were concerned that the Federal Reserve might be an accomplice of the Administration in pushing the yen higher and the dollar down) worked against the stabilizing forces in the international flow of funds.

Some analysts, however, question whether the description of Japan as a huge savings surplus country, with a natural counterpart to that surplus in capital exports (driven by low domestic rates of return), has been continuously valid. In particular, they cite the early 1980s as a period when Japanese investors had strong demand for dollar bonds and assets, and this demand was the 'tail' which wagged the current account 'dog'. The demand for dollars kept the yen at an undervalued level, which in turn fostered a huge trade surplus capable of financing the capital outflow. In turn the cheap yen and strong export demand encouraged the Bank of Japan to hold money-market rates at a high level (compared to where they otherwise would have been), which restrained domestic expenditure and contributed to the large observed savings surplus.

Three factors were cited as behind the sudden Japanese demand for dollar assets. First, at the start of the 1980s, exchange controls were lifted in Japan. Hence there was large pent-up demand for foreign assets especially from institutional investors whose portfolios hitherto had been spectacularly undiversified. Second, earthquake risk emerged as a significant factor in investment strategy, now that Japan was entering a period of higher geological risk. Dollar bond holdings could be seen as a hedge against earthquake risk. Third, liberalization in foreign capital markets added to their appeal relative to the restrictive practice ridden domestic Japanese market.

The story of the Japanese demand for foreign assets leading the Japanese current account into huge surplus is only credible in the context of considerable exchange risk between the yen and the dollar. Otherwise any slight cheapening of the yen and upward pressure on Japanese interest rates from the diversification process would have brought an elastic response in the form of capital inflows. These would have come from foreigners tilting their portfolios towards the now more competitive yen and by borrowers, especially Japanese-based, switching away from yen liabilities and towards dollar liabilities.

As a practical matter, however, there is little doubt that capital inflows into Japan have been highly inelastic. Hence some (but not all) of the giant Japanese current account surplus in the first half of the 1980s could be attributed to the strong demand (from Japan) for US assets. As a corollary, some part of the large US current account deficit in those years could be regarded as 'generated' by the surge in demand from abroad (especially Japan) for dollars. Remember this was the period of Euro-pessimism and concern about Germany being a nuclear *Schlagfeld* (battlefield), as Pershing missiles were stationed in the West to balance the Soviet build-up of medium-range nuclear missiles in the East.

Demand for dollar assets helped to sustain the US currency at an expensive price (in terms of other major investment currencies) and also to keep US interest rates at a lower level than they otherwise would have been in the situation of domestic private spending boom and budget shock that marked the first years of Reaganomics. Thus capital inflows to the USA may well have been the tail that induced a widening of the US current account deficit to well beyond normal proportion. But the whole episode presents some ambiguity. We cannot observe the rate of interest which would have prevailed if there had not been strong autonomous demand for dollar assets from abroad. We cannot reject totally, even if we do not favour, the hypothesis that foreign demand for dollars was driven first and foremost by high US interest rates which reflected the savings shortage in the US economy (bringing us back to the simultaneous determination of the current and capital account by the balance between savings and investment) rather than having any autonomous basis.

Another hypothesis sometimes advanced to back the view that capital flows out of Japan and into the US were to some extent autonomous rather than induced by savings–investment imbalance concerns the flow of direct investment. It seems that business world-wide, but most of all in Japan, suddenly wanted a new or increased stake in the USA. The foreign take-over boom in the USA took off. In practice, however, this hypothesis is hard to distinguish at first (in the early 1980s) from the view that foreigners were simply in the forefront of perceiving the great new investment opportunities under Reaganomics, and so we are back to the savings–investment imbalance as the simultaneous source of current and capital account imbalance.

In the later 1980s there was the 'outside' influence of the bubble in the Tokyo equity market. Japanese companies could print money by issuing high P/E equities in Tokyo to take over businesses selling on much lower P/Es in the USA. The arbitrage worked so long as investors in the Tokyo equity market continued to believe that Japanese management had a 'magic touch' whereby they could immediately improve the earnings outlook of business assets they acquired in the USA. The bubble-related outflow of capital from Japan into the USA tended to enlarge the US current account deficit on the one hand and the Japanese surplus on the other by promoting an overvalued dollar (and lower than otherwise US interest rates) and undervalued yen. The flow of capital was not directly dependent on a savings–investment imbalance.

A clearer case (than the US–Japanese example just described) of capital flows playing a lead role in determining current account balances (via influencing as an intermediate step the balance between savings and investment) is capital flight. One of the most dramatic examples of the phenomenon was the flight of capital out of Germany in the years 1919–21. German investors, alarmed by the spectres of heavy taxation to pay reparations to the Allies, revolution at home, and high inflation, shifted their funds abroad, especially into Switzerland and Holland (both neutral during the First World War of 1914–18). The cheap mark (which fell far below purchasing power parity) promoted an export boom, much to the chagrin of Britain. Keynes captured the resentment in his populist campaign to let Germany off paying reparations.

The power of capital flight to drag the 'trade balance' in the German example (1919–21) depended critically on 'normal' capital flows being disrupted. In many modern examples of capital flight (for example, out of Latin America in the late 1970s and early 1980s) the main accommodating flow of funds in the opposite direction is generated by domestic enterprises increasing their foreign currency borrowing in response to a widened interest rate spread (domestic rates rise relative to those on foreign currency). In the case of post-First World War Germany, borrowing abroad did not become feasible until the 'stabilization' (under the Dawes Plan) of 1924.

CAPITAL FLOW ANALYSIS

The possibility of strong autonomous influences (other than those emanating directly from the balance of savings and investment) working on the capital account, and this in turn feeding back on to the current account (and thereby the balance between savings and investment), means that market economists are well justified in searching for complex themes in the flow of capital. In their searching, economists should realize that recorded flows only hint at underlying changes in demand and supply of assets in different currencies and political jurisdictions. Over a short period of time, changes in net demand are usually reflected in price rather than observable flows. Hence at a theoretical level, capital flows are much less revealing about changes in investor taste than are, say, data on merchandise goods exports about the popularity of Japanese cars.

At a practical level, a key problem economists encounter is the paucity and unreliability of data on capital flows. The data is collected under headings and sub-headings which are usually not highly illuminating. The huge flows through offshore centres only cast a shadow over the figures collected by nation-based balance of payments statisticians. Perhaps the least reliable figures of all are portfolio flows, given the huge difficulties of tracking the trans-actions of non-bank investors both inside and outside any given political jurisdiction. The most reliable are said to be banking flows, but these are often residual or intermediary in nature (the bank acting as a channel for the flow, not as originator), rather than indicative of end-user demand and supply.

An example from the mid-1990s shows how economists can use capital flow data in their evaluation of market prices. A starting point is the US capital account. Quarterly estimates are published of this along with the other components of US international payments by the US Department of Commerce. Data is available usually ten weeks or so after the end of the previous quarter (thus data for the second quarter becomes available in mid-September). An analyst in September 1994 could have made several interesting observations.

First, the US remained (during the first half of 1994) a large net exporter of direct investment – in stark contrast to the situation at the end of the 1980s when the US was the main beneficiary of a world-wide boom in mergers and acquisitions (European and Japanese business 'buying up' the US). Second, the outflow of

US capital into foreign equities had maintained the extraordinarily high levels reached in the previous year (around $60 bn p.a.), albeit that the outflow into foreign bonds had moderated sharply (to $20 bn p.a. from $59.4 bn in 1993). Third, foreign inflows to the US T-bond market had slumped to virtually zero. Fourth, official inflows of funds were still large, but appeared to be down on the prior year's level.

The capital account data should be seen against the background of the US running a current account deficit at the same time of $150 bn p.a. – about 2.2 per cent of GDP. Several contemporary analysts saw the large outpourings of (net) direct investment and equity capital as a key element in the overall weakness of the US dollar. How, they asked, could the US finance a large current account deficit and capital exports when at the same time US interest rates and bond yields were hardly any higher than in Germany, and in real terms were well below those in Japan?

The question posed, however, was too strong. A temporary 'foray' by US investors into foreign equity markets, many of which were emerging markets in the dollar area, amounting to a net flow of less than 1 per cent of GDP, can hardly be seen as a factor of significance in the total supply and demand for US dollar assets. The question became more significant if the hypothesis were accepted that a new long-term pattern had emerged whereby US investors were now embarked on a major international diversification programme. If so, important changes in stocks could occur, say over the next ten years.

But for such a hypothesis to be treated as almost certainly correct, we must go beyond the realms of rational analysis to the psychology of booms and bust. We know that at the peak of a boom or bottom of a downswing, the normal defences against accepting highly questionable hypotheses appear to fail. The healthy sceptical response to this particular hypothesis (concerning portfolio diversification into foreign equities) would be to point out that first the data came from the most unreliable section of the capital account. Second, as much as 50 per cent of the portfolio outflow related to inflows into the Tokyo equity market – hardly a long-run stable magnitude (why should Tokyo on an earnings yield of barely 1.5 per cent attract $30 bn p.a. of US capital, when Wall Street was yielding near 7 per cent?). Third, the flow of capital, largely via mutual funds into emerging markets, carried all the hallmarks of a speculative development (salesmen selling the new funds to retail investors on the basis of many unrealistic assumptions).

The turnaround (from the late 1980s) in the direct investment account appeared to be a more substantial factor (than portfolio flows) in evaluating the dollar. But even here, market economists should have been cautious about over-interpreting the relevant data. The direct investment account spans a wide range of financial transactions many of which have nothing to do with real physical investment (the acquiring of plant and equipment). For example, if in Tokyo sentiment becomes pessimistic on the dollar against the yen, Japanese head offices may boost local borrowing of their US subsidiaries (from US banks) enabling them to transfer funds back to head office and into the yen. Correspondingly, measured direct investment inflows into the USA from Japan would dwindle. But that would have no bearing on the volume of 'real investment flow'.

Sometimes we have the situation of large real direct investment flows having only a quite diluted counterpart in currency flows. For example, the Japanese take-over boom in the USA during the late 1980s was largely financed by the Tokyo parent issuing equity-linked dollar paper in the Euro-bond market. Because the financing was by the parent (usually via an offshore affiliate of the parent) the US direct investment account reflected the gross value of the acquisitions. But net demand for dollars from Japan was only a fraction of this value. The dollar paper – usually unpackaged from the equity-warrant by investment banks – was sold to investors (many of these were banks in Japan) looking for dollar assets, and so funds were absorbed (at the margin) which otherwise would have gone into the USA.

In sum, there was an interesting story to tell about direct investment flows over the decade to the mid-1990s and this had some relevance – but not as much as at first sight – to evaluating the dollar during that period. There was no particular new addition to this by then familiar story which could be made on the basis of capital account data for the first half of 1994. By contrast, there was a new and exciting story to be told in that most 'treacherous' section of the capital account – banking flows. Inflows through the banking sector ballooned to almost $150 bn p.a. In seeking to understand what lay behind this vast flow, exchange market analysts had to sift through capital account data and other available evidence much in the nature of financial detectives. Let us see how they would have progressed to a successful conclusion.

117

First, analysts would have been aware of the contemporary 'bear market' in fixed-rate bonds and the likelihood that many international investors had decided to build up the share of deposits and other floating rate assets in their portfolios. The dwindling to near zero in foreign net purchases of US Treasury bonds (shown in the portfolio section of the capital account) was certainly consistent with that decision. Increased foreign investment in dollar deposits whether on or offshore would have been reflected in a higher level of capital inflow via the banking sector.

But analysts should have been cautious about over-stretching portfolio shifts as an explanation. Market evidence suggested that international investors were cutting dollar positions, having built up speculative holdings the year before (1993) on the basis of widespread forecasts that US economic recovery would bring exchange rate gains, and now these had failed to materialize. Moreover, desired changes in portfolio composition usually lead first to price changes (yields on the now less popular asset – in this case bonds – increasing) rather than to an observed big restructuring of portfolios.

Second, analysts should have been aware that some 'steady state' inflow of funds into the USA via the banking sector is to be expected, the source of which lies in the large grey area of the world economy reflected in the over $100 bn error in IMF payments statistics. The owners of the investment income and other types of income which accumulate in offshore centres (and such income is the main source of error in the payments statistics) can be assumed to place a substantial portion into dollar assets.

A glance at a table compiled to show the sources and uses of foreign (non-US) savings in dollars provides some general insights into 'steady state' inflows of hidden income into the dollar, some substantial share of which would normally give rise to banking inflows to the USA. We see first (in Table 5.1) that there is an estimated steady stream of 'hidden income' into the dollar from offshore centres and tax havens of around $50 bn p.a. (shown under the headings of 'international investment income' and 'invisible export payments'). Examples of hidden income include interest, coupon, and dividend payments accruing to 'unregistered' portfolios which are typically spread between a range of major international currencies of which the dollar is often the largest. Another example are earnings from exports of goods and services siphoned off into tax havens via various invoicing practices and accumulated in multi-currency portfolios.

Table 5.1 Sources and uses of foreign savings in dollars (US$ bn)

	1992	1993	1994	1995	1996
Sources					
International investment income[1]	20	20	25	30	40
Invisible export payments[1]	25	30	30	35	35
Japanese purchases of					
dollar bonds and notes[2]	5	10	5	15	20
Recorded bond purchases					
from Europe	5	10	20	15	25
Flight capital	35	40	50	55	40
Direct and equity					
investment in USA	10	60	50	60	85
Reserves of:					
Industrial countries[3]	0	40	80	65	20
LDCs[4] Fuel exporters	0	0	–20	10	5
Non-fuel exporters	40	30	15	10	15
Total	140	240	255	295	285
Uses					
Net financing in dollars by:[5]					
Industrial countries (ex-USA)[6]	–35	–100	–20	–20	–25
LDCs Fuel exporters[7]	10	20	25	25	15
Non-fuel exporters	35	55	30	50	50
US direct and portfolio					
investment abroad[8]	60	160	70	80	90
US current a/c deficit	70	105	150	160	155
Total	140	240	255	295	285

Notes:

1 Accumulating in tax havens and offshore centres, non-reported in balance of payments statistics.

2 Excludes bond purchases which are covered in the forward market or by short-term borrowings (estimated). Includes only bonds issued by non-Japanese borrowers.

3 Additions to the US Treasury's holdings of foreign currency subtract from this total.

4 IMF nomenclature is followed in categorizing LDCs. Taiwan is included under LDCs. Various asset transactions are included under this heading.

5 Bond purchases and reserve accumulation shown under sources are not netted from total. Purchases of dollar bonds and notes not under sources – for example. Taiwanese registered buying of dollar bonds – are netted. Under this heading is included borrowing in dollars by the private sector not shown elsewhere.

6 Net borrowing in foreign currency by US residents has a negative sign in forming the total under this heading.

7 Mexico is included under this heading.

8 The traditionally small but now substantial volume of US purchases of foreign currency bonds is added to this total.

When bond markets are out of favour, an especially large share of 'hidden income' being placed in dollars might well go into bank deposits. Where these are accumulated in offshore centres (rather than being placed directly in New York) they tend to have a counterpart in inter-bank lending into the USA. The same comment applies to those flows into dollars which have their source in capital flight. In the table a 'guesstimate' is made of the amount of capital flight into dollars (this is quite a separate flow from income accumulating in offshore centres) – by definition there can be no firm data in this area. (Capital flight describes funds which leave a given country primarily under the influence of considerations regarding tax, political risk, and inconvertibility risk, and often ends up in secret or disguised accounts.)

The magnitudes hinted at in the table for 'steady state' hidden inflows to dollars can hardly explain the sudden bulge of banking inflows in the first half of 1994, even if a somewhat greater share went into bank deposits than normal. A third direction in which the 'financial detective' could turn would be the accumulation of reserves in dollars by foreign central banks and governments. IMF data is a starting point – albeit that this becomes available only with a long lag. In 1993, the total reserve accumulation in dollars reported to the IMF (corrected for exchange rate changes) amounted to around $70 bn.

Only that part of reserve accumulation which goes directly into the USA (either T-bills, T-bonds, or US bank deposits) is caught under official flows by US balance of payments statisticians. Thus the official sector of the US capital account, although it has the advantage of being published with a smaller lag than IMF data, gives a less comprehensive picture of 'reserve demand' for the dollar. Reserve accumulation in offshore dollar deposits and some-times bonds (where non-US issuers of these swap their liabilities into non-dollar currencies) can be the source of big banking sector flows into the USA.

The IMF data may itself on occasion seriously understate the amount of reserve accumulation in dollars outside the USA. This would be the case when a major central bank was shrouding its operations in secrecy – perhaps in line with its intervention in the foreign exchange market. Other motives for clandestine accumu-lation include foreign policy considerations, including national security. The hidden dollar reserve accumulation outside the USA could well show up as banking sector inflows (to the USA).

In the first half of 1994, Japan was one obvious direction for the 'financial detective' to look in the search for clandestine reserve accumulation which might explain the huge inflows of capital into the USA via the banking sector. The breakdown in 'framework talks' between Tokyo and Washington in early February (the framework was to be a clear timetable for Japan to open up certain key markets to greater foreign competition – removing various 'invisible' barriers) had unleashed huge speculative demand for the yen. Yet the climb of the yen and official reserve movements reported by the Bank of Japan appeared to be only 'modestly large'.

The detective could find the vital clue in quarterly data published by the Bank for International Settlements in Basle on international banking flows. The August edition of this publication showed that Japanese banks reduced their external liabilities by $70 bn and increased their external assets by $18 bn. Furthermore, Japanese banks increased their foreign currency borrowing (mainly in dollars) from domestic residents by almost $90 bn – this was the principal counterpart to their strengthened external position.

The analysts could guess that the principal domestic resident was the Japanese government itself – and it was not difficult to get confirmation of this from the more approachable officials at supranational organizations. The story was that the Ministry of Finance had re-lent dollars bought in the foreign exchange market to the Japanese banks, who in turn had repaid their large short-term liabilities in the offshore dollar market. The resulting glut of dollar funds in London and elsewhere had presented a cheap source of borrowing to US banks who themselves were facing a rapid growth in demand for credit (from spring 1994 on) – hence the bulge in capital inflows to the USA via the banking sector.

Economists, having completed their financial detective work as described, could turn to the implications for the market outlook. First, they could warn that market rates (exchange rates and interest rate spreads) with respect to the dollar and yen were not at market-clearing levels. On the assumption that massive intervention by the Bank of Japan could not be sustained, some rates would have to adjust towards inducing private capital inflows to the USA (in sufficient magnitude to replace the official flows) – unless a big shift in expectations or perceived 'realities' had meanwhile occurred. The candidates for adjustment included lower Japanese interest rates, a stronger yen and weaker dollar, or higher US interest rates.

Second, the story unearthed carried a warning (not a forecast!) about the US inflation outlook. There was less comfort to be gained from the low rate of US money supply growth through the first three quarters of 1994. US banks had been able to hold down their supply of domestic deposits despite accelerating credit demand because of greatly increased offshore borrowing (which does not form part of the money supply aggregates). From written and also verbal commentaries it seemed that senior Federal officials themselves were not aware of the extent of hidden Japanese intervention and the monetary implications.

CURRENCY GEOGRAPHY

The discussion above about US capital flows was cast in terms of a bilateral relationship between the USA and Japan. More generally, the flow of funds internationally has to be considered in the framework of a dominant currency triangle involving the US dollar, the Deutschmark, and Japanese yen. The framework is put together using various 'geographic' terms which facilitate discussion. Subjects of currency geography include the identification of the dominant current in international capital flow and the nature of polar forces which draw one group of currencies in their motion against others.

A principle term in currency geography is 'zone'. A 'currency zone' is a set of currencies which move closely together against outsiders. More technically, changes in the exchange rate of each currency in the zone against a given big outsider (belonging to the DM–dollar–yen triangle), measured over a specified time interval, are highly correlated. The variance of intra-zonal exchange rate change is small both in absolute terms and also relative to that of trans-zonal exchange rate change. For example, most of the EC currencies during various periods of the 1970s, 1980s, and 1990s, have belonged to a zone, sometimes called the DM zone. Membership varies according to the length of time over which exchange rate change is measured. If daily, weekly, or even monthly changes are considered, the Italian lira and Spanish peseta and even the British pound could be included in the Deutschmark zone alongside 'hard core' members during several past episodes. On the basis of six-monthly changes, by contrast, only a small hard core of currencies would qualify.

There are many possible factors lying behind zonal formations. They include a high degree of economic interdependence, monetary co-ordination, similar exposure of the nation-members of the zone to one overriding political risk, and the existence of a highly volatile large outsider. On this last point the volatile US dollar has been a contributor to zonal formation in Europe – but it is not itself a sufficient condition. After all the yen does not belong to the DM zone. We have to explain also the low absolute volatility of intra-DM zone exchange rate fluctuation.

Outside Europe, the main example of a currency zone is that including the US dollar and Canadian dollar. This zonal formation is strongest when very short-term exchange rate changes are considered. It fades as the length of period over which changes are measured is increased. The basis of the Canadian dollar's membership of the dollar zone is a high degree of economic interdependence between the two nations and the pursuance of similar long-term goals in monetary policy. Outer members of the dollar zone (membership is looser and sometimes intermittent) include some of the Latin American and East Asian currencies. Occasionally the British pound could have been considered as an outer member of the dollar zone (recent examples include mid-1993 to spring 1994 and autumn 1994 to summer 1995).

Both the Deutschmark and dollar zones include a dominant currency – the Deutschmark and US dollar respectively. In our currency geography, the dollar and Deutschmark can each be described as a 'pole'. The US dollar, for example, exerts polar power over the Canadian dollar. The US dollar pulls the Canadian dollar strongly in its motion against outsiders. But the Canadian dollar exerts little influence on the US dollar. Thus in explaining fluctuations of the C$–DM exchange rate, the analyst would usually turn to the US$–DM as the main influence. But the story of the US$–DM would almost never include a Canadian element. A corollary is that fluctuations in the intra-zonal exchange rate of the Canadian dollar against the US dollar are dominated by Canadian rather than US stories.

The basis of polar power is almost always (albeit that exception exists in theory) asymmetry of economic size and related monetary dependence. The US is much more important to the Canadian economy than the Canadian is to the US economy. In particular, bilateral trade flows between the USA and Canada are a much larger share of Canadian GDP than of US GDP. Thus any event of significance for the US economy (and often thereby for the US dollar) is also of significance for the Canadian (and Canadian dollar). Moreover, the Bank of Canada, aware of the sensitivity of the Canadian economy to the C\$/US\$ exchange rate, and also of the need to at least match and hopefully better US inflation performance (essential to maintaining the huge amount of foreign investment in the Canadian dollar) tends to follow – albeit not immediately and identically – changes in US monetary policy.

In Europe the German economy does not enjoy the natural dominance of the US economy in North America. Germany accounts for just over 25 per cent of West European GDP (France is around two-thirds the economic size of Germany). Germany's economic weight is increased if we include in the arithmetic two nations which are virtually in a DM monetary union – the Netherlands and Austria (these countries together come to virtually double the economic size of France) – and if we allow for multilateral independence. For all the West European nations the inner DM bloc (Germany, Holland and Austria) is the largest trade partner. German economic 'surprises' impact on France, for example, not just via the bilateral trade relationship between the inner DM bloc and the French economy but also via the effect of the same surprise on say Italy and Britain, also important trade partners of France. Thus the emergence of unexpectedly strong recovery of domestic demand in Germany, for example, might well put upward pressure on all European currencies against outsiders (on the basis of the cyclical influences discussed earlier in the present chapter).

In practice, some of the polar power exercised by the Deutschmark stems from satellite behaviour by the French monetary authorities. Were the Banque de France to follow a much more independent monetary policy, the polar power of the DM, not just with respect to the French franc but also to the Belgian franc, Italian lira, Spanish peseta, and British pound, would be less. But during the 1990s so far (other than during the ERM crises of 1992–3), the Banque de France virtually follows every interest rate move of the Bundesbank. Thus changes in German monetary policy become changes in policy for a huge economic area in Europe. In turn, monetary policy in Italy or the UK becomes quite sensitive to Bundesbank policy because of the importance of the exchange rate between the wide Deutschmark bloc and the particular national currency. This sensitivity is an important factor in the Deutschmark's polar power over the non-bloc currencies in Western Europe.

The Japanese yen, in contrast to the Deutschmark or US dollar, is neither a currency pole nor the member of a currency zone. Both economic geography and politics play a role in the yen's isolation.

Even though intra-East Asian trade has increased remarkably in recent years, Japan and the other East Asian nations do not form an integrated economic area. Neither business cycles nor monetary conditions are generally in synchrony. The potential of military conflict between several of the nations in the area exists (China versus Taiwan or Vietnam for example).

No East Asian central bank could justify simply aping Japanese monetary policy in similar fashion to French deference to the Bundesbank. In any case, that French behaviour would have been inconceivable other than under the guise of the European Monetary System. But in East Asia there is no EC (supranational grouping of nations). And there has been less of a reconciliation between Japan and the East Asian nations with respect to wartime pasts than between Germany and the other West European nations. The isolation of the yen means that it is the smallest currency in the key triangle which dominates the world of currency trading (see Figures 5.1, 5.2, 5.3).

No more than two out of the three currencies (in the triangle) can be moving unilaterally – one rising and one falling. The characteristic of unilateral motion is the given currency moving in the same direction (either rising or falling) against each of the other two in the triangle. The exchange rate between the two currencies moving unilaterally is termed the 'axis' (of the currency world) and is named after the currency at each end. Thus if the Deutschmark is at one end (say rising against the dollar and the yen) and the US dollar at the other (falling against the Deutschmark and yen), we say that the currency world is revolving around the Deutschmark–dollar axis. The third currency, the yen, in the above example (of a Deutschmark–dollar axis) can be described as 'in between'.

Sometimes only one currency is moving unilaterally, the other two forming a pair which are moving closely together. Then there is no currency axis. Instead, the world of foreign exchange trading is dominated by a 'solostar' (rising or falling). All three currencies have enjoyed periods of solostardom, but to very different extents. For example, through the first half of 1983 the Deutschmark fell sharply against both the dollar and the yen, the yen–dollar rate remaining trendless around 240. This period of the Deutschmark as a falling solostar was marked by 'Euro-pessimism'.

A subsequent period of Deutschmark solostardom was the second half of 1989, when optimism about the German economy took off as the Democratic Republic of East Germany crumbled. In

125

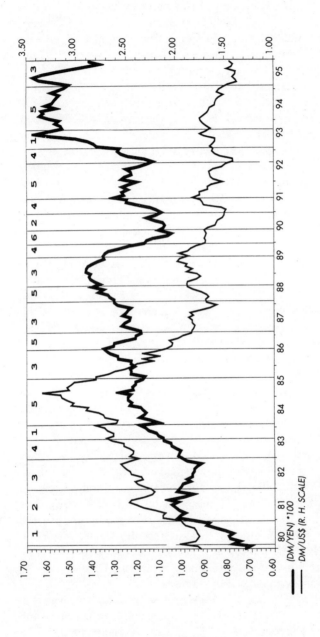

Key: 1 = DM–yen axis; 2 = $ solostar; 3 = $–yen axis.
4 = DM solostar; 5 = DM–$ axis; 6 = yen solostar

Figure 5.1 DM/$/yen triangle: the DM corner
Source: Datastream

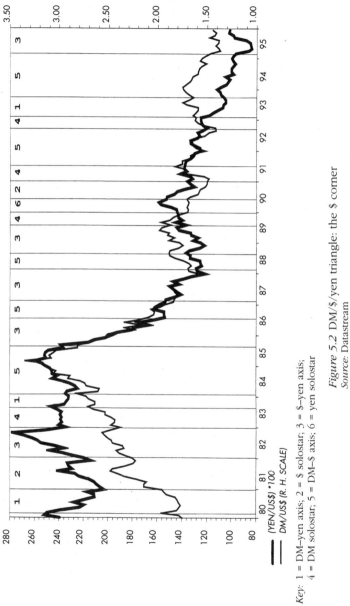

Figure 5.2 DM/$/yen triangle: the $ corner
Source: Datastream

Key: 1 = DM–yen axis; 2 = $ solostar; 3 = $–yen axis;
4 = DM solostar; 5 = DM–$ axis; 6 = yen solostar

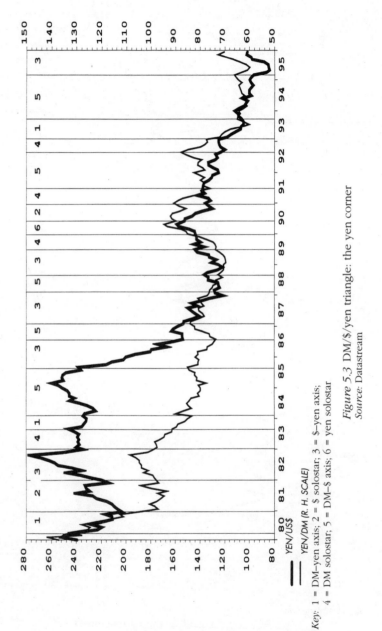

Figure 5.3 DM/$/yen triangle: the yen corner
Source: Datastream

Key: 1 = DM–yen axis; 2 = $ solostar; 3 = $–yen axis;
4 = DM solostar; 5 = DM–$ axis; 6 = yen solostar

the first half of 1991, the Deutschmark was again a solostar – this time in a downward direction – as the burdens of unification became increasingly clear and the Bundesbank delayed tightening policy sharply despite a post-unification boom. In the last quarter of 1992, the Deutschmark again fell (as a solostar), this time on evidence that Germany was in a steep recession.

By contrast, since the start of the 1980s there has been only one episode of the yen as solostar. In early 1990 the collapse of the Tokyo equity market brought an immediate weakening of the yen. Other periods when the yen has been moving in the same direction against the other two (the Deutschmark and dollar) have also seen one of those moving unilaterally (in the opposite direction to the yen). Most often the currency at the opposite end of the axis to the yen has been the dollar (five times in the fifteen years from 1980, amounting in total to four years compared to three times for a Deutschmark–yen axis, totalling eighteen months).

There have been only two episodes of dollar solostardom – and thus the phenomenon is almost as rare as yen solostardom. Through virtually the whole of 1981 the dollar swung sharply and in almost identical fashion against the yen and Deutschmark. The year started with the Federal Reserve under Chairman Volcker tightening policy ferociously as the economy began to show new strength, and short-term dollar money-market rates exceeded 20 per cent p.a. Then in late 1981 as a second US recession set in, dollar rates fell quickly and far. The US dollar followed interest rates up and then down. Second, in the last half of 1990, the dollar fell sharply against both the yen and the Deutschmark as the US economy slipped into recession and confrontation with Iraq loomed. (A third episode of dollar solostardom might be confirmed for the period late autumn 1995 to early spring 1996.)

There have been a similar number of episodes during which the axis has run from the Deutschmark to the US dollar as from the Japanese yen to the dollar – five each (with respect to the years 1980–95). Solostardom is in general less common than a currency axis holding sway. Nine years of an axis (varying between different combinations) cumulatively compares to just under five years when one of the three currencies (by far the most often the DM) has been a solostar.

Several episodes of solostardom have been associated with shock events – the opening of the Berlin Wall, the bursting of the Tokyo stock market bubble, the Volcker shock (pushing short-term

US interest rates to over 20 per cent in the first half of 1981). If we exclude these shock episodes there remain three instances of solostardom for the Deutschmark, one for the US dollar, and none for the Japanese yen.

The relative frequency of solostardom for the Deutschmark can be explained in part by a similar dependence of the Japanese and US economies on exports to Europe in contrast to a much greater 'dollar dependence' of Japanese than European exports. Specifically Japanese exports to North America come to almost 3 per cent of GDP (on the basis of 1994 data). Exports to East Asian nations, most of which may be considered as in the outer dollar zone, come to a further 2.5 per cent of GDP. European exports to North America run at just over 1.5 per cent of GDP, and to East Asia 0.75 per cent of GDP.

Hence changes in US economic prospects and in the dollar's international value have a considerably greater influence on Japan than Europe. A differential impact of US 'news' on both areas means that the yen and Deutschmark should be affected differently. When the dollar is moving, both the yen and Deutschmark are unlikely to be together at the opposite end of the pole. Either the currency world would be revolving around a dollar–yen or dollar–Deutschmark axis. Periods of a dollar–yen axis have sometimes been marked by trade confrontation between Washington and Tokyo, when the US is pressing for action to cut the Japanese surplus. The Deutschmark, as the world's number two investment currency, is at the opposite end of the axis to the dollar, sometimes when the investment appeal of the US currency is in flux.

By contrast to the asymmetric influence of a 'moving dollar' on the yen and Deutschmark, a symmetry exists between the importance of Europe for the USA and Japan. Exports from each to Western Europe run at just below 2 per cent of GDP. Hence a sudden change in German economic perspectives which puts the Deutschmark at the centre of attention in the currency markets could push the dollar and yen together to the opposite end of the pole.

The relatively high degree of economic interdependence between Japan and the dollar zone means that there is indeed a significant chance of the dollar and yen being stable against each other when the Deutschmark is in motion. Periods of quiet for the DM–yen or DM–dollar exchange rate, by contrast, are extremely rare, a factor which lowers the chances of either the yen or the dollar having a period of solostardom.

The extent of economic interdependence between Japan and the dollar zone is also a factor in why a yen–Deutschmark axis has been observed so little. If the yen is 'in motion' because of some change in Japan's 'situation', there is likely to be a 'mirror image' situation in the USA but not Europe. Take the example of Japan running a huge trade surplus and its economy growing at only a sluggish pace. The USA, whose imports from Japan run at near 2 per cent of GDP and whose exports to Japan are close to 1 per cent (in addition exports to other Asian countries exceed 1 per cent of GDP), would usually be at the opposite end of the policy confrontation with Japan rather than Europe (whose exports to Japan represent 0.5 per cent of GDP and imports near 1 per cent). Pressure from the US Administration for yen appreciation usually has the side effect of raising investor concerns about the safety of the dollar itself as a store of value, also causing it to fall against the Deutschmark.

There is an alternative example of a change in the Japanese 'situation' – a sudden shift in Bank of Japan monetary policy. In the portfolios of Japanese investors the US dollar is typically a closer substitute than the Deutschmark for the yen – meaning that a sharp fall, say, in Japanese interest rates would trigger a much bigger investor response with respect to the dollar than the Deutschmark. (The experience, however, of large flows of funds between Japanese yen and Deutschmarks in 1995 suggests 'substitutability' is far from constant.) Similarly many investors in East Asia see the yen, rather than the Deutschmark, as the principal alternative investment currency to the dollar. Thus the monetary shift should have a bigger impact on the dollar than the DM, causing the dollar to be at the opposite end of the pole to the yen.

By extension, a German monetary surprise is unlikely to have its main impact on the yen. The dollar is a closer substitute than the yen for the Deutschmark. For most holders of Deutschmark investments, the US dollar rather than the yen is the principal alternative currency in their portfolio. In particular European investors have little natural interest in the yen as a core holding in their portfolios. The US dollar rather than the yen is likely to be the principal gainer or loser from a strong unilateral move by the Deutschmark in the currency markets induced by a big shift in German monetary policy (or by a shift in perceptions of the Deutschmark's safety).

Two early episodes – both very brief – of a Deutschmark–yen axis (during the years 1980–95) relate to the early stages of US economic recovery (autumn 1980 and summer 1983) from an immediately prior recession – a situation which, as we have already seen (Chapter 4) can simultaneously buoy the yen and weaken the Deutschmark, the US dollar being in between. The next example of the currency world revolving round a yen–Deutschmark axis (the yen rising, the Deutschmark falling, and the US dollar in between) was a full decade later in the first half of 1993. This episode could be explained by the coincidence of US–Japan confrontation on trade with gathering pessimism on European economic prospects. Huge budget deficits and recession in most West European nations contrasted with an evident gain of momentum in US economic recovery coupled with decisive action by the new US Administration (President Clinton) to slash the budget deficit.

The eruption of a crisis in the European Exchange Rate Mechanism (ERM) in summer 1993 brought the period of a yen–Deutschmark axis to a close, as a new episode of Deutschmark–dollar axis dominance started, during the first few months of which the US dollar was falling unilaterally, the Deutschmark rising unilaterally, the Japanese yen in between. Later the Deutschmark and US dollar switched positions – the mark falling and the dollar rising unilaterally. If we consolidate the first three quarters of 1993 into one period, we would have a rare instance of the yen performing as a solostar – rising strongly against a trendless mark–dollar exchange rate.

Such consolidation, however, serves little purpose and handicaps the economist in his attempt to detect the strong current of money flow. There were distinct big stories driving funds through the first half of 1993 from the third quarter. The cartographer of currency market history should be fully aware of the contemporary driving stories when he divides his charts into a period of time when the currency world was revolving around a particular axis or dominated by a solostar. Otherwise every minor turn in any of the three key exchange rate series – for the DM/$, yen/$, and yen/DM – could bring a new sub-period into being. The cartographer in effect studies three pairs of charts – one for the dollar corner (of the dollar–DM–yen triangle), one for the yen corner, and one for the Deutschmark corner.

The dollar chart portrays two series – the yen/dollar and DM/dollar exchange rate. The yen chart shows the yen/dollar and yen/DM exchange rate. And the DM chart shows the DM/dollar and DM/yen exchange rate. During periods of currency world domination by the DM–dollar axis, the yen is an in-between currency, and so in the yen chart the yen/dollar rate and yen/DM rate go in opposite directions; in the Deutschmark and dollar charts, by contrast, both series go in the same direction, with a clear, non-flat, trend. Similarly during periods of dominance by the yen–dollar axis, the Deutschmark is an in-between currency, and so in the Deutschmark chart the DM/yen and DM/dollar series go in opposite directions, whilst in the dollar and yen charts both series go up or down together (not on a flat trend). Finally, when the DM/yen axis holds sway, the two series in the dollar chart move in opposite directions.

Periods of solostardom for any of the three currencies are identified by the two series on that currency's chart moving in the same direction, whilst in the other two currencies' charts one series will be flat (the exchange rate between the non-star currencies) and the other series (the exchange rate with the star currency) will have a strong trend. Thus when the Deutschmark is a solostar, both series in the Deutschmark chart, the DM/yen and DM/$ move in the same direction (with a clear upward or downward trend); in the dollar chart, the yen/dollar series is on a flat trend, whilst the DM/$ series has a clear non-flat trend; in the yen chart, the yen–dollar series is flat whilst the yen/DM series has a clear non-flat trend.

Currency cartography does not just involve breaking the past into distinct episodes. Market economists, in practising currency cartography, are particularly concerned with the present and future. They seek to determine the present situation. Which axis is now dominant or is there a solostar? How long is the present situation likely to last and what axis or solostar will come next? As in the analysis of business cycles and growth cycles the foreseeing or even early recognition of turning points – from one formation to another (for example Deutschmark–dollar axis to yen–dollar axis) – is particularly difficult.

The rationale for market economists putting effort into futuristic or speculative cartography is that investors' performance should be improved thereby. The investor who recognizes, for example, where the dominant axis now lies (if anywhere) and has above average insight into coming changes in phase, should be well placed to achieve superior performance. Yes, it is useful information to know the most recent history as drawn by the cartographer. Yes, longer history can help the investor have a feel for the likelihood of different patterns of currency motion (whether domination by any of the three axes or a solostar performance). But eventually the investor must speculate on what is the current state (which axis is the currency world presently revolving around or which is the present solostar?) and what might come next. The Royal Flush in currency trading comes to the speculator who takes the correct view on the movement of the correctly identified axis or solostar.

6

NEW LIFE AS A STRATEGIST

Economists looking for highly paid jobs in international finance had a new opportunity by the early 1990s – apply for the position of 'chief strategist' with a major global investment house, Yesterday's market economists who had maybe somewhat tarnished reputations as seers in the currency and bond markets had a new opportunity to prove their high worth. 'Strategists', in contrast to 'market economists' (the title widely given to economists practising in financial markets), have to focus on producing 'ideas' for the traders and salesmen (in their organizations) to follow.

High-flying strategists would not have much time or direct incentive to reflect on the deeper problem of how a so-called 'neutral' portfolio should be divided between various asset classes, even though concepts which are familiar to them from their training as economists should be useful towards finding a practical solution. Neutral investors have no strong speculative views (about how a particular asset price might move a long way from the path now discounted for it – either explicitly in a forward market or implicitly). They 'simply' want to get the best balance possible (given their own situations and tolerance for risk-bearing) between risk and return.

The practical solutions to the neutral 'selection problem' are qualitative rather than arithmetically precise. There are no big fees to be earned or income to be generated by proffering advice in this area. Even so, for the ultimate investor (as opposed to the professional fund manager, running in competition against others with performance measured over short periods) the discovery of the 'neutral portfolio' is essential to efficiency (getting the best trade-off between risk and return). Most investors do not even embark on the voyage of discovery, in large part because of 'information costs' (including the cost of acquiring knowledge).

It would not be commercially viable, for example, for the private banking department of any investment house to provide detailed input to each client taking account of his/her own particular circumstances. At best, the general principles of neutral portfolio composition could be set down in a generally available form (as illustration, a chapter in the department's investment 'manual' for clients), and those who are sufficiently motivated could proceed to acquire further knowledge about optimal portfolio diversification.

HOW FAR TO THE HORIZON?

In the standard simple model of portfolio selection taught in finance courses at business school, risk is measured in one dimension – the variance of returns for the probability distribution from which these are generated. Returns are of course measured with respect to a given time interval. But the probability distribution is assumed to remain unchanged from one interval to the next, and in each interval the 'gamble' starts afresh, independent of the result of the gamble in the previous period. Because investors are risk-averse, high risk assets are priced in the market to yield higher expected returns than low risk assets. But the market compensates only non-diversifiable risk (measured as the co-variance between returns on the given asset and on the market portfolio).

The simple model is subject to a number of criticisms. For example, investors do not measure risk in just one dimension (variance). They are concerned to identify returns under various imaginable states of the world (scenarios) – for example, war, peace, recession, high inflation. Moreover, even when focusing simply on the supposed probability distribution of returns, they may see this as quite different from the normal shape in the finance textbook (in particular the distribution may be non-symmetric around the mean return line, and other measures of risk in addition to variance be relevant to decision-taking).

A second criticism is that the simple model does not acknowledge that risk can only be estimated. We may know what the variance of actual monthly returns from a diversified portfolio of US stocks has been over the past ten years and what the average return has been. But in no way can we be confident that the probability distribution now 'generating' returns is approximated by these observations. The distribution might have changed through time – and could indeed change remarkably on occasion from one period to the next. It is possible that the distribution of returns changes in a non-random fashion through time. (For example, a big positive cumulative return over several periods may mean the probability distribution of future returns moves into an asymmetric shape – a small risk of a big negative return not matched by a significant possibility of a big positive return. This asymmetry is an important consideration in foreign exchange risk diversification.)

The nature of shifts through time in the probability distribution of return is a key consideration in assessing how the neutral portfolio should vary according to the length of the intended holding period. Where returns in each period are independent of those in the previous period, and the distribution from which returns are drawn is unchanged and normal, then risk – as measured by variance of returns as expressed at an annual rate – diminishes, albeit at a decreasing rate, the longer the holding period. By contrast, the expected rate of return (again expressed, say, at an annual rate) remains constant as the holding period is extended.

Hence an investor who is optimizing his/her portfolio distribution with respect to say a date six months hence will be biased much more to assets conventionally regarded as low risk than one assuming, say, a five-year period. In constructing the neutral portfolio the investor should consider what is the appropriate time interval in his/her case. As illustration, an investor who is saving to buy a house within the next one to two years has a well-specified 'horizon date'. By contrast, an investor considering the neutral position for a portfolio meant as a nest egg, only to be touched in his/her own lifetime in the event of an emergency, and otherwise intended as a bequest to children, would reckon with a 'horizon date' perhaps two decades or more into the future.

In practice, the second investor described does not have only one date on which he/she focuses in his/her optimization calculation. He/she is looking at a probability distribution for, say, each five-year period into the future describing the amount of the portfolio which he/she might wish to consume. For example, for years one to five, there might be a 10 per cent probability he would wish to consume 20 per cent or more of the portfolio (with a mean estimate of say 2.5 per cent). For years six to ten, the probability might rise to 20 per cent with a mean estimate of say 8 per cent. And by years fifteen to twenty, the probability (of 20 per cent or more of the portfolio being consumed) might be up to 50 per cent with a mean estimate of 25 per cent (consumption includes handing on as a bequest). By weighting the midpoint of each five-year period by the mean estimates (expressed as proportions) the investor can calculate a horizon date. He/she would probably calculate then a shorter adjusted horizon date to take account of the 'risk' that his/her desired consumption would be in excess of the mean in the earlier periods.

The amount by which risk (measured in terms of, say, variance of annualized per cent returns) declines for each, say, year's lengthening of the horizon diminishes. Where the probability distribution of annual returns is constant and normal, the decline in risk for extending the horizon from one year to four years (risk halved) is double that from extending by a further sixteen to twenty years. Hence the importance of precise calculation of horizon data (to deciding the allocation of the neutral portfolio) diminishes the further ahead we look. Our hypothetical 'nest egg' investor does not have to be overly concerned whether his/her horizon date is fifteen, twenty or twenty-five years. For simplicity of discussion we could call him/her a long-run investor, in contrast to the short-run investor whose horizon may be one year. Others are in an intermediate zone, where differentiation by horizon still has some importance.

Just as the individual consumers with 'atypical' tastes (liking, for example, to have leisure time during the week rather than weekends, and liking summer resorts best in winter) is at an advantage in the labour or goods markets over the 'conformer', so the investor with an exceptionally long horizon date is at an advantage compared to the great majority of short-term investors. The risk premium set on equities, for example, should be relatively generous for the long-term investor, who sees less risk in that asset than the 'average investor' in the marketplace with a horizon of say one to two years.

One particular type of asset – fixed-rate (or zero-coupon) bonds – has a structure designed to appeal to long-term investors. Take for example a pure-discount ten-year bond, whose redemption value (ten years from now) is fixed in real terms (as illustration, each $1,000 bond bought at issue – for a market price well below $1,000, allowing for the normal time discounting – will pay back $1,000 multiplied by a factor equal to the US price level then divided by that at the start). The investor whose horizon is ten years into the future would find this asset to be of zero risk. (There would be some residual risk, however, if the horizon were continuously rolled forward; at the end of year one, the horizon may now be nine and a half years ahead, rather than nine years, in that the risk of premature consumption being necessary within the first year did not materialize.)

The pure-discount indexed bond is not found in practice. The nearest actual bond to the theoretical construct is the indexed coupon bond issued by various governments. There is a small element of uncertainty as to the cumulative returns (real) to be earned over the lifetime of such bonds. The coupon income received in each sub-period (usually once or twice a year) has to be reinvested, and the yield on new indexed bonds (with a maturity at the same horizon date or for a rolled forward horizon date), is unknown at the start. But this source of uncertainty is likely to be of a 'second-order' nature. In practice there is the difficulty of non-availability of a continuous spectrum by maturity of indexed bonds.

Indeed, even in countries where governments issue indexed bonds, these account only for a generally small share of outstanding debt. Most issues are conventional nominal fixed-rate bonds which promise a given nominal sum at maturity and fixed nominal coupon payments once or twice a year. Where inflation risk is low or non-existent, these are as attractive to the long-term investor as would be indexed bonds. By contrast, where inflation risk is substantial, a ten-year fixed-rate bond would not appear as a low-risk asset at all, even to the long-term investor. Its appeal would be as a highly speculative, trader-type asset.

Bond risk (especially in the case of non-indexed paper) is quite different from equity risk. A ten-year nominal bond, for example, can be viewed as a one-year cash note, plus a forward purchase of nine one-year notes, starting successively one year from now, two years from now, right up to nine years from now. At the end of year one, the cash note has expired, and the one year forward purchase evolves into a new one-year cash note; the portfolio of forward positions shrinks to eight in number from nine. At the end of year two, a new one-year note comes into existence, and the forward portfolio shrinks to seven contracts etc.

The real return on the one-year cash note in any one-year period turns wholly on inflation. Higher-than-expected inflation in the previous period is likely to go along with raised inflation expectations for the future and also a raised uncertainty about inflation (a bigger variance for the probability distribution from which the actual inflation rate is drawn). As regards the portfolio of forward positions, higher than expected inflation last period will also mean a raised variance of returns in the present period. Moreover the expected real principal value of the outstanding forward positions would decline at an accelerated pace as inflation estimates for the future increased.

For example, if over the period of time from the issue of the bond (end of year zero) until the end of the second year, long-run inflation expectations rise from 2 per cent p.a. to 6 per cent p.a., then the expected real principal value of the one-year forward note bought for years nine to ten would fall by almost 30 per cent. Thus the portfolio of forward contracts shrinks in real size through time not just because of natural expiry but also because of accelerated erosion of value by higher than expected inflation. Yes, there may be a 'fair bet' on the portfolio of forward positions each period, and the risk of several bets (in annual per cent terms) should be less than one. But the bets are taken on a smaller and smaller amount of real capital at wider and wider variances of possible return. So the early bets are much more important than the later bets.

That contrasts with the situation for equity investment. Just because returns in the present period have been negative does not normally lead to a downgrading (progressively bigger) of the importance of future returns. And there is no shrinking of the size of the bet in the case of equities through portfolio contraction (the analogy of the shrinking portfolio of forward contracts). The exception to these two observations is the aftermath of an equity market crash. A 50 per cent fall, for example, of the equity market over six months would leave the real (and nominal) value of the equity portfolio on which future one-period (say six-month) bets were taken heavily depleted. Even if these bets were to remain unchanged in nature from before (in terms of the probability distribution of annual per cent returns) the first bet would have been the most important (being on a much larger principal value).

Even in the extraordinary case of equity market crash, the long-term investor can look forward to many subsequent periods of still substantial 'bets' which might go the other way. There is not the progressive scaling down of future bets as was hypothesized in the bond market case (via a rise in inflation expectations). In general we can say that where inflation expectations and inflation risk are substantial the long-run investor is at much less of an advantage relative to the short (in terms of risk exposure) with respect to conventional bond investment than to equity market investment.

A particular appetite of the long-run investor for fixed-rate nominal bonds is dependent on low or zero inflation.

INTERNATIONAL DIVERSIFICATION

Inflation risk can be reduced through international diversification. For example, the investor with a ten-year horizon can reduce the exposure of his/her fixed-rate bond portfolio to inflation risk by spreading the mix over several low inflation monies. The problem is that introducing several currencies into the portfolio may have the side effect of exposing the investor to something new – real exchange risk (an exchange rate changes in real terms if the change in the nominal exchange rate is more or less than what can be explained by differential inflation alone). The importance of real exchange risk for any particular investor depends on the distance to his/her horizon (at an annual rate real exchange risk diminishes the further ahead is the horizon) and on the geographical spread of his/her consumption (the more the investor is a 'citizen of the world' the less subject he/she is to exchange risk).

Real exchange risk arises from the fact that the given foreign currency (say Swiss franc) might fall by more in terms of purchasing power with respect to our (US) investor's shopping basket (assumed here to be the same as that used for calculating the US price level) than to the domestic (Swiss) investor's shopping basket (assumed to be the same as that for the Swiss price level) as would be the case if the Swiss franc rose by less against the US dollar (or actually fell) than its better inflation performance would justify (arithmetically). Then, even though inflation might be less in a given period in the foreign currency (Swiss franc) than the domestic (US dollar), the benefit of that superior performance could be offset by exchange rate change.

The investor whose shopping basket is 'international' rather than nationally based is less exposed to real exchange risk. Such investors buy traded and non-traded goods from different currency areas (for example, North America, Europe, and Japan). So long as they hold key currencies in much the same proportion as the areas from which they buy goods, they are not exposed to real exchange risk. Yet if all these key currencies are of 'reasonably' low inflation risk, they are able to obtain a lower overall exposure to inflation risk for their portfolio by virtue of its spread.

Of course it is the spread of consumption (by currency zone) at the horizon date which is crucial to the investor's exposure to real exchange risk. Typically long-term investors can contemplate a wider spread than short-term. They might well imagine (equivalently, they put some significant probability on the scenario) that in one or two decades from now they or their children will be resident in another currency zone. Some institutional investors may be unsure of where major capital investment will be effected several years from now (Europe, East Asia, or North America) and so a diversified portfolio of currencies (between the US dollar, Deutschmark, and yen principally) would be less exposed than a purely domestic one to real exchange risk.

Even long-term investors whose consumption is almost certainly going to remain concentrated in one given currency zone are much less exposed to real exchange risk than short-term investors (where risk is measured at a per unit interval rate). Note that we are discussing here non-discounted real exchange rate change. Sometimes bond-yield spreads between currencies are clearly different from mainstream inflation expectations, and so they discount some real appreciation or depreciation of one currency against another. For example, when the dollar was spectacularly high against the Deutschmark in 1984 and early 1985, real US bond yields were far above German – on the basis of consensus inflation expectations – and so a depreciation of the dollar back to a more normal level was discounted.

Much short-run volatility in real exchange rates is attributable to transitory factors which are self-reversing ('white noise', cyclical disturbances, for example). Moreover, there is a well-known tendency for exchange rates to 'overshoot'. A shift in asset demands by final investors can lead to a big fluctuation in the exchange rate which is partially reversed later when trade flows are generated in response. The trade response is greater in the case of two countries belonging to the same currency zone (USA and Canada) than between two countries in different zones (for example, Germany and the USA). Hence intra-zonal exchange rates generally fluctuate by less in real terms over long-run periods than do trans-zonal exchange rates. As a low inflation risk money, the Deutschmark has a built-in advantage over the US dollar as a constituent of European investors' bond portfolios.

As the investor's horizon shortens (this sometimes happens with ageing – but not always, where the focus is passing on to the next generation) real exchange risk becomes more important – both in absolute terms at an annual per cent rate and in relative terms compared to inflation risk. For an investor with a ten-year horizon whose consumption is concentrated in one currency zone, inflation risk in his/her domestic money (measured cumulatively over the ten years) might well loom larger than real exchange risk incurred in adding another low inflation international money to his/her bond portfolio (note that there is little basis for an empirical estimate of the probability distribution of non-discounted ten-year real exchange rate changes as there are so few non-overlapping ten-year periods for the purpose of study). That may well not be the case when the comparison is made over a three-year horizon. If the investor's horizon does indeed shorten (rather than moving forward as he/she passes through life), then the neutral bond portfolio would require restructuring.

Real exchange risk need not be a wholly negative phenomenon for the investor – it might be negatively correlated with some other risks. For example, bad news on domestic inflation (much higher than expected) might have a high chance of being accompanied by a substantial real exchange rate gain on holdings of foreign currency (where the gain is measured cumulatively up to the horizon date). The rationale for this negative correlation is that a deterioration in the quality of a given money (higher inflation risk) should mean that it becomes cheaper relative to competitors whose quality is unchanged. The cheapness may come at first in the form of a substantial rise in the real interest rate, but should eventually take the form of a real exchange rate decline (for the now poorer quality money).

The negative correlation between inflation and the real exchange rate may have its source in an initial disturbance to the real exchange rate fuelling inflation rather than a rise in inflation spurring a real depreciation of the national currency. As illustration, suppose a troubling current account deficit emerges which seems to indicate a national loss of competitiveness in key export sectors (lack of sufficient technological progress, poor design?). The national currency depreciates. Most probably the central bank would not seek to hold the price level to an unchanged path, but would accept some blip up to accommodate raised prices of traded goods, whilst trying to ensure that a 'vicious circle of inflation' does not develop.

A third source of negative correlation can involve a simultaneous disturbance to the real exchange rate and inflation expectations (but not to present inflation). Suppose investors suspect that the central bank (US Federal Reserve) is over-reflating the economy and thereby sowing the seeds to an inflationary upturn say twelve to eighteen months from now. Then the exchange value of the dollar would fall immediately, in advance of the inflation upturn. The resulting real and nominal exchange rate gain on foreign currencies would provide some compensation for the immediate loss on domestic bonds (Treasury bonds). Once inflation becomes apparent, however, the real exchange rate gain could be reversed (unless the deterioration in monetary quality is seen as a long-term feature), meaning that by the horizon date there may be no residual real gain on foreign currencies.

In addition to the above examples of offsetting movements in real exchange rates and inflation, there are many examples of unrelated random shifts in each. The far from perfectly negative correlation between real exchange risk and inflation risk means that on balance it (real exchange risk) is a limiting factor on the scope of international diversification to reduce risk of real return in a bond portfolio (where return is measured cumulatively up to the investor's horizon date).

Sometimes the claim is made that the limiting factor of real exchange risk can be 'got round' by hedging currency risk in the short-term forward exchange markets. For example, the German investor could hedge holdings of US T-bonds by selling dollars forward say six months for Deutschmarks (the amount sold equal to the present market value of the T-bond holding). On closer examination, however, the claims are misleading.

The short-term forward cover (rolled-over every six months, adjustment being made for change in market value of the holding) as proposed does not provide a full currency hedge. The only way of hedging the T-bonds fully against currency risk would be to take out a set of forward contracts with maturities and amounts corresponding to each and every coupon and principal payment. But such hedging would simply transform the T-bonds into Deutschmark fixed-rate bonds, albeit with a coupon stream somewhat different from the conventional German bond.

In fact, a position in T-bonds 'hedged' simply with a short-maturity forward currency contract is equivalent to a holding of, say, six-month floating rate Deutschmarks plus a notional long position in a series of forward one-year dollar interest rate contracts (starting respectively six months, one year six months, two years six months, etc. up to the horizon date). If the returns from this portfolio of forward contracts (measured over each sub-period) are highly correlated with unexpected declines (measured relative to expectations at the original starting date) in real short-term German interest rates, then the hedged position in T-bonds has some merit as a candidate for inclusion in the German investor's portfolio.

In practice, a high correlation is not found. A hedged portfolio of T-bonds is much inferior to a position in Deutschmark bond futures as a means of reducing risk of accumulated returns up to the horizon date (the combination of Deutschmark floating rate assets and the long position in Deutschmark bond futures is equivalent to a holding of Deutschmark fixed-rate paper). True, the hedged portfolio provides some diversification with respect to inflation risk (German and US risks may well be similar, but they are not perfectly correlated). But the reduction in exposure to German inflation risk obtained is considerably less than for the case of unhedged holdings (of T-bonds) in that the (German) investor (in the hedged T-bond portfolio) is fully exposed to German inflation risk within each six-month period.

In sum, hedging is no magic wand with respect to the limiting factor of exchange risk on the potential for international diversification in the fixed-rate bond portfolio. Investors with a horizon far into the future are unlikely to have such confidence in low inflation persisting throughout (the period of time until then) that they would put most of their money-denominated wealth (in contrast to real assets – for example, equities and property) into fixed-rate bonds. Rather, they would hold a mix of floating rate nominal assets (for example, bank deposits, certificates of deposit, commercial paper, floating rate notes) and fixed-rate bonds. Inflation risk exposure is less on the floating rate portion (than fixed-rate), in that an upward revision in inflation expectations would be reflected usually in a rise of rates obtained at the next fixing date.

Inflation surprise in the present period for which the rate (say, six-month) has been fixed can be considerable – inflation turning out to be significantly greater than what was built into expectations at the start of the period. Inflation surprise usually brings an upward revision of inflation expectations with respect to the next and future periods. But this upward revision may not be reflected in an immediate rise in money-market rates. The central bank might obstinately refuse to accept that inflation pressures have built up and hold its key rates pegged at a low level. Or, in an extreme case, the central bank may be wilfully accommodating higher inflation. Thus unexpectedly high inflation in the present period may be followed by one or more periods during which the expected real rate of interest (calculated as the actual interest rate less the expected rate of inflation) is exceptionally low.

Unpredictable fluctuations in real interest rates (as measured at the start of each period using current inflation expectations) through time (from one period to the next right up to the horizon date) and unexpected inflation within each period (before the next setting of rates) are the sources of uncertainty as to total real return from a floating rate portfolio (cumulated up until the horizon date). Both risks can be reduced by spreading the floating rate portfolio between currencies, but, as in the fixed-rate portfolio, an undesirable side effect of currency diversification is the assumption of real exchange risk.

Note that real interest rate risk can be attributable to other factors than short-term rate pegging by the central bank (as described above). The investor may be concerned, for example, that over a long period real rates may become very low or negative as a reflection of (unexpected) economic stagnation. A shortage of new investment opportunity might go along with a savings glut. Alternatively, real rates may be depressed by a shift towards a much tighter fiscal policy. Real rates of interest (nominal rates less expected inflation over the period in question) are far from perfectly correlated across currencies, and so there is scope for reducing real rate risk via currency diversification (the real return risk of any candidate currency for inclusion in the portfolio must not be abnormally high).

Cumulative real interest rate risk to the horizon date (say five years ahead), measured as the difference between what the capital sum would have grown to if real interest rates in each sub-period (say six months) were as expected at time zero (at the start of the five years), and what the final sum would have been if real interest rates in each sub-period were as expected at the start of that six-month period, might well increase less than proportionately with the distance to the horizon. Equivalently the risk expressed as an annual average should diminish the further ahead the horizon. But the rate of diminution may not be very large – and nothing like as fast as the decrease in real exchange risk as horizons are extended.

Any diminution of real interest rate risk (expressed as an annual average) with horizon extension is due to a tendency for some shocks to be offsetting. For example, if the central bank keeps its short-term interest rate peg unchanged despite a rise in inflation expectations (meaning a low or negative expected real interest rate in the present), then most likely in a future period 'monetary overkill' will be required to bring inflation down, implying exceptionally high expected real rates. Alternatively, a move down of the expected real rate during a recession may be balanced later by abnormally high real rates during a boom.

By contrast, a decline in the expected real interest rate which is attributable to a secular change such as shrinking of investment opportunity or increased personal savings has no tendency (by definition) to reverse itself before the horizon date. Indeed, the secular fall in real rates may occur as a progressive decline over several years, meaning that the risk of the expected real interest rate for year ten as seen at the start of year ten being far below the same expected real rate as seen at time zero is (much) greater than for a similar comparison with respect to year five.

The importance of real interest rate risk to long-term investors (and the declining importance of real exchange risk with distance to horizon) means that they have a considerable interest in currency diversification. Inflation risk is less of a factor to the long-term investor in monetary assets than in fixed-rate bonds, in that short-term rates are continuously refixed and usually reflect shifts in inflation expectations (from one sub-period to the next). Thus inflation risk in the floating rate portfolio stems from a series of one-period 'throws of the dice' (actual versus expected inflation) and should diminish substantially (expressed as an annual average) as the horizon is extended further into the future.

As is the case for the bond portfolio, the long-term investor whose consumption (or that of his children) might well be spread between different currency zones would not be greatly troubled by real exchange risk and has maximum scope to reap the benefits of real interest rate risk reduction and inflation risk reduction from currency diversification. Real interest rates may well tend to be more closely correlated between currencies in the same currency zone than between those lying in different zones. A high degree of economic integration for countries lying in the same zone would explain that closer correlation (business cycles more synchronized, secular changes in investment opportunity similar). Hence in the monetary portfolio there might be more emphasis on trans-zonal diversification than in the bond portfolio.

Investors for whom real exchange risk looms larger (those whose consumption at their given horizon date is concentrated in one currency zone) can see some partial offset in a negative correlation between real exchange rate risk on the one hand and inflation and real interest rate risk on the other. The negative correlation seems to be most significant in the case of investors with short-term horizons rather than long. Take the case of an inflation shock in the present period, in the form of inflation being significantly higher than expected, raising fears that monetary policy has been too lax in the recent past and that raised inflation lies ahead. An immediate real exchange rate gain might well be made (on foreign currency as the domestic currency falls steeply).

The gain might not last long if the central bank moves swiftly into 'overkill mode', raising its interest rate peg to far above the new higher inflation expectations. Then the national currency might rise back temporarily to its pre-inflation shock level or even higher. Several periods further ahead the currency might fall back sharply as overkill gives way to neutrality and then stimulus (as the economy enters a post-inflation recession). The low rates at that time match the high rates during the period of overkill and mean the investor cannot count on a floating interest rate income alone to provide compensation over a long period for unexpected inflation. A real exchange rate gain (on foreign currency) subsists only if the domestic currency remains below its pre-inflation real level even when the economy returns to full employment. That might be the case if it has suffered a permanent loss of reputation as a safe store of value.

An alternative case of inflation shock is where this is led by the exchange rate. A first example is where weakness of the domestic currency appears as one early symptom of monetary policy being too easy. By the time a significant jump in inflation expectations occurs (as a critical amount of evidence is to hand), the real exchange rate of foreign currencies may have risen substantially. Again, none of this gain on foreign currency (in real terms) may subsist over the long-run.

A second example is a small open economy (Belgium) which has pegged its currency to a large neighbour (Germany) being 'forced to devalue' (perhaps a fundamental lack of competitiveness has shown up in a stubborn high rate of unemployment and this has been the catalyst to a speculative attack on the parity). The devaluation would bring an almost immediate rise in the domestic price level and a rise in inflation for some periods ahead. So long as the devaluation is successful (meaning that not all of the initial competitive advantage is eroded by subsequent inflation) then by definition some real exchange rate gain persists (and this provides compensation for the unexpected inflation). Detracting, however, from the bonus 'real gain' on foreign currency holdings is the extra real income obtainable on the domestic money during the post-devaluation period (when monetary policy is highly restrictive).

A surprise devaluation is not a mainstream occurrence, in contrast to real interest rate shock. As a first example, take the case of a country (USA) entering a sharp cyclical downswing (whilst the rest of the world is in a milder recession or still growing). The big fall in expected real income from that country's currency could be matched (from the viewpoint of domestic investors) by a big gain on foreign currency. But that gain could melt over the long-run as the depression ends, US interest rates rise towards a normal level, and the exchange rate of the dollar appreciates (reflecting its narrowing interest rate disadvantage). Only if the cyclical downturn led into a prolonged period of stagnation (unparalleled elsewhere in the world economy) would it have been the source of a 'permanent real exchange rate gain' relevant to investors with a long-term horizon.

A second example of real interest rate shock stems from a central bank following a deliberately inflationary policy, or ignoring evidence of raised inflation expectations in the marketplace (sticking to its own lower forecasts). The big real exchange rate gain which the domestic investor would earn as the currency slumped could again peak early in the subsequent inflation saga. The profile of the cumulative gain through time including its eventual erosion (not necessarily total) can be seen in the example of inflation shock (as above).

The conclusion that long-run investors should not count on much dilution of real exchange risk in their diversified monetary portfolio via a negative correlation with inflation or interest rate risk does not jeopardize the whole construction effort so long as real interest rate risk is indeed important.

INTRODUCING EQUITY AND REAL ESTATE

Except under highly inflationary conditions, the real value of an equity portfolio (income reinvested, and normal rebalancing through time to take account of new entries and exits to the equity market – see Chapter 1) at any horizon date in the short or medium term (up to five to ten years hence?) is less predictable (can vary within a wider range) than that of a money or bond portfolio. The greater risk of the equity portfolio follows from the lack of anchor to value (in real terms) in the form of a large principal repayment at a fixed date in the future, and, in the case of conventional bonds, of fixed coupon payments in the interim.

A well-diversified portfolio of equities produces a stream of corporate income, some share of which will be paid in cash (dividends). The remaining share is reinvested by the collection of corporate managers involved (in all the various corporations corresponding to the equity holdings). As we have seen already in Chapter 1, the expected growth rate of the earnings stream through time averaged over a long period (twenty years?), excluding what results from such reinvestment, might be quite low (in the case of advanced industrial nations), even possibly zero, when account is taken of the process of creative destruction – 'blue chips' decaying whilst new businesses only enter the mainstream equity universe once a track record of entrepreneurship has been established. But the range within which an average growth rate could lie (calculated over, say, ten years) might be wide – the outcome depending for example on whether the starting year turned out to be the peak of a cycle before a long recession or the start of a long golden period of non-inflationary yet substantial economic growth.

As illustration, the cumulated real income, including dividends, retained earnings, and earnings from reinvestment in new equities or within the corporation (corporate earnings should be calculated net of inflation as described in Chapter 1), from an initial $100,000 investment might lie anywhere between $30,000 and $180,000 (in real terms) ten years from now at a 95 per cent confidence level. The 'residual' value of the equity holding at the horizon date (ten years hence) is the market value of the original equity placement, without taking account of subsequent income reinvestment – in the form of retained earnings or otherwise – that has taken place in the interval (thus we look at the total value of the portfolio less the cumulated income mentioned of anywhere between $50,000 and $200,000). Illustratively, this real residual value, at a 95 per cent confidence level, may be $40,000 to $140,000. Hence the total value of the equity portfolio, including all earnings however reinvested, may lie between $70,000 and $320,000.

By contrast, a portfolio of floating rate notes over ten years whose initial value is also $110,000–140,000 would also grow illustratively to somewhere in a range of $110,000–140,000 at a 95 per cent confidence level. The expected rate of return on these figures would be just over 2 per cent p.a. That compares to an expected rate of return on the equity portfolio of 5 per cent p.a. The range of possible rates of return within the 95 per cent confidence interval would be –3 per cent p.a. to +12.5 per cent p.a. for the equity portfolio and 1 per cent to 3.5 per cent p.a. for the bond portfolio. The premium between the two expected real rates of return (in favour of equities) is around 3 per cent – a risk premium which is well within the range of historical experience as determined by empirical research. (The range of possible outcomes for portfolio performance in the example above is also consistent with estimates of standard deviations of equity returns found in the same research.)

Indeed the argument for including equities in a passive portfolio is that their expected rate of return is considerably higher than that on money-market assets. Historical experience is grounds for investors having a considerable degree of confidence in the proposition that the expected return on equities does indeed contain a substantial risk premium. But investors can do more than just rely on historical experience. They can seek to determine whether equities are indeed now priced at a level likely to yield a good return in the context of current economic and political prospects. Here the market economist offers the service of going through the type of appraisal exercise already outlined in Chapter 1, in particular using 'consensus' estimates of prospective earnings growth to calculate forward real earnings yields.

The decision of how much weight to give equities in the port-folio is dependent on the distance to the investor's horizon and also on his/her tax status. The risk of an equity portfolio (measured as, say, variance of six-month returns expressed at an annualized rate) diminishes (at a decreasing rate) with respect to horizon extension. Thus equity-type assets are more attractive to the long- than short-horizon investor.

Earnings yields are calculated usually net of a standard rate of corporation tax. But the investor should consider carefully on what tax basis he/she should be ranking net yields and whether the comparison faced is different from the 'average' faced in the marketplace. For example, an international investor operating through an offshore centre and not having to report income to any fiscal authority would compare post-tax earnings yields on equities with gross (non-taxed) returns on money and debt instruments. In calculating post-tax earnings yields he/she must make adjustment for the fact that dividends under most regimes are subject to a withholding tax on top of corporate taxation.

As illustration, if dividends average 30 per cent of post-corporate tax (real) earnings and the rate of withholding tax is 15 per cent, then net earnings yields calculated after deduction of corporate tax should be reduced by around 4.5 per cent. Thus 6 per cent net (real) earnings yield becomes 5.7 per cent when adjustment is made for withholding tax. This would be compared with 2 per cent (real) on money-market assets. By contrast a domestic tax exempt US investor (not subject to withholding tax) would see comparative returns of 6 per cent and 2 per cent. A high-income taxable US investor might compare a net yield on equities of 5.3 per cent (assuming a 40 per cent tax rate on dividends) with 0 per cent on money market (tax is levied on nominal interest income, which is higher than real). In sum, the risk premium on equities varies (not by a great deal in the illustration given) according to the 'tax bracket' of the investor.

How do investors assess the extent of their own risk aversion? There is no alternative to a hard look at the range of possible real values of their wealth at the horizon date which would follow from different combinations of a diversified holding of equities and of a holding of money together with bond market assets. Investors have to decide which probabilistic picture they are most comfortable with. Inflation risk, for example, is greatest in the case of the bond portfolio. If investors have a particular distaste for inflation risk – perhaps because the probability distribution from which cumu- lative inflation over the next, say, ten years is drawn is so subjective (compared to equity risk which is assumed to be much more stationary and capable of being estimated than inflation risk), or perhaps because they are highly averse to bearing the small risk of a serious break-out of inflation (which would reduce the real value of outstanding bonds by much more than equities) – they may largely shy away from bonds (in favour of money-market assets and equities).

Market analysts, when they discuss the risk premium on equities, tend to take the yardstick of net earnings yield less the yield on long-term government bonds. The procedure can be faulted. The inflation element in both is quite different. Net earnings yields are converted into real yields by adjusting corporate profits for 'capital consumption' and 'stock valuation' effects of changing prices (see Chapter 1). Nominal yields on bonds are converted to real by deducting inflation expectations over the lifetime of the instrument (for which there is no objective measure).

Suppose we arrive at a subjective estimate of the expected real yield on ten-year government bonds of say 3 per cent and compare this with the expected real earnings yield over a ten-year period on equity (6 per cent in the example above). We would have then a 'risk premium' of 3 per cent. But the term 'risk premium' is misleading. The real value of a portfolio of ten-year bonds together with cumulated income at maturity most probably lies within a considerably wider range at the 95 per cent confidence interval than the real value of a portfolio of floating rate notes (ten-year inflation risk is assumed to loom larger than cumulative interest rate risk and short-term inflation risk). The better measure of risk premium on equity is to take the real return from a money-market portfolio expected over the medium term, say five to ten years (this does not involve staking a view on ten-year inflation) and compare this with the prospective real earnings yield.

The much higher risk of returns from equities than from money market assets (under normal inflationary conditions – scenarios of hyperinflation danger are assumed to be of insignificant probability) means that their presence in a portfolio cannot be justified by appealing to the 'need' of diversification. Trying to reduce inflation risk in a money-market portfolio by diluting with the stronger but different risk of equity is as futile as a US investor seeking to reduce risk of a US T-bond portfolio by diluting it with Italian lira bonds. The justification for adding equity to a monetary portfolio is quite simply higher yield. Of course, equity is not the only high-yielding asset which can be added to a portfolio to boost returns. Real estate is another. And there are clear benefits in terms of risk reduction in diversifying portfolio holdings between several classes of high-yielding assets (of which the most important are equities and real estate).

Some commercial real estate is held by large quoted corporations that specialize in the development, letting, and management of such assets. Some other real estate is held by corporations whose main activity lies elsewhere. Thus investors in a well-diversified portfolio of equities already have a position in real estate markets. But much real estate wealth is outside the large quoted corporate sector. Correspondingly many investors have holdings in real estate which extend beyond their equity portfolio.

One example of extended holdings are those in pension funds. Under several tax regimes income accruing in the pension fund is tax free. Income received via equities is at a disadvantage (compared to interest or rental income) in that corporation tax already paid by the corporation is not refundable to the pension fund (under UK rules, however, a share of corporate tax – the so-called dividend tax credit – is refundable with respect to distributed earnings). Hence it is tax-efficient for pension funds to hold real estate directly (rather than via corporate holdings) and the perceived returns should be attractive relative to those seen by fully taxable investors.

The large pension funds concentrate their investment in commercial real estate on certain prime assets, the characteristics of which are large unit value, secure income (low risk of default or non-occupancy), modernity (no big refurbishment, development, or other works to manage). They hope to manage their real estate portfolio as passively as possible, with minimum outgoings to intermediary agents. By contrast, some private investors go into real estate in the role of owner-manager.

These private investors are not simply seeking an improved trade-off between return and risk obtainable by passive outsiders – indeed, they extend their holdings of real estate well beyond that point. It makes sense for them to concentrate on 'non-prime' properties – so as not to pay 'premium prices' for advantages they do not seek or cannot derive. They hope through their business acumen to be able to make a good salary as manager and also an above average (for the sector) net rate of return.

Commercial real estate has particular attractions to many owner-managers (in comparison to other possible direct business ventures). For example, the operation is capital intensive and does not require significant staffing (a million dollar net income might require just one accounts clerk and secretary plus a personal computer). The hours (or days) of work can be chosen flexibly to suit the owner's preferences (he/she does not have to 'mind the shop'). The assets are marketable in contrast to much of the asset base of a distribution or manufacturing company (the latter cannot readily liquidate custom-built machinery or work in progress – in contrast, the real estate company can sell off its assets one by one). The income (net of the owner's salary) may be subject to favourable tax treatment (for example, a 'small company' lower tax rate).

Finally, the appeal of physical ownership itself – whether to the owner-occupier, private investor, pension fund, or other types of institutional investor – should be considered. The appeal can take a number of forms, most of which come under the headings of 'land' and 'bricks and mortar'. We have all heard or experienced the sentiment that 'given all the uncertainties of life – both personal and collective – a direct holding of land and buildings is a desirable safe-haven'. There are no untrustworthy layers of corporate empire to come between the owner and ultimate assets (as in the case of equities), and no fleeting goodwill which may be 'gone the next day'.

Such sentiments are often hard to rationalize. Yes, the value of any one equity may be highly sensitive to the vagaries of corporate management and effervescent goodwill, but in a diversified port-folio of many equities much of such risk should be 'washed away'. Any particular piece of real estate is itself subject to a package of highly specific risks (developments in the neighbourhood, shifts in buying patterns, the building of new highways – to mention only a few). And no, investors in commercial real estate – if the worst comes to the worst – are not going to take up occupation them-selves or turn into subsistence farmers.

There is one special category of investor for which the 'simplicity of direct land ownership' does have real meaning. This is the investor who spans several generations. Examples include institu-tions or collective entities which have a life of their own – monar-chies, dukedoms, universities, the Roman Catholic Church. The advisers to the monarchy may seek a safe store of value as if they were taking a part in *Sleeping Beauty*. One hundred years from now, what assets in their portfolio today would still have substan-tial value, irrespective of a whole sequence of interim investment decisions? Land in prime positions of the metropolitan centre and highly fertile agricultural areas stand out as obvious candidates (gold is another – see next section).

In the language of portfolio theory, advisers to these 'permanent institutions' have an exceptionally long horizon (say 100 years) with respect to part of the total holding. When they look forward to what real wealth may persist into the far distant future, prime land stands out. By contrast, a portfolio of equities held today would almost certainly have been replaced almost completely, as new corpo-rations enter the equity universe which are unknown at present. Active management is essential to equity portfolio construction over the very long run, and it may be incompetent. The monarchy's advisers can see in land an asset which is relatively safe against incompetence by future advisers and whose real value 100 years from now (together with accumulated income in the interim) might well lie in a narrower range (at say a 90 per cent confidence interval) than that of a diversified equity portfolio (allowing for the additional risk of mismanagement).

THE SEARCH FOR SAFE HAVENS

Gold, like land, has a special appeal to the trans-generational investor. It has the distinct advantage of being a highly liquid asset. Thus sovereigns and national treasuries typically hold a significant share of their wealth in gold. But interest in gold extends far beyond this particular category of investor. For example, the yellow metal is a principal form of saving in many countries (especially China) where the national money is inconvertible (not freely tradable). Foreign currency banknotes may also be hoarded in such political jurisdictions, but they suffer from a substantial opportunity cost (in the form of interest forgone) and are subject to obsolescence risk (if old notes lose validity) and forgery risk (can the investor be sure of the note's authenticity?). They are also usually bulkier to store (not, however, in the case of 1,000 SF notes).

Gold is in part a consumer good for some investors – for those who derive any enjoyment from the wearing of jewellery. Gold when combined with the labour input of craftsmen can form objects of considerable beauty. 'Uses' of gold jewellery can be extended beyond aesthetic satisfaction to impressing potential business or social contacts and winning their respect (or trust in credit and other personal transactions). Gold is far from being the 'barren relic', as described by Keynes, for a wide range of holders. It comes closest to being barren, and even then not completely, for international investors who hold bullion bars in bank vaults (or warehouses).

These investors have no income in the form of jewellery enjoyment and business or social uses to cumulate up until their horizon date, say, ten to twenty years into the future. For them, the attraction of gold is as a 'bad news good' (an asset which yields an especially high return in certain identifiable bad states of the world). These (bad states) include a bout of inflationary monetary policy in all the key currency countries (so interest rates there fall to negative levels in real terms); or asset freeze orders being used in a situation of economic warfare (for example investors resident in a political jurisdiction on the verge of becoming an international outlaw might fear that their assets in the form of money deposits or bonds would become subject to a freezing order imposed by the US and its G-7 partners); or a cataclysmic event such as the dawning of a new Ice Age where 'paper assets' might be worthless and gold would function as money.

In addition to the utility derived from gold as a hedge against imaginable bad states of the world occurring it may also be appreciated as an asset whose returns are uncorrelated with those from the market portfolio (including equities and real estate). Note, however, that zero correlation (with market returns) is not enough to make gold special as an asset – money-market returns may well show little correlation and be much less risky than returns from gold. And there is no strong *a priori* case to be made for strong negative correlation of returns between gold and the market portfolio except with respect to the rare periods when calamity looms.

In principle, the hedge quality of gold should mean that it is priced at a level where its expected rate of return (averaged across all possible scenarios in each future period) is below that on so-called near riskless assets (for example US T-bills from the viewpoint of US investors). In practice, investors (and analysts) have no way of satisfying themselves as to the range within which prospective yields on gold lie. Unlike for equities or real estate or bonds there is no independent income stream which can be assessed (analogous to earnings, rents, or coupons). The history of past returns on gold provides little basis for estimating the present probability distribution for gold returns with any degree of confidence (almost certainly the probability distribution is non-stationary through time).

Some analysts claim they can project a long-term band within which the price trajectory to be followed by gold will lie – and that this could be a substitute for the independent 'check' on returns to be expected on average, otherwise unavailable – from studying in detail the outlook for mining costs and jewellery demand. But the bands are so wide, and the level of 'reasonable' confidence in the identified trajectory so low, that no independent source of evaluation can be identified. The lack of knowledge about the probability distribution from which gold returns are drawn, and in particular of the expected rate of return, is a negative feature – but not so negative as to mean investors should exclude the asset altogether from their portfolios. The special protection against certain bad states of the world is much sought after. The problem for the investor is how much protection to buy when its price cannot be specified (for any particular period) even in probabalistic terms except within quite wide limits.

In practice, the investor may meet the dilemma by specifying a largely subjective probability distribution of returns including the expected return. The resulting subjective estimate of the price paid for gold's protection cannot be placed on a parity with prices known with certainty or specified in terms of a fully known probability distribution. The subjectivity involved means that the investor should put a 'load factor' on this (again, arrived at subjectively) and buy less than otherwise.

There is the further question of in what form the pure investor (not jointly 'consuming' jewellery income) should hold gold. The alternatives range from physical ownership in a bank safe (or warehouse) to gold-indexed bonds to a long position in gold futures or swap market contracts. The trade-off involves income versus safety. The investor can be most certain of the protection to be gained in the case of direct ownership (no danger of default, gold-index clause being broken, or paper claims – including the gold claim – becoming worthless). But he/she sacrifices income.

Note that income forgone is usually considerably less than money-market rates times the outstanding value of the gold holding. Interest rates on gold paper of various forms in a contemporary context are well below money rates. For example, the gold interest rate on a three-month bill issued by a triple A rated borrower (principal and interest payable in gold or indexed to gold) would be close to zero. Otherwise present holders of physical gold would storm into the gold bills, still maintaining sufficient residue in metallic form to satiate their appetite for protection against certain bad states of the world where they would be unable to convert paper gold into gold.

The most common form of paper gold found in practice is long positions in futures contracts. Typically the futures price is at a premium above the spot rate which is very close to the money interest rate for the same maturity. On this price basis (between spot and futures) holders of the physical metal could not gain significantly from selling in the cash market and switching into a long futures position (they could gain only if the premium were much less than the interest rate). Nor could treasurers succeed in making a margin above money-market rates by simply buying physical gold spot and hedging (going short) in the futures market.

If an international crisis erupted and investors suddenly aimed to hold a larger share of their gold assets in metallic form, then it is conceivable that the spot price of gold could rise relative to its futures price (equivalently gold interest rates would rise). But such a turnaround has not been witnessed in recent history. Much older histories date back to the pre-1914 world, when the international gold standard reigned supreme. Then metallic gold (as distinct from paper gold) yielded various important services for which there is no counterpart today (especially as coinage, and as high-powered money in the banking system). Under the gold standard the gold interest rate (or default-free short-term paper) was by definition the same as the money interest rate. Banks and non-bank investors did not move out of metallic gold (at the margin) into paper gold (despite the interest incentive) for many of the same reasons as they now hold non-interest bearing reserves or banknotes.

Under the gold standard, forward and spot prices for the metal would be virtually the same (so long as there were no doubts as to the continuing convertibility or par value of the currency in question – say dollars). Any hedge property of metallic gold would be paid for – along with other services – in the form of interest forgone. In modern portfolio theory jargon the expected rate of return from metallic gold was less than from the riskless money-denominated asset (for example, US T-bill). In today's world, paper gold has a more extensive hedge function (than under the gold standard). The paper has some strong likelihood of rising in price in certain bad states of the world. The expected return on both paper and metallic gold should thereby be significantly less than that on Treasury bills.

If, however, the futures price is equal to market expectations of where the spot price will be at the given maturity date, then it would seem that the expected return on gold is the same as the money rate (given the relationship already defined between spot and futures prices under the contemporary financial system). If the expected return is less, then it must be the case that the futures price of gold is somewhat above market expectations. High risk uncovered arbitrage would exist in the form of rolling over short positions in futures contracts. But given the highly subjective nature of the probability distribution of returns from gold, and the potential price volatility, it is not surprising that such arbitrage fails to occur in practice other than possibly in the form of producers' keenness to take short positions in the futures markets against gold production far into the future. Deciding whether or not to hedge future gold production requires no abnormal amount of boldness, in contrast to the open arbitrage of going short in a hedge asset which may well jump in price in many bad states of the world – so inflicting large loss on the short-sellers when they can ill-afford it.

Gold is perhaps the most famous 'hedge asset'. Some distance behind is the Swiss franc (from the viewpoint of non-Swiss investors). The hedge property – no more than for gold – cannot be demonstrated by any simplistic analysis based on past co-variance of franc returns with world stock market portfolio returns. Rather, investors can identify – at least in very broad brush form – bad states of the world where the Swiss franc could be a better store of value than other assets. These states of the world are not general for all investors.

For example, an investor resident in a Deutschmark-zone country may be concerned about the risk that the Deutschmark's present high reputation could erode – perhaps due to a Bundesbank mistake or because of ill-fated attempts to harmonize monetary policy in the run-up to European Monetary Union. In these scenarios the Swiss franc, as an independent currency outside the EC of intrinsically lower exchange risk than the dollar from the perspective of a Deutschmark-zone-based investor, should gain strongly in value. Indeed, already in summer 1995 there was anecdotal evidence of a large flight of capital out of Germany into the Swiss franc on the part of investors fearful that European Monetary Union would take place on schedule in 1999, which would mean the death of the Deutschmark and its replacement by a new money of uncertain quality.

Amongst Europeans, Italian investors may be especially impressed by the Swiss franc's record of strength during periods of economic and political turmoil at home. By contrast, UK-based investors may see a much smaller, if any, hedge role for the Swiss franc, not least because the pound over long spells behaves as an outside member of the dollar zone and rarely behaves as a Deutschmark-zone currency. Non-European investors, especially from 'volatile' political jurisdictions, may see the Swiss franc as safe against asset freeze, in contrast to risks attaching especially to the US dollar and Deutschmark.

Outside the group of traditional hedge assets, including the Swiss franc and gold, 'collectables' are sometimes mentioned as an additional category. Rare stamps and fine art are examples. These are not hedges in any conventional sense of the word. In bad states of the world, luxury consumption in the form of enjoyment of the fine arts would surely run at lower levels than in an (affluent) good state. Rather, collectables should be considered as having a dual role in the well-diversified portfolio – first, satisfying a particular consumption demand (from the stamp collector or art connoisseur) and second, providing useful risk spreading because their total returns are far from being perfectly correlated with those from an equity market portfolio; and yet the probability distribution of returns from a diversified portfolio of collectables may well have an expected value and variance not very different from that of equities. Finally, the return from collectables may be substantially tax free (unlike dividend income for many investors).

As for gold (but unlike equities) an objective basis for assessing the value of collectables (as a category) is missing (for equities the basis is projections on corporate earnings over the long-run in the economy). 'Earnings' for collectables are a stream of aesthetic enjoyments, analogous in the case of gold to 'joint enjoyment' – in various proportions according to the particular owner – of the beauty of jewellery and of protection against various types of disaster. But aesthetic enjoyment (or sense of safety against disaster) does not come in standard units with a price tag.

In principle, the price per unit of aesthetic enjoyment may be somewhat less volatile than that of the 'sense of safety' – given the greater extent to which perceptions of the present degree of safety might fluctuate through time. But that speculation about relative price volatility of an immeasurable magnitude is impossible to translate into a method of appraisal. Instead, some analysts base long-run price projections for collectables on the hypothesis that demand for aesthetic enjoyment is likely to rise faster than income given its luxury nature. Assuming the supply of collectables to be fixed (a strong assumption when account is taken of new collectables emerging – today's promising artist becoming a future master, for example), the real value of a diversified holding over a long period might be expected to grow substantially faster than, say, OECD economic output – perhaps by 5 per cent p.a., but that begs the question of whether the 'starting price' was reasonable (no independent appraisal is possible analogous to equity level appraisal – see Chapter 1).

The investor in collectables should consider income return both in the form of expected asset-price gains and of aesthetic consumption. Only the multi-millionaire can afford to hold a well-diversified portfolio of fine paintings. One or two paintings only have a high variance of return. Hence 'poor' millionaires can only justify fine art in their portfolio if they derive far above average enjoyment from its consumption. At the opposite end of the pole, the billionaire may none the less justify a small diversified holding even though his/her rate of return is thinned by 'a poor capacity to consume beauty'. The justification is found in overall risk reduction. But, of course, even the billionaire must carefully consider the liquidity disadvantages of art in assessing returns and risk. On the other hand, he/she can stretch the meaning of consumption to include 'enjoyment' and use of demonstrating conspicuous wealth.

Investors who have a taste for rare stamps can reap portfolio diversification advantage at a much lower level of wealth (than is the case for fine art). A 'poor' millionaire might hold five rare stamps for example. By definition a stamp is one of a class rather than unique and so its value is easier to appraise. This is an advantage to the investor in that there is less of a 'random factor' in what price is achieved at a decided sale point, and at all times a fairly reliable estimate of achievable sale price can be included in his regular portfolio valuations. Finally, storage and transport costs are insignificant in the case of stamps, unlike for fine art.

7

CONFESSIONS OF
AN ECONOMIST

Could my advice help generate superior performance for my clients? Or am I in a niche area of the entertainment industry – providing 'disc-jockey' commentary on the latest economic news, writing astrological reports about the future, and telling eloquent stories about the latest twist of market prices along their random walk? The serious practising economist would surely despair if indeed the evidence pointed in an affirmative direction with respect to the second hypothesis. But he/she should none the less confront the questions. Intellectual honesty and wisdom requires that the economist becomes aware of both the extent and limits of his/her ability.

It is not, of course, just the economist or any other 'professional' who should revisit the fundamentals of their practising knowledge. There is the story of the famed 90-year-old yeshiva scholar who is asked to address the congregation of students on the most solemn evening, Kol Nidre, of the Jewish year. They wait in awe, expecting a puzzle to be revealed requiring great Talmudic knowledge for its solution. Instead he starts off: 'This evening I am going to talk about the existence of God.'

The economist, unlike the yeshiva scholar, cannot assume anything as a matter of belief. It is not a question of religious principle or revelation whether economics has anything useful to say about the likely behaviour of financial markets. Usefulness and relevance must be demonstrated by available evidence. But as in the spiritual world, 'deepening' of experience – which is the basis for greater wisdom – can be achieved via a process of confession (critical self-evaluation).

THE STORY-TELLER

Successful market economists should be able to tell a good story. They must compete for readers (and listeners) – and they are off to a promising start if the narrative can be made exciting. But they should also know when there is no story to be told – and, indeed, that can sometimes be a story in itself. They should be wary of becoming philosopher-commentators who no matter what happens spin a story of profound rationality on the part of market participants. If they always have 'rational' explanations at the ready, they risk becoming comic characters in the vein of Voltaire's Pangloss – the philosopher in the novel *Candide* who continues to demonstrate that no matter what terrible event he encounters, 'it was all for the best.'

An example of there being no story to tell was the Kobe earthquake. This devastating event in Japan (January 1995) brought live an image of tragedy to television screens throughout the world. Within days, estimates appeared in the financial press of the total damage in the region of $100–200 bn (as much as 4 per cent of GDP). Many bond and currency analysts churned out revised forecasts of higher yields (on Japanese government bonds) and a weaker yen (smaller trade surpluses as exports were disrupted and imports increased to meet reconstruction needs).

In fact, the real story to tell in January 1995 was that whatever market influence the Kobe earthquake had would be small over the medium term compared to other influences. After all, if we take the mean estimate of total reconstruction at 3 per cent of GDP over a period of say five years, and allow for the fact that some of the private spending component might have a direct counterpart in lower alternative spending (medium-size corporations rebuilding plant might well trim back plans for other capital market expenditure in compensation), then the overall impact on the balance between savings and investment in the economy could be quite small compared to even modest changes in the propensity to spend by either corporates or individuals.

There are opposing examples of sophisticated commentators priding themselves on perceiving that there is no story to tell – but in fact a very big change is under way, at least in the investor's 'state of mind'. An example might have been economists in the early to mid-1980s who wrote (and spoke) sceptically about the current vogue hypotheses of the US economic miracle under

Reaganomics and of Euro-sclerosis (the West European economies' lack of dynamism). In the long-run, their scepticism may have been partly justified, but in the short and medium term they should have acknowledged that there was an important story to tell, at least about the climate of expectations.

Panglossian market economists would claim that expectations, whatever they were, have validity at the time. Moreover, they might invent the expectations which fit the market facts and then try to attribute those expectations to a large body of investors. Hence they would remain true to the gospel of the market always being dominated by rational expectations – just as Dr Pangloss always demonstrated Liebnitz's general principle of optimism to be valid.

Examples of overstretched attempts by economists to attribute rationality to market pricing, making them blind to the occurrence of a bubble, include Irving Fisher's notorious justification of Wall Street pricing in early 1929, the stories written in 1989 to justify the Tokyo equity market at 40,000 (on the Nikkei index) or well-known US analysts spinning an economic tale of why the US dollar at 3.40 against the Deutschmark in early 1985 was 'fair value'. Searching for a story to justify an absurd price level is a pitfall for the economist trained in the theory of rational expectations. The biggest pitfall is to be driven, out of respect for the 'collective wisdom' of the marketplace, into a large change in fundamental view about the political and economic outlook just when the bubble is about to burst.

Yet arrogance towards the judgement of the market has also been the 'undoing' of many an economist. Bubbles are the exception not the norm. Some academic economists scoff at market economists who earn rich rewards for 'simply writing the script for a random walk by market prices'. But drawing out what indeed the 'market is saying' – or, equivalently, describing the constellation of scenario building by market-participants which lies behind present prices – is indeed a useful function in at least two respects.

First, market efficiency may well increase in consequence of well-written analyses being presented of the views behind present pricing. Some investors may be alerted to new scenarios or alternative probability weightings (to their own) with respect to various well-known scenarios, which lead them in turn to change their own outlook. An example was the sustained fall in US T-bond yields from late autumn 1994 onwards. (Ten-year T-bond yields at end-1995 were more than 200 basis points down – or just below 6 per cent – compared to autumn of the previous year.) The good narrator of the random walk (followed by T-bond prices) would have told readers early on that a growing number of market-participants were adopting as their central (most likely) scenario the US growth cycle (starting in 1992) having already peaked.

Second, in describing the dominant consensus the market economist might strengthen some investors in their willingness to assume a contrarian position in the marketplace. For example, some economist commentators writing the script for the random walk of the yen during its surge of early spring 1995 drew attention to a dominant view found amongst the yen bulls that, so long as Japan has a big current account surplus, its currency must come under upward pressure. Investors who suspected that the link between current account position and currency strength was unreliable and who were convinced anyhow that the Japanese surplus was shrinking fast might have been encouraged to sell their yen holdings.

Not all scripts for the random walk are as insightful as those just described. Indeed some scripts are simply third-rate fiction. An example is the market economist author writing an 'explanation' for his/her weekly report of the latest wriggle of US bond yields and the dollar when in reality there is no explanation at all. Market prices can move within a range where no market-participants have a strong enough view to take counter-positions (based on a return to an 'equilibrium level'). Price fluctuations within that speculative desert are meaningless.

Yet the economist hard up for a story sometimes stoops to inventing an explanation which has no basis in researched attitudes or facts. For example, the economist pressed for a story behind today's 2-pfennig jump of the dollar against the Deutschmark might tell his/her friendly newspaper correspondent that the move is symptomatic of growing confidence in a US economic rebound. But he/she may not have any reliable evidence of such a change of viewpoint in the marketplace – rather it is a completely unproven hypothesis, which, along with many others could fit the facts.

It is easy for even the proficient scriptwriter to get over-excited by the day-to-day sub-plots at the expense of portraying the bigger picture. Economists can become the excited chroniclers of the daily calendar of economic data releases and of public statements by senior officials. In their excitement, however, they risk becoming transformed into the buzzing insect of Isaac Bashever Singer's well-known parable. In this, Singer compares our understanding of divine purpose to the ability of the insect crawling through the pages of *War and Peace* to comprehend Tolstoy's message. The economist transformed into an excited chronicler can lose all power to comprehend the bigger picture.

The sirens drawing market economists into the band of excited business-cycle chroniclers offer fame and large rewards. The vast amounts of dollars which Wall Street firms spend on forecasting the business cycle can be understood in the light of the impressive excess returns which could be made from success – especially in the equity market. Jeremy Siegel concludes from a study of New York Exchange prices over the past thirty years that an increase of 4.8 per cent p.a. in portfolio returns could have been achieved by predicting business-cycle turning points four months in advance (moving into bonds before the cycle peak, and equities before the trough).

In turn, the potential interest amongst investor readers for stories on the business cycle make these easy copy for economic journalists. They can 'get away' with writing hyped-up accounts of minor fluctuations in data. Consider, as example, the headline in a major US newspaper in late July 1995 'US data point to a slump'; in question was a 0.1 per cent fall in durable goods orders in June when all other indicators published around the same time suggested a rebound from a very mild growth recession might already be under way.

The market economist who as story-teller successfully navigates past the sirens of 'short termism' may develop undue passion for a hypothesis (sometimes of his own creation) about the long-run. We could go as far back as Malthus, who not only developed an elegant model of 'impoverization' based on agricultural production increasing arithmetically and population geometrically but also wrote as if this 'model case' *were the only possible future reality.* In the 1940s, Keynes not only described a possible economy where the *rentier* investor would die (rates of return falling to zero) but boldly foretold the imminence of that reality. In the early to mid-1980s, when the dollar was scaling dizzy new heights, some market economists became enthusiastic converts to the 'belief' that huge capital flows into the dollar were being driven by a 'life-cycle' motor – the bulging pre-retirement generation in Germany and Japan putting their current excess savings into the US where population ageing was much more modest.

Turning a model case which the economist finds fascinating into a prediction of reality is a pitfall for the economist who remains enthusiastic about his/her subject. Enthusiasm for ideas may also lead the economist into excess subjectivity. Examples include the 'monetarist' economist who is too quick to predict that the Federal Reserve is making a big inflationary error, without a sufficiently exhaustive analysis of the present situation, because he dislikes the 'philosophy' of the present leadership.

Alan Greenspan, the successor as Chairman of the Federal Reserve to Paul Volcker, was disliked by many liberal monetarist economists because he threw overboard money supply targeting in any effective sense and replaced it with a highly discretionary operating procedure. The key Federal funds rate, rather than being allowed to float freely, became tightly pegged – with adjustments only being made immediately following Open Market Committee Meetings. It seemed to many monetarist economists that the Federal Reserve had reverted to an obsessive concern with fine-tuning the business cycle rather than respecting a medium-term monetary rule. Yet much of Mr Greenspan's 'discretionary management' proved to be well timed and inflation remained at a low level throughout the first five years of the business upturn starting in spring 1991. Monetarist antagonists who already in 1994 were demonstrating that the FOMC was making a dangerous error of policy (in the direction of inflation) sounded a fake alarm.

Another illustration of strong opinion tainting analysis has been the tendency of economists who see European Monetary Union as a costly and unwelcome project, to argue also that it has very low probability of ever occurring. But the analysis of probability of occurrence should be conducted quite independently of any critique of merit – except in so far as there is evidence that policy-makers are likely to change their assessment of the project's costs and benefits. Just because the market economist is convinced of his/her own cost–benefit analysis does not mean that this is going to influence the probability of any particular outcome. The good market economist must seek to understand fully the arguments which have been put forward and accepted by policy-makers.

Of course, as in any profession, some economists cross the frontier from healthy modesty about the extent and relevance of their knowledge to complete cynicism about their purpose. At one extreme are the efficient marketeers who believe that all is in vain – whatever insight economists believe they have about the direction of markets it is already fully discounted in market prices (equivalently, there are enough market-participants trading on the basis of good economic analysis so as to make its value negligible). At the other extreme are the 'irrationalists' who have despaired of the attempt to provide economic justification for market movements and turn instead to concepts found in group psychology or to examining the 'tea leaves' of past market episodes.

Market efficiency and group psychology should certainly be familiar concepts to market economists. But if they still sincerely believe in their purpose they cannot accept that efficiency in its strongest form holds (meaning absolutely no return – other than by chance – over the short, medium, or long-run to good research). Whilst economists should be ready to learn from psychology, the mental processes by which investors may change opinion and how they may be influenced by changes in others' opinions (as reflected in market prices), this should not justify throwing economic analysis overboard. If they are going to be successful in maintaining and building a following, it is going to be as economists, not as chartists or psychologists.

In seeking to market themselves, economists should be aware of the comparative advantages of geography. Great literary writers usually base their works in the very small part of the world they know well. Otherwise their novels would lack authenticity. Similarly, British economists working in London would have a hard job setting themselves up as the principal experts on the German economic and political outlook. Investors, traders, and other readers (or listeners) would assume that German economists living in Germany of equal experience and capability would be at an advantage – having a wider range of contacts 'on the spot' with whom they can exchange information (including anecdotes) and test ideas. True, economists outside Germany have equal access to data releases and publications – but not to 'hearsay' evidence. Foreign economists do not have the same opportunity to test speculative hypotheses about the future against criticism of other economists and experts who are specialists in the same area (the German economy).

When it comes to evaluating the influence of economic and political scenarios on market prices (in contrast to drawing those scenarios up) the nationally based analyst is at a lesser advantage. Market prices are determined in simultaneous equilibrium internationally. An evaluation of the prospect for German bond yields should include an analysis of foreign markets and the nature of their link to the German market. The relevance of a German base is perhaps least in assessing the Deutschmark's prospects within the key yen–dollar–DM triangle.

By contrast, in the case of exchange rates outside the yen–dollar–DM triangle, a national base may be a good starting point for story-telling credibility. An analyst in Toronto has an advantage in talking about the Canadian dollar compared to a London analyst. The advantage is rooted in the satellite relationship that often exists between a small currency and a big neighbour (see Chapter 5). The Canadian dollar is often dragged along by the US dollar against other currencies, but not conversely. Thus the Canadian dollar–US dollar exchange rate is much more influenced by Canadian than US developments.

The market economist based in London has a comparative advantage in 'story-telling' based on easy access to anecdotal evidence as to what the big international fund managers concentrated in the City are doing. What are their present fears? What are the scenarios with which they are preoccupied? Is there a vogue hypothesis about the long-run which is strongly influencing their decision-making in one area of international investment? The anecdotes are useful to international investors in other centres who are looking for 'points of disagreement' with present market pricing as a basis on which to take speculative positions, or who are simply trying to satisfy themselves that there is no bubble phenomenon presently at work.

Anecdotes are one form of narrative for market economists. But they are not the basis of stardom. Ambitious market economists are in search of inspiration to make a 'revelationary' story. But they should be aware of the message in Kafka's famous parable (*Die Prüfung* – The Test). This is about a servant (of whom? – most likely of God) in search of work (the meaning to life). He wonders why other aspirants (for work) appear to be successful without making as much effort as himself. Then one day he enters the inn and finds someone already sitting at the place where he usually chooses to watch all the comings and goings of possible 'employers'. The stranger introduces himself also as a servant, and says that they have met before without speaking to each other. The stranger asks a series of unintelligible questions which our servant cannot answer. As the servant despondently gets up to go, the stranger says 'stay, that was only a test; the person who does not answer the questions passes the test'.

Indeed, the best stories can come as inspiration when the economics writer is not in a 'state of search'. But he will not be open to them unless he has striven to develop his sensitivity.

Furthermore he must not suppress any new idea in embryo because it does not seem to fit with convention. Writers with weekly or more frequent publishing schedules to meet cannot count on the good fortune of the story being there just when needed. Sometimes writers can strike lucky in the form of picking up a chance comment made in a conversation or article. Other times they have to work harder – for example, finding an explanation for a puzzling trend. An illustration was writing the first article attributing dollar strength in the early to mid-1980s to the behaviour of Japanese investors.

A short-run but high-risk road to fame is aiming to write and trumpet the 'right' story just when a major market turn is occurring. The same story trumpeted six months early can land its author the tag of notoriety. For example, at any point during 1994-5 the economist could have written a provocative article to the effect that yen strength owed little to the so-called mega current account surplus of Japan. Instead the infernal machine of yen appreciation was manufactured in Washington – by the 'harping' of the Administration on the unacceptability of Japan's bilateral trade surplus (with the US) and the fear this fanned amongst investors that the Federal Reserve would seek to drive the dollar lower via easy money. The Bank of Japan put power behind the infernal machine by running an inappropriately deflationary monetary policy.

Economists who wrote that story in early 1995, and predicted that before long the US Administration would have to back-pedal on trade confrontation and the Bank of Japan radically ease its monetary stance, would have faced ridicule during the subsequent 'yen bubble' of early spring 1995 – even though they were proved correct by late summer that same year. By contrast, if they had saved their articles for publication in May or June, pointing out moreover that so far in 1995 the current account surplus had dwindled to 2.25 per cent of GDP from over 4 per cent just two years before, they would have been acclaimed.

No market economist can hope that each article he/she writes will be equally provocative. Directions in which he/she can look for composing articles of interest include cross-sectional comparisons (why does the Japanese current account surplus at 2.5 per cent of GDP create such tension in the currency markets, whilst a Swiss surplus of 8 per cent of GDP goes along with a much smoother determination of the exchange rate?). Another standard direction in which to turn is history. For example, in summer 1994, for want of any more 'grabbing topic', the market economist could have written about the present US growth cycle upturn already being two years old and comparing that with the length of previous post-war upturns. 'Juice' could have been added to the article by speculating on how good a guide history might be to the course of the present cycle.

The lowest form of writing for market economists is providing the script for a particular piece of business, in a case where their own opinions are very different from what is in the script. Yes, it is feasible for an economist to make a living by scriptwriting stories on demand for the financial production department. But stardom and its rewards never come from such scriptwriting. The activity is hazardous in that the economist loses credibility if the market strategy ends up in tears. The economist who under business pressure finds himself/herself 'compelled' to write a script does best to state quite clearly that he/she is putting the 'pro-case' for the strategy but that a counter-case exists (without elaboration). Moreover, in the script the economist does not have to say that he/she is convinced by the pro-argument.

THE RESEARCHER

Market economists, as researchers, must be careful to 'remain cool'. If they join the crowd of traders in becoming excited by the latest hot piece of information, they lose all perspective. The latest conversation, the latest seminar, the latest story on the Reuters screen, the latest business trip – these should all be ranged carefully against an array of other information rather than being the catalyst to an immediate revision of opinion coupled with a portfolio shift recommendation. Market economists should have some serious self-doubt if they are finding themselves excited ahead of each piece of weekly or monthly piece of economic data to be released. Such excitement is surely coming at the expense of enthusiasm about medium-term or fundamental analysis where the economist's 'comparative advantage' should lie.

None of this means that market economists should become cold as regards latest developments, retiring into the ivory tower of some 'academic' economists. They are part of the marketplace and should be alive to the continuous shifts in mood and excitement there. But they must not forget what part they are playing. They are not traders. They are not fixated spectators (analogous to the addicts of sports programmes on TV). Their prime role is that of evaluator, and that requires much work in the fields of information gathering and analysis, speculative scenario building, and eventually story-telling.

The market economist, in communicating with other market-participants, should be aware of what role the latter are playing. So if he/she is speaking to a group of fund managers, including proprietary traders, and there has been a piece of hot news just that morning (for example, a surprise sharp fall in German money supply), then the economist should certainly refer to it – but not throw overboard the remarks which he/she had prepared about the medium term. Similarly, if the economist has just paid a visit to the Bundesbank or Federal Reserve, or done 'the rounds' of large market actors (for example, the life assurance companies) in Tokyo, he/she can delight an audience by relating the latest anecdote or 'inside tip'.

But the market economist should surely be on guard against becoming convinced that anything picked up on his/her 'travels' is new. (Indeed, one large Dutch investment group is reputed to have it as a rule that analysts should make no new strategy recommendations during a 'silence period' following a business research trip.) After all, anything the market economist learns about 'current moods' in a centre just visited has surely long been discounted in the marketplace.

Travel has many purposes for market economists – but the gaining of hot information is not one of them. They can be stimulated by discussion with insightful conversation partners. They may be able to discover the dominant views and concerns which are determining prices in important asset markets. On reflection they can take issue with that consensus and make their disagreement a central element in the story about medium-term market prospects. Economists writing (or speaking) about a market based in a foreign centre (for example a London-based economist writing about the US T-bond market) should remember that their comparative advantage is 'international perspective', not immediate access to hot information and market anecdote.

Most market economists would confess to having broken these strictures about foreign travel at some point in their careers with unfortunate consequences. Take European economists visiting New York in November 1994. They would have picked up from their discussions with 'opinion formers' the 'information' that this business cycle was at last taking a conventional form. Wholesale price inflation was already strongly rising. With a normal lag, retail price inflation would follow wholesale price inflation. The Federal Reserve, despite all the talk of pre-emptive action, had tightened no earlier in this cycle than previous cycles. Money-market rates would rise to 8 per cent or more by summer 1995.

If these European economists had returned and related this story enthusiastically as a guide to action, their clients would have been sorely misled. In fact, the US growth cycle upturn was expiring just around this point, and a growth recession had already set in. The economists were latecomers to the already discounted wisdom of the consensus. A better presentation for them to have given on their return would have been to relate the consensus with a strong warning attached (to the effect that this was most likely already discounted in market prices and money was not to be made from its recognition at this point). Then they would have moved on to discussing whether the consensus scenario could be wrong, and lone opinions of dissenting economists could have been mentioned. They might then have proceeded to give their own balanced views, expanding on the reasons for their disagreement with the consensus.

The European economists on their return (home) could also have excited interest by relating the substance of any 'provocative discussions' they had succeeded in having with senior officials at the US Treasury and Federal Reserve – a type of discussion that would very rarely if at all be initiated by a journalist and reported in the newspaper (partly because the official would be much more on his guard and partly because the journalist might not be sufficiently on top of the subject matter at an academic level or market level to have the immediate follow-up question to hand).

Economists, in their interviews with officials, are seeking to assess how 'sure' the latter are in their present policy and how they might react to changed circumstances. The economists feel their way towards this objective, carefully avoiding questions which seem to be seeking pointers to immediate action in prospect (these are sure to cause officials to 'clam up'). Indeed this search for the level of self-confidence and how opinion may change underlines economists' questions to other market analysts. Their audiences back home would be interested in a report to the effect – yes, this is what the leading analysts are saying and writing, but my sense is that their level of conviction is not high and they could well be moving on soon to this new mainstream scenario. As 'outsiders' they can tell the story. In New York, leading economists would encounter practical obstacles to regular 'rundowns' of other Wall Street economists being a part of their presentation work.

Sometimes a business trip produces little substance for an interesting story. Perhaps senior officials could not be drawn this time into a free-ranging discussion. Perhaps market analysts were remarkably confident in their mainstream views. Better to come back with low-key findings than feeling under pressure to make a bigger story or longer story than there is. The same principle holds with respect to research through time. Historical insights can sometimes help illuminate the present situation and point the way to possible scenarios for the future. At other times, however, the 'laboratory of history' cannot be used to any extent, and the telling of a historical narrative is no more than pointless fill-in in the story being told – a bit like the sports reporter punctuating a commentary on the present match with references to contests of one, two, or three decades ago.

A number of different types of references to the laboratory of history can be made by the market economist. One is 'shock-simulation'. For example, when the Tokyo equity market bubble burst in early 1990, analysts turned back to the Wall Street market collapse of 1929. Subsequent big errors in monetary policy by the Bank of Japan could be likened to those of the Federal Reserve. On both occasions the central bank effected a series of modest interest rate cuts rather than aggressively expanding the monetary base. Modest rate cuts were not sufficient to prevent either a contraction in money supply (as in the US example) or a sharp slowdown in monetary growth to well below trend (Japanese case). The question could be raised as to whether the eventual emergence of the Japanese economy from its deflation of the early and mid-1990s would 'require' a currency devaluation in similar nature to that of the dollar in the period 1933–4.

A second example of shock simulation was found in the efforts of some contemporary observers to predict the outcome of oil price shock (the first big shock of 1973–4 saw a quadrupling of prices). An obvious question was whether the world economy had ever faced such a shock before. The nearest historical example was the payment of reparations by Germany after the First World War. The victorious powers imposed an annual reparations bill on Germany, this being similar, as a proportion of its (then) economic size, to the oil tax which the oil-importing countries were now to pay to OPEC.

175

The German experience was not encouraging, in that hyper-inflation and later slump had had some link (of highly arguable extent) with the reparations question.

On closer examination, the German experience provided little basis for predicting catastrophe in the wake of the oil price quadrupling. None of the importing nations were surely going to follow a 'passive resistance' policy (as pursued by the Weimar Republic) of demonstrating their inability to pay oil tax at the cost of sending their economies into hyperinflation and default. Unlike in the case of Germany, recycling of surplus funds held by the tax recipients promised to be smooth. OPEC nations had every reason to invest their surplus in prime international monies issued by the oil importers. By contrast, French and British investors in the early 1920s had little reason to park funds – other than on a highly speculative, short-term basis – into the German currency in the early 1920s.

How were investors who read such a historical analysis (in say late 1973) better placed than those who did not? First, they could have more confidence in optimistic assessments of the outcome this time round. The analyst proffering advice had done more than sketch out an optimistic central case – serious contemplation had been given to bad outcomes and these had been rejected. Second, they were forearmed against pessimistic accounts they might meet in the press and elsewhere, and it could be that these would include superficial reference to the disastrous post-First World War experience of Germany.

A third illustration of shock simulation was the re-examination of the 'Reaganomics' period in the USA which some market analysts undertook when confronted with the surprise announcement (February 1990) of early monetary union between West and East Germany. Would the explosion of the German budget deficit and consequential upward pressure on interest rates mean the Deutschmark would rise strongly (on the assumption of the Bundesbank retaining firm monetary control), similar to what had happened to the dollar in the early to mid-1980s (when nuclear rearmament and tax cuts brought a big increase in the US Federal budget deficit)?

Some economists hypothesized solely on the basis of theoretical considerations (capital account strengthening – as domestic interest rates rise – by more than the current account weakens) that the Deutschmark would strengthen. But the reference to an at least partially similar 'real life' example in the laboratory of history could have strengthened their case. Clients of the market economist presenting a currency outlook would also have been impressed (and hence have more confidence in his/her view) by an account of the exploration into differences between the historical episode and the present and how these (the differences) influenced the economist's judgement. In particular, the economist might have suggested that the 1:1 conversion promised for GDR-marks into Deutschmarks would mean that monetary conditions accompanying the budget explosion would at first be easy – and this could delay the Deutschmark's upturn (until the Bundesbank shifted policy).

A different type of reference to the 'history lab' from the examples of shock simulation just described is the testing and developing of a general hypothesis which can be forcefully applied to a present situation in the marketplace. For example, the market economist can test a hypothesis about how a lack of synchrony between the US, European, and Japanese business cycles influences exchange rates within the key DM-$-yen triangle. Drawing on such historical evidence adds weight to the market economist's prognosis for the triangle in a present period of, say, US economic recovery at a time when the Japanese and European economies are in a downturn.

Another kind of reference to the laboratory is the simple rejection of a popular hypothesis in the marketplace. For example, mention has already been made of the popular view during 1993–5 that the yen was being driven ever higher by the mega Japanese current account surpluses. At a theoretical level, there is no simple connection between the size of the current account balance and the direction or level of the exchange rate. But the market economist seeking to warn clients against accepting the popular view in the marketplace could strengthen his/her case by pointing out a stark counter-example in the economic history book. In particular, Great Britain ran a current account surplus in excess of 10 per cent of GDP throughout the two decades up to the outbreak of the First World War, and yet that was consistent with an almost perfectly smooth fixed exchange rate (under the gold standard regime) between sterling and other major currencies.

Rejecting popular views by a quick reference to history is perhaps the easiest use of that laboratory. Some other simple references are unfortunately downright misleading. Take for example those analysts who in summer 1993 defended thirty-year T-bond yields falling towards 5 per cent on the hypothesis that inflation had now been killed and pointing to the low level of yields prevalent during previous historical episodes of long periods without inflation. But during these previous episodes the dollar had not been a wholly fiat currency (having instead some link to gold), and investors (in these earlier episodes) had not a long period of recent peacetime history when inflation had run at a virulent pace to which they could point as evidence of risks in-built to discretionary monetary management.

Some enthusiasts on very long cycles in economic development find themselves able to put pen to paper detailing how the present situation fits into that framework. The Kondratieff cycle is the longest in the literature, lasting between forty-eight and sixty years. But too few of such swings have been observed to prove or disprove their existence. They are without practical use in the evaluation of market prices (except in the extraordinary circumstance of a large number of investors becoming convinced that the world economy is in, say, a thirty-year weak phase, meaning that equity returns would be much more modest than in the previous thirty-year period). The best that can be said for the Kondratieff cycle is that the possibility of its existence (unprovable) should put investors on their guard against simplistic 'historical' analysis which underlies much of the finance literature – in particular the assumption that the expected rate of return to equity capital is constant through time.

In sum, historical knowledge should add to the wisdom of the market economist. But wisdom should not mean a dulled sense of enthusiasm about the present. Yes, economists should keep their cool in the excited atmosphere of the trading floor and not become obsessed spectators waiting with great anticipation for the next piece of routine data or the next scheduled press briefing by the Bundesbank President. They should retain the capacity to become stirred – and much more so than their trader colleagues – by the rare bolts from the blue which really could be of great significance for the future. They should be excited by the possibility that they are 'piecing together a new economic trend' from pieces of information not yet generally recognized as carrying significance, and that they will be amongst the first to trumpet the new reality.

WRONG ADVICE

Good market economists may well not be highly successful investors. But consistent success in investment almost always depends on good use of first-class economic input into decision-making. Exactly when to take the plunge and open a position, when to cut the position, how big a position to take – these are all questions which transcend economic analysis itself. Good economic input serves to widen the range of serious investment strategies to be considered and to improve the investor's appraisal of risk and possible returns. Economists who claim that super-normal investment performance is virtually guaranteed by simply reading their analyses overstate their function.

Good market economists present well-thought-out scenarios and well-considered – albeit highly subjective – probability assessments of their likelihood of occurrence. They should state clearly what their degree of confidence is in these estimates and the scope (under present circumstances) of their probabilistic vision. The good investor does not ask the market economist for portfolio advice – unless of course they are one and the same person. Indeed, the investor who is an able market economist avoids the problem of trust. The investor depending on outside economic advice might always be unsure of the effort the economist has put into answering the question – whether he/she has been lazy and not updated his/her probabilistic vision. Or worse, is the economist still pedalling an analysis of the situation which is already out of date with his/her latest views, but for political or presentational reasons he/she does not want to change (for fear, perhaps, of being charged with a too-quick change of mind).

Market economists do indeed face a general problem in presenting the future in probabilistic terms. They know that many clients do not warm to being given a kaleidoscope of possible different scenarios with probability estimates and a confidence level thrown in. These clients would see the combination message as confusing and suspect that the economist was simply trying to cover all options so as not to be faulted subsequently. Such clients prefer a simple bold message 'told straight'. If the investor wants a full message, he/she should tell the market economist so, quizzing the economist carefully about the next most likely scenario.

Machiavelli's comment to his ideal prince on how he should choose advisers can be transposed to the large owner of liquid wealth. 'There are three classes of intellect to choose between – one which comprehends by itself; another which appreciates what others comprehend; a third which neither comprehends by itself nor by the showing of others. The first is the most excellent. The second is good. The third is useless.' The investor who is not a trained economist should know how to extract the best advice from economists and how to use it.

The accusation that economists, by outlining a 'scenario-tree' rather than one central case, are simply providing themselves with a parachute should the investor client lose money does not stand up to examination. Probabalistic vision can be faulted by subsequent events. Take for example the economists who took the popular view in autumn 1994 that the US growth rate would continue above trend in 1995, inflation would accelerate, and money-market rates rise to 8 per cent plus. Some of these economists mentioned alternative scenarios – most often the next favourite was a slowdown starting in the first half of 1995 and culminating in a hard landing (actual recession).

In reality, the US economy had already slowed down in winter and spring 1995, US bond yields fell sharply through the next six months, and money-market rates edged lower. But by late summer 1995 it seemed that economic rebound rather than a hard landing lay ahead. Economists who revisited clients in summer 1995 to whom they had presented their views late in 1994 could each defend their then positions by saying, 'at least I warned you of the scenario which did indeed occur (slowdown) as my second most likely case'.

Critical clients would respond by saying 'but why was it your second most likely rather than first most likely case?' Economists could respond in a number of ways. First, they might point to the weakening of car and home spending during the first half of 1995 and say this was all unpredictable quarter-by-quarter white noise. Clients might be unsatisfied with that explanation, being aware of alternative analyses back in autumn 1994 which stressed the likelihood of some retrenchment in interest rate sensitive sectors of the US economy. Economists would have to admit that others had had a greater insight, but they could validly say in their defence that their declared confidence level (in the central or any other scenario presented last autumn) was low, precisely because the assessment of monetary conditions and their influence on spending is notoriously difficult over short periods.

Second, economists might put the blame on the Mexico shock, arguing that their central case would have been correct if it had not been for Mexico getting to the brink of default and the knock to the US export sector from the slump in Mexican demand. But did this same economist mention a Mexico shock as at least a risk-factor in autumn 1994? After all, by then the writing was surely on the wall – and the subject of internal memos within the US Treasury Department, even if 'watchdogs' at the IMF remained remarkably optimistic.

Failure to mention the possibility of a shock before it occurs, and to draw this possibility to the attention of the investor client is a fault in the economist's probabilistic vision about which the investor can complain subsequently with some validity. The analyst who did not warn clients back in November 1989 when the Berlin Wall came down that a German budget deficit explosion and monetary union (between the two Germanies) were at least possibilities had faulty probabilistic vision. Likewise a failure of analysts already in 1972 and early 1973 to warn of the possibility of a forthcoming oil shock was a fault.

Some economists might admit to themselves that they did indeed glimpse the possibility of these shocks but that they failed to give them mention in their presentations. That is symptomatic of another fault to which almost any market economist must confess at least once in their professional life – failing to beat the drum when they are groping near a hypothesis full of market consequence. An example of this is the economist who, confronted with the alarming budget deficit data for Italy in the early 1990s, concluded that the only way a big improvement could be achieved without subjecting the economy to slump was to engineer or permit a big devaluation of the lira (so that a strong impetus from the external sector would offset fiscal deflation). But in the heyday of ERM when spontaneous 'convergence' was being widely acclaimed, the economist may simply not have written the story up.

Market economists operate in the marketplace. It takes considerable boldness to advance a view which is totally at odds with prevailing conventional wisdom – if economists are wrong they risk ridicule. Economists are influenced by the revealed consensus of market opinion apparent in market-prices. Hence it is rare to find economic predictions of an exchange rate or interest rate which within six months or a year is far distant from that in the forward rate. A big movement in the market-price would most probably bring a change in the market and economic forecasts of virtually all analysts.

In self-defence, economists could say that market-prices move most often because of the arrival of new information. And that is new information for economists too. So why should they be ashamed of 'going along' with the market-price. There is much of merit in that argument. But economists should not just be like vessels on the changing tide of market outlook. They should on some occasions be in advance of the change in market outlook. Best of all, they should be able to trumpet, albeit rarely, a major disagreement with market pricing and be proved correct.

It is easy to trumpet hypotheses about the long-run which have little relevance to present market valuations and will not be subject to an early test. But that is not the way in which market economists earn a following. Clients cannot be expected in 1995 to reward some bold assertions about the demographic time-bomb due to hit Japanese public finances from 2000-on unless this factor can be shown to be of importance already in investor evaluation of, say, long-maturity Japanese government bonds (JGBs). Yes, the arithmetic was superficially stunning – Japan's budget deficit expanding by 8 per cent of GDP between 2000 and 2015 on account of unfunded social security liabilities. But the deterioration was due to start only in the last five years of a ten-year benchmark JGB bought today (1995) and amounted (during that second five-year period) to barely a cumulative 2.5 per cent of GDP. Any effect on present JGB valuations of that modest far-off deterioration – which could yet be corrected by counter-measures (new taxes, cutting pension entitlements) was bound to be small.

Sparring about long-run hypotheses can be a neutral and possibly entertaining activity for market economists. By contrast, a quite clearly negative act is advocating a course of investment, perhaps under pressure to perform, without undertaking adequate research first. For example, economists, as investors, in 'a moment of exasperation' may have converted funds out of US dollars in early 1993 (where money rates were only 3 per cent p.a.) into Canadian dollars, where rates were some 200 basis points higher. They would thereby have allowed themselves to be carried along by the tide of other investors seeking to salvage their level of investment income by going into the 'northern dollar'.

If, however, economist investors had done a basic amount of research they would have been aware of considerable risks in the switch (from US into Canadian dollars). In particular, the existential question of whether Canada would hold together was looming on the horizon. The failure of the Mulroney government's constitutional initiatives towards resolving the Quebec problem had given new wind to the nationalist cause in that province. Already in the federal election of autumn 1993, the federal wing of the nationalist party, the Bloc Quebecois, had gained a big majority of seats in Quebec. A year later the Parti Quebecois won the provincial parliamentary elections, with a promise of a referendum on withdrawal from the Federation within a year. This catalogue of uncertainty took its toll on the Canadian dollar, far outweighing any income advantage over the US dollar.

WHO WILL BE THE JUDGE?

How can we judge the performance of the market economist? There are several levels at which judgement can take place. An investment bank employing a market economist is interested in the economist's capacity ultimately to generate revenue. The bank's management might consider that having a visible high-quality research function is a 'must' for convincing certain large institutional investors to put business their way. The management might believe further that a reputation in research raises the perceived quality profile of their operation generally. A further consideration could be that the investment bank's various trading operations should gain from in-house access to a top market economist.

The management in appraising at regular intervals whether their hired economist is 'up to standard' could first form their own view as to whether the quality of his/her research is exceptional. Second, they might be influenced by feedback from the other market-participants in similar positions to themselves (other senior managers) as to how their economist's output is viewed. Third, they might digest comments from their sales and trading departments as to how useful the economist's input has been. Finally, they could take note of press coverage and general media recognition (articles or books the economist has published and how they have been received).

At a different level from an employer weighing up performance is a particular investor's judgement of the input received from a given market economist. The investor might well go through a check-list of questions. How good have been the most likely scenario projections – both as to economic variables and market-rates – which the market economist has made? If the economist has been good at predicting market rates, has success been due to luck or skill (was the underlying scenario correct – or was the forecast rescued by offsetting coincidence)? If wrong, was the error due to sloppiness, poor research, failure to spot key data already available, or bad luck? How good has been the economist's probabilistic vision? (How far ahead did what actually happen appear on his/her screen. If wrong on the central case, did eventual reality at least appear as an alternative possible scenario?) How frequently does the economist update his/her views and is it with good reason? Is the economist any good at trumpeting gross misvaluations in the market just near a turning point? Is he/she approachable and a good communicator?

It is not surprising that many investors fail to comprehensively judge economic advice in the manner described. But simplistic proxy-judgements have every prospect of being downright misleading. For example, in the foreign exchange markets, some academic economists have conducted periodic surveys as to which of their colleagues working in the marketplace have consistently forecast better than, say, the three-month forward market – with a total time-span for the examination of, say, two years.

At best the survey reveals which economist has skill in advising the investor who is determined to 'take a given size of bet' on exchange rates once every three months with no tailoring of positions in between. No allowance is made for differing levels of expressed confidence in the forecast for each interval. Economists who make a big bang once in the two years and correctly, whilst expressing low confidence in their forecast the rest of the time, are not distinguished from non-discriminating colleagues. Thus the key question of what size of position the investor decides to take in light of advice proffered is left out of account, as is intra-period changes of opinion. At worst, the survey reveals a winner who has no more claim to superiority than the lottery stall which has sold the most winning tickets.

A third level of judgement is self-judgement and in principle this could be the most comprehensive, especially in the case of the investor who is his/her own principal economist. His/her check list of question might start with, 'what episodes are you proudest of (including popular fashions in investment which correctly you refused to follow)?' 'What episodes are you most ashamed of, and how do you explain these failures?' 'Have you made significant mistakes in long-term strategy (for example, what proportion of the portfolio to hold in equities, real estate, or bonds)?' 'Looking at the good decisions, were you insufficiently bold?' 'Looking at the bad decisions, are there lessons you can draw for the future?'

Finally, there are the unfavourable 'populist' judgements about economists as a group, not yet totally dismissed from public consciousness. Take the quip 'consult 10 economists and you get 15 different opinions'. The comment makes no distinction between weather forecasting and economic forecasting. Top weather forecasters, all with access to the same instruments, should come up with the same range of scenarios with the same probabilities attached (20 per cent chance of rain, 80 per cent likelihood of a midday temperature of around 30°C). Economic forecasters in contrast have to portray a much wider range of scenarios over a long period of time which transcends the two dimensions of humidity and temperature. By listening to a cross-span of top economists, able investors should not get confused but should be able to expand their own probabilistic visions and improve their own assessments of risks and returns.

Then there is the well-worn comment to the effect that if the economist were any good he/she would be living it up in the South of France. Well – some successful economists who are also good investors and who have been prepared to take big risks are indeed living there – or in other parts of the world they find desirable. But other economists toiling in offices in Manhattan, the City, or elsewhere, might none the less be worth listening to! Perhaps they themselves have not been highly successful investors. They may not have been prepared to take big gambles. Their insights – and prompting – could substantially improve the performance both of the bigger, bolder players, and also of the more modest.

GLOSSARY

Bubbles

In the history of markets, there are various episodes where prices have been described (in retrospect) as taking off from economic reality, rising to levels far above what appears to be consistent with reasonable views about the future. These episodes are generally called 'market bubbles'. Examples include Tulipmania (in the Netherlands from 1634 to 1637), South Sea Bubble (1720), railroad shares in Britain in the second half of the 1830s, foreign currency in Germany immediately following the First World War, US equities in the late 1920s, and the Japanese stock and land market bubble of the late 1980s.

Market bubbles are inconsistent with pricing dominated by rational expectations (where prices reflect a sober balanced assessment of the economic fundamentals). Some economists have sought, though, to develop market models in which bubbles could be consistent with *rational behaviour* by speculators. These so-called 'rational bubble models' depend on a mathematical formalization of the well-known greater fool theory. In practice, none of the rational bubble models have been demonstrated to fit well with any of the episodes.

Perhaps market economists and commentators are too quick to label contemporary periods of large price action as bubbles. In fact, to prove a charge of bubble against the markets is a highly difficult, but not impossible, task.

Capital flight

Outflows of capital driven by fear (for example, of political change, war, the introduction of exchange restrictions, or irresponsible monetary policy) or by the reality of high taxation – these are all illustrations of what could be called capital flight. The operative force behind capital flight is not a fine weighing up of different scenarios and a calculus of expected returns across these. Gross fear or gross tax differences are the prime movers.

Currency geography

This is not as yet a recognized term in economics but has been developed here. Currency geography includes such topics as identifying zones of co-movement (dollar zone, DM zone), dominant poles, determination of which axis the currency world is revolving around.

Diffusion indices

These have become increasingly popular in the monitoring of business conditions both in the USA and Japan. The index is made up of a number of components – a rise in a component month-on-month registers as +100, no change as +50, and a fall as 0. An average of all the components above 50 is treated as an indicator of economic strength. In the USA, the most followed diffusion indices of current business conditions are those published by the National Association of Purchasing Managers, both on a regional and national basis.

Dirty floating

A currency is in a 'dirty float' on the foreign exchange market if its rate is being influenced by massive official operations. For example, there have been various episodes in recent history of dirty floating for the Japanese yen. The term 'dirty floating' should not be applied to the case of a currency whose central bank follows a monetary policy highly dependent on exchange market conditions but which does not engage in large-scale purchases or sales (in the currency markets).

Euro-sclerosis

A term first born in the early 1980s to fit the diagnosis of the European economies suffering from a lack of 'flexibility and dynamism' in comparison to the USA and Japan. Rigid labour markets, lack of progress in the high technology field, over-regulation by government, were all part of the complaint.

Federal Reserve Open Market Committee (FOMC)

The Committee is formed from Governors of the Federal Reserve Board in Washington plus a selection (based on a complex system of rotation) of regional Federal Reserve Bank Presidents. Every five to six weeks the Committee meets to determine the course of monetary policy. Decisions, if any, are announced in terms of changing the degree of reserve pressure on the banks together with an equivalent of what this means for the Fed funds rate. Technically the FOMC gives instructions to the open-market desk of the New York Federal Reserve Bank which operates for the whole system in the money and bond markets.

Fundamentalist

Some market economists, when asked to assess the likely movement in a given asset price over a specified period, restrict their whole analysis to a consideration of fundamentals – the economic and political outlook and how this might vary from the average case already discounted. Such market economists are called fundamentalists. By contrast, some other market economists incorporate 'technical factors' into their assessment of at least short-term price movements. Technical factors include a wide range of possible subjects – including chart-points, trend lines, and highly complex time-series analysis.

Hedge asset

An alternative more popular name for this is 'bad news good'. A hedge asset is one which has a high probability of yielding a 'good return' if a specific bad state of the world occurs. For example, gold is widely viewed as a hedge asset with respect to war risks or inflation. The Swiss franc is sometimes seen as a hedge asset with respect to German political and monetary risks. In its heyday as a petro-currency, sterling was considered to be a hedge asset against oil crisis.

Inflation shock

A significant upturn in recorded inflation is usually unforecast at the time it happens – hence it can be described as an inflation shock. It is well within the 'historical norm', for example, that when US inflation pressure builds up, an acceleration of the recorded quarter-to-quarter rate by around 2 per cent p.a. takes place within a six-month period. Sometimes a coincidental factor in inflation shock has been a jump in primary commodity prices – including in particular those of food and energy.

Intermediate target

According to textbooks of monetary economics, the 'ideal' central bank set itself an ultimate aim of policy – for example, low inflation and 'full employment'. Towards achieving the ideal, the central bank sets itself an intermediate target, the pursuance of which is meant to increase the chances of success. Common intermediate targets include a monetary aggregate or an exchange rate.

International money

Some currencies enjoy a wide use as money by non-residents of the country of issue – whether as a medium of exchange, store of value, or unit of account. Such monies are called international. The extent of international usage depends on such factors as economic size of the country in question, the regional pattern of its trade (a dominant trade partner of a group of other countries), and quality of the given money (how low inflation, what degree of liquidity?). The three 'big' international monies are the US dollar, Deutschmark, and Japanese yen. The Swiss franc enjoys large international use relative to its size, but most of all with respect to the store of value function.

Leading indicators of inflation

Some econometricians claim to be able to put together a composite index of leading indicators (including for example commodity prices, vendor delivery times) which has some predictive power with respect to inflation six to twelve months into the future. A well-known index in the USA is that of the Center for International Business Cycle Research at Columbia University.

Money supply aggregates

These fall into three main categories. First, the base or high-powered money stock includes only liabilities of the central bank – bank notes and deposits of the banks (reserves) at the central bank. Second, narrow money comprises base money plus deposits with the banks which can be identified as used primarily for transaction purposes. Third, broad money comprises monetary base plus narrow money plus deposits and (on some definitions) money-market assets which are essentially pure investment (rather than to be used for transactions). Typically, there are several broad monetary aggregates depending on the range of assets included. In the USA, the two broad money supply aggregates are M2 and M3 (the latter broader than the first).

Natural real rate of interest

This is the level of interest rate, expressed in real terms, at which the economy would be in overall equilibrium (inflation stable and a high level of resource utilization). The natural rate of interest varies through time according to the extent of new investment opportunity, private propensity to save, and the budget deficit. Most discussion of the natural rate of interest begs the issue as to the maturity. Is it a three-month rate, one-year rate, or longer, that should be the benchmark for measurement? Most probably a medium-term maturity which reflects an average interest rate which the saver can expect to receive and the borrower (capital spender) pay up to their standard horizon-date (for planning) is best.

Open economy

An open economy is one where the traded goods sector is of significant size. Equivalently, imports and exports are a large share of GDP. A small open economy is one where the traded goods sector is especially large (for example, Belgium).

Playing the yield curve

In the context of a very positive-sloping yield curve many banks and investors may be ready to play the yield curve. Rather than accepting low rates on short-term, money-market assets they obtain

higher rates by extending maturities. They may aim to keep a
constant longer maturity by rolling over, say, what was originally
five-year paper, after one-year into new four-year paper. Banks
may substantially expand their government's bond holdings by
issuing deposits in the money market. In all cases the so-called
'arbitrage profit' from playing long rates against short is in fact a
speculative activity. The running income from long versus short
would be eroded by capital loss if short-term interest rates moved
as discounted in the term structure of rates.

Probabilistic vision

This is a new term (found first in the present book) to describe the
looking into the future mapped out as a scenario tree branching far
out into the distance where each branch is heightened in colour by
the extent of its probability of occurrence. Vision can be improved
by training. And at any time the market economist's efficiency in
using his/her power of probabilistic vision can vary.

Public good

A public good is one whose consumption cannot physically be
restricted to 'paying users'. Examples of public goods include 'clean
air' and national defence.

Rational expectations

The central idea of the theory of rational expectations is that
economic agents, who have to forecast the future, use the available
and relevant information, including macro-economic theory. If
markets are dominated by rational agents, then non-discounted
price changes must be explained by new information or by a
revised perception of the meaning of existing information. Rational
expectations are not consistent with group psychological influences. An individual economic agent may gain confidence in
his/her own assessment of available information from the fact that
many other agents are evidently of the same opinion.

Rental yields

This is a term used in the real estate market. It is calculated as the
current rent payable under the existing lease divided by capital value.

Scenario

Economists make use of scenarios in their attempts to describe what the future could be like. Each scenario is based on a different set of key assumptions. Furthermore, the economist attaches subjective probability assessments to each scenario. Strictly scenarios are built for a given period in the future (say three to six months from now). A scenario-tree spans several periods in the future.

Speculative desert

Some market prices can move within a range without triggering any corrective pressure from speculative action. The term 'coined here' to describe that range is a 'speculative desert'. In the economics literature, a related term for this phenomenon is 'range of agnosticism'.

For example, Euro-dollar futures rates for dates three years and more ahead may 'stray' by at least 10–20 basis points from present levels without triggering any new speculative interest. The 'straying' may occur simply in consequence of random market factors. Speculative views about interest rates a long time ahead are too weakly held and too imprecise to provide a source of strong absorptive power for the market (with respect to random fluctuations in supply and demand).

Speculator

A speculator exposes his capital to an increased degree of risk in order to extract profit from a perceived present mispricing in the marketplace. Examples of speculative action include putting a far-above-average proportion of one's portfolio into a particular asset – say Italian lira bonds – in the expectations that these will yield an exceptionally good total return over the period in question as the market comes to terms with changed economic fundamentals (which the speculator believes he has perceived ahead of his market peers). We can distinguish short-, medium-, and long-term speculation according to the length of time over which speculators expect they will hold their positions so as to reap profit.

Term structure of interest rates

To a given yield curve (joining yields at different maturities) there corresponds a term structure of interest rates. For example, from a yield curve joining one-year interest rates to two-year rates, and up to ten-year rates an implicit term structure of one-year rates spot and forward respectively, one year, two years, and up to nine years can be formed. The term structure of interest rates can readily be compared against expectation for interest rates (one-year in the example given) up to the horizon.

Traded/non-traded goods

In international monetary theory, goods and services are divided into two main types. First, internationally traded goods enjoy low transport costs (per unit value) and sell for around the same price in all markets. Second, non-traded goods and services cannot be transported effectively and they can sell at very different prices internationally. An example of a pure traded good is gold or oil. A haircut is a typical example of a non-traded good. In practice, of course, many goods and services fall between the two opposite definitions. Some goods may be effectively traded within one area (for example Western Europe) but not world-wide.

Yield curve

This joins the yields for differing maturities from short up to long. For example, in the US T-bond market, the two- to ten-year yield curve joins the yields for two-year maturities up to ten years. A uniformly steep yield curve usually reflects some expectation of short-term interest rates rising, and conversely. Yield curves can also be put together for swap markets.

INDEX

Deutsche mark: crash of Spring 1991 40; era of the floating DM–$ rate 96; exchange rate with dollar and US bond yields 23, 97, 142–3; how influenced by US business cycle 94–5; *see also* Bundesbank

earthquake: risk of in Tokyo 64–5
equities: risk premium on 153; role of – in a portfolio 151; sensitivity of price to business cycle 91–3; valuation of 3–6; *see also* Japanese equities
ERM: shake-up, 1993 35, 132

Federal Reserve: mistakes of in the 1930s 82
Federal Reserve Open Market Committee (FOMC): its pegging of Fed funds rate 18; policy errors of 35; pre-emptive policy in 1994 173
flow of funds analysis 119
freedom of information 32
Friedman, Benjamin on economists 85
Friedman, Milton 82; view of the Federal Reserve in the 1930s 82–3

German unification 32, 73–4, 83; how economists responded to the news of 176, 181
gold: its role as a hedge-asset 160–2
gold bloc 68
gold window: closing of 26; *see also* Bretton Woods
Governor Mieno 24; errors of his policy 99–100
Greenspan, Alan 168–9
growth cycle: defined 77; of 1995/6 in USA 77; role in currency fluctuations 94–5

hedge funds 23
hyperopia 58–64

inflation: and rational expectations 54; expectations of in the bond market 21; inflation is dead? 59 inflation hedges 152–3; equities are not 152
inside story: how useful? 34–5

Japanese capital flows 101, 111–13; secret reserve movements 121; through the banking sector 117
Japanese equities 8; crash of 1990 24; interlocking shareholdings 8–9; P/Es of 63; *see also* Tokyo markets
Japanese yen: and the business cycle 99–100; flows between the yen and the DM 131–2; its position in currency geography 124; relationship to DM and dollar 99
Joseph's dream 49
journalists: versus economists 36–7
judge: who will be the – of economists? 183–5

Keynes: a tawdry truism of 49
Kondratieff cycle 177–8

land: *see* real estate
leading indicators 55
long-run views: sensitivity to market prices 51

Machiavelli 179; relevance to economic advice 179–80
market efficiency 165
Mexico shock 24, 77–8, 181
monetary policy: and intermediate targets 56

natural disasters: and the business cycle 83–4
natural rate of interest 17
news: overproduction of 43–8

oil price shocks 71–2
opinion polls and currency fluctuations 70–1

polar power 124; *see also* currency geography
political risk 69
populist 184
portfolio strategy: benefits of international diversification in money and bond portfolios 141–9; measuring the horizon date 136–40; passive strategy 151; role of equities in 152–3
probabilistic vision 1
PROFEX 3–6

rare stamps 162
rational expectations and the business cycle 79
Reaganomics and its influence on the dollar 175–6
real estate: and the business cycle 73, 86; nature of value 10–11; rental yields 12; residential 14–16; role of – in the well diversified portfolio 154–6
real exchange risk 142–6
real interest rate risk 146–7; shock 148
researcher: economist as 172–8
Russia: market reaction to 1993 crisis 48

safe-havens: collectables are no 161–2; search for 161–2
Samuelson, Paul: premature heralding of business cycle end 75

shocks: and market response to 71–4; monetary and non-monetary distinguished 83–4
solostardom in currency markets 130
South of France: as destination for economists 185
speculative desert: concept defined 166
story-tellers: the economist as 164–72
strategists: difference from economists 135–6
Swiss franc: as hedge-asset 160–1
Switzerland: referendum on EEA in 1992 45; similarity to Japan with respect to balance of payments 111–2, 170–1

Tokyo markets: and earthquake risk 64–5
travel: what purpose in for economists 172

Volcker, Paul 100

Wall Street: crash of 1929 24; catalyst to the crash 40
Warniski, Jude 40
world wars: market crisis ahead of 66–7

yield curve analysis 17, 89, 52, 90; related to business cycle 90; playing the yield curve 21